ANCIENT ROME IN EARLY OPERA

ROBERT C. KETTERER

Ancient Rome in Early Opera

UNIVERSITY OF ILLINOIS PRESS

URBANA AND CHICAGO

© 2009 by the Board of Trustees
of the University of Illinois
All rights reserved
Manufactured in the United States of America
C 5 4 3 2 1

∞ This book is printed on acid-free paper.

Library of Congress Cataloging-in-Publication Data
Ketterer, Robert.
Ancient Rome in early opera / Robert C. Ketterer.
p. cm.
Includes bibliographical references and index.
ISBN 978-0-252-03378-0 (cloth : alk. paper)
1. Opera—17th century. 2. Opera—18th century.
3. Opera—Roman influences. 4. Operas—Literary themes,
motives. 5. Rome—History. I. Title.
ML1700.K47   2008
782.1—dc22   2008012687

To my mother
Margaret Cary Ketterer
and the memory of my father
John Joseph Ketterer

Contents

Acknowledgments

The process of writing this book has taken me in directions that no one who knew me two decades ago would have predicted, since I was anything but an opera fan. That group includes my parents, to whom this book is fondly and gratefully dedicated. Opera was always part of the musical life of their household and some of it must have stuck. It also includes my wife, Margaret Riggs Ketterer, who makes all things possible and has so often held the fort while I spent time at National Endowment for the Humanities seminars, conferences, and research libraries; and my sons Andrew and David, for whom the final chorus of Vivaldi's *Catone in Utica* became the official morning wake-up music during their grade school years. I can still drive all three of them from the room by putting an opera on the stereo, but this project could never have been the joy it was without them.

Don Cameron took me to a production of *Suor Angelica* in Ann Arbor that got me thinking about the connections between classics and opera. He has since supplied information and inspiration from his apparently limitless fund of knowledge about nearly everything and has been made to attend more baroque operas than he might otherwise have done. I hope the experience was as much fun for him as it was for me.

One of the attractions of an interdisciplinary project is the interaction it provides with colleagues from different intellectual spheres. At the University of Iowa I must first thank three successive chairs of the Classics Department: Jack Holtsmark, Helena Dettmer, and John Finamore. Their patient and unfailing support, financial and moral, made this project possible. All my colleagues in Classics, but especially Carin

Green (who loves opera) and Mary Depew (who doesn't), have been unflagging with their encouragement. Further afield, my colleagues in the Department of French and Italian, especially Geoffrey Hope, Downing Thomas, and Cinzia Blum, educated me about early modern France and Italy and helped occasionally with translations. In the Department of Music, Michael Eckert since the beginning was a dependable reference source, as was the staff of Iowa's Rita Benton Music Library, Ruthann McTyre, Susan Malecki, and Amy McBeth. Francesco Dalla Vecchia patiently produced the music examples. I owe particular thanks to Roberta Marvin, who generously included me in so many of her ambitious projects to promote opera studies at Iowa, encouraged me in projects of my own, and was always ready with information, advice, and friendship.

Fellowships at two Aston Magna Academies funded by the National Endowment for the Humanities and directed by the indefatigable Raymond Erickson jump-started my study of the early modern period and its music. Through Aston Magna I met many people who contributed to my understanding of the subject at hand and wrote letters of support, including Ellen Harris, Lowell Lindgren, Ellen Rosand, Ruth Smith, Donald Burrows, Anthony Hicks, David Hurley, Robert Holzer, and, as a result of these connections, Wendy Heller and John Roberts. After the 1997 Academy on Handel's England, the board of directors of the American Handel Society asked me to join them, and gave a classicist a foothold in the musicological world, providing direct contact with the people studying eighteenth-century opera. I offer each of them my heartfelt thanks for their knowledge and comradeship.

Wendy Heller, Lowell Lindgren, and Ruth Smith read and commented on individual chapters of this book at very busy times in their own lives. Their conversations over the years were crucial in helping me form my own ideas. I hope they will forgive me at places where I didn't take their advice, possibly to the detriment of my arguments. My two very generous readers for the University of Illinois Press, Ellen Harris and Richard Tarrant, helped enormously in shaping my arguments and saved me from some of my own failings. Bill Regier, my editor at the University of Illinois Press, is a genius at supportive encouragement and judicious setting of deadlines. Without him this project would not have materialized. My research assistant Jason Osborne produced the Index Locorum and provided a fresh eye during the final stages of proofreading.

Finally, I wish to thank the organizations that funded my research. At the University of Iowa, the Department of Classics, the College of Liberal Arts and Sciences, the Division of International Programs, and the Division of Sponsored Programs have provided a steady source of support. The Newberry Library Renaissance Consortium at Iowa and a Newberry Library short-term fellowship made possible frequent trips to Chicago and a month's stay at the Newberry, in particular to use the Howard Mayer Brown libretto collection. A Music & Letters Trust Award enabled me to take a Grand Tour in 2001 to relevant archives and museums. The Gladys Krieble Delmas Foundation helped fund a crucial stay in Venice in summer 2006 to tie up loose ends. My debt to their collective generosity is great, but I hope in some measure discharged by what follows.

ANCIENT ROME IN EARLY OPERA

1 Ancient Rome in Early Opera

Beginning in 1643 with Monteverdi's *L'incoronazione di Poppea*, the producers and consumers of opera in Italian became increasingly interested in subjects taken from classical Roman history. For the next century and a half, among the many thousands of librettos produced on a large variety of historical, epic, and mythological subjects, hundreds involved plots and characters from Roman history and legend.[1] Almost all the composers we think of as in the mainstream of the baroque, including Handel, Vivaldi, Albinoni, Telemann, and Alessandro Scarlatti, wrote music for these texts and at times even used them to vie with one another for public attention. In the mid-1660s, Venetian operas with the titles *Mutio Scevola, Scipione affricano, Pompeo Magno, La prosperità di Elio Sejano, La caduta di Elio Sejano, Il Tito,* and *Eliogabalo* were all part of a vigorous game of one-upsmanship among opera houses, librettists, and composers. In 1721 a *Muzio Scevola,* its libretto a distant descendent of the Venetian *Mutio Scevola,* was produced, with individual acts set by the two most popular composers in London, George Frideric Handel and Luigi Bononcini, in what may have been a deliberately staged talent contest.[2] But toward the end of the eighteenth century, operatic interest in Roman history began to dwindle, giving way to other stories from modern history or remoter myth, and the early operas about ancient Rome were largely forgotten. More recently, with the considerable interest in earlier operas made possible by the baroque revival of the twentieth century, Monteverdi's *Poppea,* Handel's *Giulio Cesare* and *Agrippina,* and Mozart's *Clemenza di Tito* have reached the mainstream. But these are only a small percentage of the enormous body of operatic work featuring historical Romans. Stories about Rome clearly addressed issues for the operatic audience of the baroque in a way that they have not done since.

This book examines a selection of the early operas in Italian written on Roman historical topics. It takes a roughly diachronic approach, discussing the operas or groups of operas in the order of their first performances, beginning with Monteverdi's *L'incoronazione di Poppea* and concluding with operas of the 1790s, including Mozart's *La clemenza di Tito* and Cimarosa's *Gli Orazi e i Curiazi*. Specifically, I want to argue that Rome provided early modern Europe with impressive aural and visual presentations of two important myths, which I call the myth of the clement prince and the myth of liberty. Here I am employing T. P. Wiseman's simple definition of myth as "a story that matters to a community, one that is told and retold because it has significance for one generation after another." Myth by this definition need not be fantastical or involve the gods but may be historical or pseudo-historical, as are most of the plots of operas in this book. As Wiseman notes, "If it matters enough to be retold, it can count as a myth."[3] Looked at in this way, the histories of Scipio Africanus, Julius Caesar, or Emperor Titus were vital myths for the early moderns, as were the larger story patterns of ancient virtue and liberty, which were abstracted from the specific histories.

What I will call the myth of the clement prince, descended from the stories of clemency associated with Julius Caesar and the emperor Augustus, assumes that a monarch who can control himself and unite his people under a just rule constitutes the best kind of government. It is a myth that justifies the position of the divine right king or emperor. In various transformations this story resonated with producers and audiences almost unchanged until well into the nineteenth century. The myth of liberty, by contrast, wishes for the throwing off of that monarchic power or the assertion of national independence from external rule. The paradigm was the story of Lucius Junius Brutus, who led the revolt that expelled the Tarquin kings and established the Roman Republic. Brutus's heirs were Cato the Younger and Marcus Junius Brutus, both of whom opposed Julius Caesar.

A link with antiquity was part of the deep social structure in early modern Europe. Operas in the seventeenth and eighteenth centuries did not simply take ancient Greeks and Romans as their subjects. They told those stories in dramatic and literary modes that were consciously adapted from the ancient world and addressed issues the baroque era recognized it shared with that world, especially with the Romans. Even operas based on subjects other than those from the Greco-Roman world, such as Xerxes or Montezuma, share these fundamentally classical structures and modes of thought.

I have argued elsewhere that early opera was "Roman and not Greek," despite statements by the inventors of opera that they were trying to reproduce the affective power of classical Greek dramatic speech and music and despite the insistence by subsequent generations of theoreticians that Greek tragedy, at least as it was defined by Aristotle's *Poetics* and Horace's *Ars Poetica,* was the model on which opera should be based.[4] My argument was deliberately tendentious in order to make the point that we should not take the generic and cultural claims for opera at face value, but I continue to believe that the form owes far more to the Roman heritage than to the Greek. A broader approach, however, might suggest that early opera was "Hellenistic, not Classical," or "imperial, not democratic." Aristotle's *Poetics* describes tragedy that was written for and about the democratic polis of Athens. Even in Aristotle's day (384–322 B.C.E.), the three great tragedians of the fifth century—Aeschylus, Sophocles, and Euripides—were dead and their works were considered classics, not contemporary literature. The Macedonian conquest of the Greek peninsula by Philip II and his son Alexander the Great wiped out democracy as anything but a form of very local town governance. Alexander's wider conquests and their aftermath brought a Greek-like—that is, Hellenistic—culture to the entire eastern end of the Mediterranean. It also established the image of a superhuman king as the accepted form of ruler for large geographical areas. For the next two hundred years, Seleucids, Ptolemies, and Antigonids would dominate most of the Levant, Egypt, and Balkan peninsula, until the Romans finally united the entire Mediterranean basin under one imperial government. Hellenistic literature, especially that produced by writers of the court and library in Alexandria in Egypt, was inevitably a response to two forms of authority, the giants of classical Greek literature and the Macedonian god-kings of the Hellenistic empires. In this context the Hellenistic writers produced the erotic epigram, the panegyric hymn, and melodramatic historiography, which were to become models in turn for the Roman literary response to an overbearing literary heritage and irresistible political authority.[5]

The Roman Empire itself might be regarded as the last and greatest of the Hellenistic kingdoms. The Romans had from their beginnings been influenced by Greek culture through immigration and trade, particularly with the Hellenized but unliterary Etruscans to the north. Their first expansionist successes beyond their local mountain ranges brought them into contact with Greek-speaking peoples in southern Italy and Sicily, the descendants of Greek colonists of the seventh and sixth centuries B.C.E.

The earliest Roman literature, dating from the third century B.C.E., is already and unavoidably Hellenistic, comprising "modern" Latin versions of Homer and tragedy as well as adaptations of the comedies of Menander and his contemporaries. For as long as they could, Romans asserted their cultural autonomy and republican liberty, even to the point of sticking twenty-some knives into Julius Caesar in 44 B.C.E. when it looked as if he wanted to be declared a Hellenistic-style king. Caesar's heir and successor Augustus was cagier in his approach to power than Caesar himself had been, and after defeating Antony and Cleopatra in 31 B.C.E., he claimed he was restoring the Republic and traditional Roman society. But Augustus was systematically concentrating control in his own hands and setting the course for imperial government for the next three centuries. When he died peacefully at the age of seventy-six, he was declared to be a god in Rome itself. His successors kept the power but were not always so reticent about denying their own divinity while they were still alive. The idea of the Hellenized divine principacy found its expression in such very different people as Caligula, Domitian, and Hadrian.

The result was an imperial literature in both Greek and Latin that had to respond to the reality of autocratic power. Under Augustus there was some room for disagreement: The historian Livy's account of the civil war between Augustus's great uncle Caesar and Pompey the Great earned him the wry nickname "Pompeianus" from the emperor but did not get him into trouble.[6] Livy was unswervingly patriotic but acknowledged that Roman history was not a uniformly positive series of events, and his approach to history was didactic: "In that record you can find for yourself and your country both examples and warnings; fine things to take as models, base things, rotten through and through, to avoid."[7] Vergil's great celebration of Rome and Augustus in the *Aeneid* is shot through with famously dark passages that suggest the underside of imperial destiny. A mild expression of resistance to the Augustan program has often been detected in the erotic poetry of the day, which seemed to fly in the face of Augustus's efforts at moral reform after the excesses of the late Republic. Ovid and Propertius are notable in this regard.[8]

As the expressions of imperial power by Augustus's successors became more overt and sometimes oppressive, however, literary responses became correspondingly more extreme. They can be nauseatingly fulsome, as are Statius's *Silvae* or certain letters of Pliny the Younger. Elsewhere they are scathing, as in the more caustic passages in Lucan and Tacitus. Sometimes the former approach appears to imply the latter: Lucan dedicated his *Pharsalia,* an epic on the fall of the Republic, to the emperor Nero in euphuistic terms that still have critics debating whether it was meant as toadying or satire. But the fact of an emperor, good or bad, had to be accepted and dealt with. In a more realistic mood, Tacitus recognized the possibility of a beneficent monarchy, and in his *Dialogue on Orators* he meditated on the role the public speaker could play in a world where republican liberty had been effectively eliminated. Greek writers, too, with experience of the Roman imperial government, "who never denied their Greek linguistic and cultural background, but still identified completely with the political and historical tradition of Rome," produced assessments of Roman history that were syntheses of the inherited Greco-Roman tradition and became textbooks for late antiquity.[9] Cassius Dio, a Greek of the second and third centuries C.E. from Asia Minor, served in the inner circles of the Roman imperial court and wrote a history of Rome in eighty books that complements the extant histories in Latin. A century earlier, Plutarch of Chaeronea, a Greek contemporary of Tacitus who admired Rome and had friends in the imperial court of Trajan, produced his highly influential *Parallel Lives* and *Moralia*.[10] Like Livy, Plutarch thought the history he inherited was suitable for both examples and warnings to his own world. His stories above all became the myths of power, villainy, and heroism that sustained the European imagination from antiquity to the end of the eighteenth century.

The imperial reception and synthesis of the ancient historical tradition that included Livy, Plutarch, and Dio as well as Tacitus, Suetonius, and others supplied rich veins to mine for the plots of baroque operas. Like the inhabitants of the Mediterranean world under the Roman empire, most early modern Europeans had to negotiate their lives in response to a king or emperor or pope. Early opera functioned in a world of patronage far more like that of Hellenistic Greece and imperial Rome than democratic, classical Athens. Opera was first created in the context of late Renaissance court celebration. The men in the late sixteenth century who were contemplating the ways in which they might recreate the affective power of Greek tragedy in Italian musical drama were working for northern Italian dukes who paid their bills and gave them places and occasions to put on their shows. The first operas helped to celebrate ducal weddings and birthdays, and so from the very beginning there was a tension between the purpose of opera and the form and spirit of the Greek tragic model. The social occasion for opera was officially joyous and reflected in real life the essence of comedy; that is, marriage and the assurance that social order would continue. The violent stories of the traditionally dysfunctional Greek families were unsuitable for the context, and the earliest operas were set instead to pastoral myth from the pages of Ovid and Vergil: Apollo and Daphne, Orpheus and Eurydice, or Bacchus and Ariadne.[11]

There is of course plenty of room for pathos in these stories, and the pathos was popular. An arrangement of Ariadne's lament from Monteverdi's *Arianna*, for example, became a household favorite in mid-seventeenth-century Italy. But genuine tragedy was another matter. Taste was moving on from the blood and thunder of Spanish and English tragedy of the sixteenth century. The late romances of Shakespeare such as *The Tempest* or *A Winter's Tale* already show the trend. The earliest operas in fact tend toward tragical-comical-pastoral: While Apollo's beloved Daphne is turned into a laurel tree and Orpheus's Eurydice is lost at the last moment, the conclusions of the operas go on to exalt the male lover. Through the power of his poetry and music, he "sublimates his defeat in love into a poetic statement about the power of art to overcome the limitations and frustrations of life," as Barbara Hanning has put it.[12] Even Monteverdi's semidramatic "Il Combattimento di Tancredi e Clorinda" (1624), which musically presents onstage battle and death, still manages to end in bliss. In Tasso's *Gerusalemme liberata*, from which the text is adapted, Tancredi falls in love with the female warrior Clorinda, kills her in single combat, and in consequence goes mad from grief. Monteverdi's version ends not in madness but in Clorinda's vision of heaven, sung on a strikingly original resolution in the music that set a fashion for other composers.[13]

In all this there are still visible traces of the Neoplatonism that was an integral part not only of Renaissance philosophy and art but also of political self-presentation, not least in Florence, where opera was invented. The Medici associated themselves with Apolline sun imagery, which signified the centrality of their position to the state and their rule as the source of prosperity and light. In this context, love is a Platonic vector for transfiguration to a higher plane of existence. The hero's or heroine's metamorphosis, whether it be into a tree, like Daphne, or a deity, like Orpheus and Ariadne, created the happy ending that celebrated at the same time mythic transfiguration, a ducal wedding, and the power of music.

During the years that the Pilgrims were establishing Plymouth Colony and Galileo was getting into trouble with the Inquisition, the new genre of opera, or *dramma per musica* as it came to be called, spread from the courts of northern Italy to papal Rome, where, under the patronage of the Barberini family, the stories of saints and martyrs were dramatized to music.[14] These operas, too, could confront death, but like the story of Clorinda, they ended in transfiguration and religious bliss.

They were not yet popular entertainments, however. Opera only found a wider audience when the Republic of Venice began to produce it in public, commercial theaters as part of its popular carnival festivities, where all of Europe came to celebrate. There, in a venue run by a senate rather than an autocrat, one might have expected that the drama of the Greek city-states could find a new expression. But such was not the case. In the first place, the Venetian aristocracy was notoriously jealous of its own authority, and although Venice was a republic, it was not a democracy. Unlike either Pilgrim Separatism or Galilean astronomy, opera was clearly an expression of the entrenched structures of power, not least because it was those structures that could afford to produce it.[15]

Furthermore, the season of carnival was famous for the overturning of social norms, and the triumph of the disadvantaged on stage is generally comic rather than tragic. Opera had been established to celebrate happy occasions in an age that no longer valued violent tragedy, and stories in which imperiled lovers overcome hardship and opposition in order to live happily ever after became the pattern for the genre. So when the source material from which the libretto was adapted did not readily lend itself to a happy outcome—if, for example, there were no lovers involved or if the protagonist came to a violent end—the story was changed, sometimes quite abruptly, to give the opera its requisite erotic interest and happy ending, or *lieto fine*. This remained the rule for *dramma per musica* and the eighteenth-century *opera seria* that developed from it. The seventeenth century, after all, was the age in which Nahum Tate could change the ending of *King Lear* to eliminate the deaths of both Lear and Cordelia, a revision that continued to be popular into the nineteenth century. Addison's *Cato* (1713) complements its meditations on republican liberty with a decidedly un-Roman romance between Cato's daughter Marcia and the Numidian prince Juba.

Consequently, in opera's first phase, roughly from 1600 to 1690, Ariadne is of course saved by Bacchus, and Ulysses and Penelope are happily reunited to sing a love duet, but in addition, Jason marries Hypsipyle, not Medea. Scipio Africanus falls for a Carthaginian princess named Sophonisba while campaigning in Spain, Arminius the anti-Roman freedom fighter captures Agrippina in the German forests but subsequently saves her husband Germanicus's life, Nero apologizes and reinstates Octavia as empress, and so forth.[16] Even the worst Roman emperors—Caligula, Domitian, Heliogabalus—were shown to repent and survive, in preference to dramatizing their violent historical deaths.[17] If all of this seems laughable to the classically trained, it was, after all, celebratory entertainment and supposed to be amusing at some level. Sir Philip Skippon, an English visitor to Venice in 1664, was not in doubt about opera's fundamental nature: "The operas of Venice are comedies acted in carnival time, with a great deal of magnificence and curiosity."[18]

When critics began to object, it was not because the source stories were altered but because the librettos failed to follow Aristotelian unities as they were then perceived and used overblown diction derived from the baroque poetry of Giambattista Marino to decorate an uncontrolled multiplicity of incident. One practitioner of the genre, who also obviously regarded opera as a descendant of ancient comedy, put it thus:

> This is a genre of poetry that has returned to the first nature of drama in regard to song, but as to the rest, to a different culture, following the pleasure of the age according to the nature of our time. It does not recognize any more today Epicharmus as its father, nor Sicily as its homeland, nor Aristotle as its lawgiver. Every usage is changed, even depraved novelties are pleasing, as Scaliger said in regard to Plautus's *Amphitruo*. If the Crateses, the Aristotles, the Aristophaneses, the Terences were alive today, maybe they'd change their way of thinking. Of the two purposes that Horace taught us [instruction and pleasure], only pleasure remains for poetry. In this day and age, people don't need others' compositions to learn how to live in the world.[19]

The critical challenge to this freewheeling attitude toward classicism coincided with a change of taste at the end of the seventeenth century. In Italy, that change was expressed most prominently by the intellectual society that called itself the Arcadian Academy.[20] Founded first in Rome in 1690, its members were dedicated to the purpose of expunging the excesses of the previous decades from Italian literature and answering French criticism that Italian poetry violated the canons of good taste. Initiates took pastoral names and advocated simplicity in literature; the movement spread to most of the cultural centers of Italy.[21] The opera libretto, as one of the most conspicuous Italian poetic texts of the day, came under their scrutiny. A series of Arcadian poets, including Silvio Stampiglia, Apostolo Zeno and, most definitively, Pietro Metastasio, produced a new style of libretto meant to conform more closely to Aristotelian ideals. They read Corneille and Racine, eliminated overtly comic elements in opera to favor the heroic and pathetic, and controlled the unruly and unrealistic aria to make it contribute as much as possible to the drama. Nevertheless, the love interest was maintained, as it had been in French drama, and the happy ending remained firmly in place.[22] This operatic form was entirely in the spirit of the age and eminently exportable. The poets mentioned above, for example, began writing in Italy, but they all ended up in the court of the Holy Roman Emperor in

Vienna, where the celebration of established autocracy was their principal duty.

Metastasio's librettos became both a staple and a model for the opera until nearly the end of the century and were still being produced sporadically in the early nineteenth century. These librettos suited not only the court at Vienna but also almost any venue where there were patrons rich enough to fund a musical drama that might flatter their position or class. The fundamental celebratory function of opera inherited from the Renaissance court performances remained intact. Inevitably the dramatic values and moral intent of Metastasian *opera seria* succumbed to the elaborations of adapters and singers in answer to audience demand. When reformers such as Gluck and his librettist Calzabigi proposed to force it once again into a form that resembled more accurately the supposed purity of the Greek model, they nevertheless either chose the romantic plays of Euripides that skated close to modern notions of comedy—*Alcestis* and *Iphigenia among the Taurians*[23]—or fixed the endings: Gluck's Orpheus is reunited with Eurydice by Amor after all; his Iphigenia is not sacrificed at Aulis, and the marriage with Achilles goes forward. In the earlier serious operas of Mozart, Neptune prevents Idomeneus from sacrificing his son, and Sulla repents of his crimes, relinquishing the woman he has been pursuing to her intended. The bare bones of the plot of Mozart's "tragic" *Lucio Silla* are scarcely distinguishable from those of his comic *Die Enführung aus dem Serail.*

There were, naturally, exceptions to the patterns of the Arcadian reforms. Librettists in the eighteenth century regularly adapted less-tidy seventeenth-century librettos that retained traces of their carnivalesque origins. (Handel's operas are frequently of this type.) And from time to time the happy endings were compromised or even eliminated. The *scena ultima*, or last scene, of Busenello's *La prosperità infelice di Giulio Cesare* (1646) is a *lieto fine* in that it shows the conspirators' celebration of Caesar's assassination, but the treatment of the dictator's character in the libretto calls their joy into question.[24] Purcell's *Dido and Aeneas* (1689) ends in death and lament; Cato gasps out his death throes on stage in the first version of Metastasio's *Il Catone in Utica* (1728). Operas on the subject of Tamburlaine and Mithridates of Pontus include the suicides of Bajazet and Mithridates. But these were exceptions that proved the rule. In the case of *Il Catone*, Metastasio was induced by public outcry in Rome to revise and change Cato's dying speech on stage to a reported offstage suicide. Vivaldi's setting of 1737 for the spring season in Verona eliminates the death altogether. As a rule, *dramma per musica* dealt with death and tragic feeling in the internal scenes, and while these may inject an ironic or mournful tone into the joyful conclusion, they generally do not cancel it.

The "serious" qualities of what came to be known as *opera seria* resulted instead from the genre's interest in character and in temporary risk rather than disastrous outcome. Rheinhard Strohm has suggested that "a regular tragedy had to arouse terror and pity in the spectator, which required that at least one character, who enjoyed the spectators' sympathy, had to be thrown into misery. But the intrigue against this hero could fail and its perpetrator be punished, allowing for a happy ending without neglecting the effects of pity and fear. Tragic heroes and heroines were, in a sense, more indispensable than tragic actions: the personalization of the tragic was a dramaturgical principle which opera has successfully absorbed to make it one of its own major characteristics."[25]

But the happy ending was not the only reason Skippon could call these dramas comedies. At the center of the conflict in any comedy derived from the Greco-Roman tradition is an obstruction of some sort whose function is to keep young lovers apart.[26] The dramatic process of the comedy is to rid the lovers of this obstruction and unite them in some satisfactory way. The earliest operas, appropriate to their roots in late Renaissance celebration, made the prince the lover and the romantic triumph his unification with a princess. The first five years of opera in Venice (1637–42) featured the union of numerous famous pairs of mythic lovers: Andromeda and Perseus, Peleus and Thetis, Apollo and Daphne, Venus and Adonis, Ulysses and Penelope, Ariadne and Bacchus, Aeneas and Lavinia, and Jason and Hypsipyle, all of them concluding with some kind of happy resolution.[27] This dramatic pattern could have bizarre repercussions, as we will see in the first "Roman" opera produced in 1643, *L'incoronazione di Poppea,* in which Nero and Poppea overcome the obstructive forces of virtuous action and legitimate marriage to unite with the blessings of Venus and her son Amor.

As the librettists explored the possibilities of historical drama on the opera stage, however, a new pattern emerged. The authority figure began to appear as the obstruction to the final unification of lovers, often because he himself desires the young woman in question. Already in 1651 with Cesti's and Sbarra's *Alessandro, il vincitore di se stesso,* Alexander brings about the happy ending through a crisis of conscience that results in the beneficent use of power, manifesting itself either as mercy *(clementia)* or sexual self-denial *(continentia).* This story pattern, which I am calling the myth of the clement prince, has its origins in a constellation of ancient stories and philosophical treatises attached particularly to generals and rulers of the Roman world.

Clemency as a virtue in a conqueror and leader was associated most notably with Julius Caesar, who deliberately created his own myth with his famous commentaries on the Gallic and civil wars. In the generation previous to Caesar's, the reactionary Cornelius Sulla and his associates had solved their political problems by use of terror and legalized political murders known as proscriptions. Notoriously, Sulla had at one point assured the anxious senate that only a few malcontents were being executed even as his troops were slaughtering seven thousand captive Samnites in a nearby square. Caesar, by deliberate contrast, publicly forgave his political enemies, sometimes multiple times, during the civil war with Pompey. Caesar may well have been sincere in his gestures of forgiveness, as he himself had barely escaped Sulla's proscriptions, but there were doubts, and Cicero called his mercy "treacherous" (*insidiosa*).[28] Whatever the motives, Caesar certainly exploited his actions for what he hoped was political advantage, elevating *clementia* to public policy; the senate even dedicated a temple to *Clementia Caesaris*.[29]

In the chaos following Caesar's assassination, Caesar's heir Octavian and his colleagues reverted to brutal means of eliminating their enemies, including proscriptions; Cicero was one of their victims. But when at long last the Roman civil wars came to an end and Octavian became the emperor Augustus, he chose to adopt a Caesarean *clementia* as one of his official virtues.[30] This move is expressed in Anchises's famous advice to his son Aeneas in the underworld (*Aeneid* 6.851–53), "You, Roman, remember to rule the nations with your power (this will be your skill), and impose the custom of peace, spare the humbled and beat down the haughty."[31] A generation later, the younger Seneca enshrined Augustan clemency as a philosophical exemplum in his treatise *De Clementia*, where he reports Augustus's decision to forgive Gnaeus Cornelius Cinna, who had conspired against his life. This episode is the inspiration for Corneille's *Cinna, ou La clémence d'Auguste*, which was in turn the source of inspiration for Metastasio's long-enduring libretto *La clemenza di Tito* (see chapter 8).

Related in spirit to this imperial *clementia* are the stories of the sexual continence of Alexander and the family of Darius and of the elder Scipio Africanus in Spain. In each case the conquering general refused to indulge himself with beautiful captive women, protecting them instead. Alexander is not otherwise famous for his *clementia*: In Seneca's *De Clementia* (1.25) he is cited as a negative example for having thrown a close associate to hungry lions. But after the battle of Issus, he captured the family of King Darius and treated them with consideration. Scipio, after the siege of Cartagena, returned the young woman with her ransom

Figure 1. Giambattista Tiepolo. The Continence of Scipio. Prado Museum. Photo courtesy of Scala, Art Resource, New York.

money to her betrothed. These episodes of Alexander's and Scipio's magnanimity became favorites, interpreted by Veronese and Tiepolo, to name
only two early modern painters (figure 1).[32]

The choice of clemency and virtuous action over personal gratification is also informed by the philosophical exemplum known as the
Choice of Hercules. Prodicus of Ceos (fifth century B.C.E.) apparently invented the story that the young Hercules had to choose at a fork in a road
between Virtue and Pleasure; he chose the former as the means to true
honor and distinction. The story was retold by Xenophon (*Memorabilia*
2.21.34) and then by Cicero (*De Officiis* 1.32.118). The episode was a favorite in early modern iconography, for it accorded well with the popular
Neostoicism of the seventeenth century, for which virtue and endurance
in the face of adversity were prime *desiderata*.[33] The Choice of Hercules
often stands behind the ubiquitous choices by operatic kings and heroes
for virtue and clemency rather than enforce their own desires.[34]

Thus what I have called the myth of the clement prince accords
well with the celebratory and comic structure at the root of opera. From
the second half of the seventeenth century until the end of the eighteenth, this myth largely replaced the Neoplatonic transfiguration as
the structuring idea for *dramma per musica* in general and for those on
Roman themes in particular. The clement ruler, in essence, became the
divinity that customarily appeared ex machina at the end of operas in
the first half of the seventeenth century. Already in *L'incoronazione di
Poppea*, Busenello combines the older and newer patterns. Nerone, in
an ironic reminiscence of Senecan teaching, forbears to execute Ottone
and Drusilla for the plot against Poppea's life, makes them a couple, and
then sends them into exile. This frees the way for the transfiguration of
Nerone and Poppea by Amore and Venere, who appear in the final scene
and declare Poppea to be Venus on earth. As we will see, the shift to the
story of the clement prince is made more definitely in Cavalli's *Scipione
affricano* of 1664, although the comic and erotic elements threaten to
overpower it. It is with the coming of the reforms of the 1690s, particularly with the court operas of the Habsburgs, that the Neostoic sermon
comes truly to the fore.

That shift is gradual, however, and the older, Neoplatonic pattern
of the prince as the successful lover continued to be viable in the eighteenth century, especially in adaptations of the older seventeenth-century
librettos; *Giulio Cesare*, revised for Handel by Nicolà Haym from a 1677
Venetian libretto, is a notable example. Most often, however, a Roman
general or emperor steps back to allow the happy union of his subjects,
recognizing that his responsibility (*officium* in Latin) is the greater. In

a seeming paradox, therefore, serious opera was structurally Stoic comedy, its happy ending meant to encourage good behavior in princes while providing entertainment for their subjects.[35]

However, Roman Stoicism had a second, more tragic strain to it that is also already observable in Monteverdi's *Poppea*. At the north African town of Utica in 46 B.C.E., the Stoic republican Marcus Porcius Cato committed suicide rather than surrender to Julius Caesar. He immediately became a martyr to the cause of the Republic, motivating Julius Caesar to write a bad-tempered treatise titled *Anticato* in an effort to debunk his memory. But that memory persisted to haunt both Caesar and his heirs. Marcus Brutus helped assassinate Caesar partly out of a sense of Stoic duty to oppose tyranny. In the early empire, Cato remained the model for a series of Stoic champions of republican liberty who in their turn were suppressed and often killed by the emperor. The most famous of their number was Seneca the philosopher, the sometime adviser and tutor to the young Nero, who was forced to commit suicide in the wake of the unsuccessful Pisonian conspiracy. These Stoics became martyrs to a lost republican cause, a symbolic last-ditch stand against the emperor's power.

In seventeenth-century opera the Stoic martyrs become adviser figures; Seneca himself appears in operas about Nero. There is a Cato in Cavalli's *Scipione affricano*, and Marcus Brutus appears in the final act of Busenello's *La prosperità infelice di Giulio Cesare*. The republican Stoic, present but subordinate in the seventeenth century, then emerges as a central figure in the eighteenth. As I will suggest below, the historical Cato was a model for the actions of a character in Zeno's 1713 *Scipione nelle Spagne*. Metastasio's *Il Catone in Utica* was inspired in part by Addison's spoken drama *Cato*, also of 1713. As we saw, the sight of a dying Cato onstage was suppressed—by public taste, as it happened, rather than official censorship—but the revised version of the opera was very popular, set by more than twenty composers in the course of the century. Finally, Marcus Brutus returns at the other end of our chronological period, in Sertor's 1789 *La morte di Cesare*.

The Stoic champions of liberty had thus been present in opera since the mid-seventeenth century as opponents to the prince; arguably they were anticipated by the Christian martyrs defying pagan authority in the Barberini operas in Rome. Rebellious figures such as Arminius, the German tribal leader who effectively kept Rome from crossing the Rhine, appear in the early eighteenth century. But it is not until the coming of the age of revolution that they temporarily emerged as consistently central figures, bringing with them a sense of tragedy lacking in mainstream *opera seria*. From the middle of the eighteenth century, operas appeared about Junius Brutus, founder of the Roman Republic, and Julius Sabinus, leader of a Gallic revolt against Vespasian. By the 1790s, overtly antimonarchical pieces like Tarchi's *La congiura pisoniana* were being written, inspired by French revolutionary dramas. This fashion quickly faded when the excesses of the Reign of Terror became known, and was replaced by more generally patriotic pieces like Cimarosa's *Gli Orazi e i Curiazi*, which asserted the hard-nosed Roman patriotism of the citizen without challenging established authority. At the same time, Mozart's version of the very conservative, monarchical *La clemenza di Tito* was finding an audience. The first decades of the nineteenth century continued to see operas on ancient themes, but 1815 was a turning point in more ways than one, and slowly historical Romans as subjects ceased to engage the creators and consumers of opera.

In the meantime, they had had a long run. The following chapters chart that run with representative Italian librettos performed in Italy, England, Spain, and Austria from 1643 to 1797. French opera, unlike French spoken drama, did not represent historical Romans, and so Paris is not discussed except insofar as Corneille and Racine influenced the writing of Italian librettos. The operas I have chosen hardly exhaust such a large field, but by selecting texts about certain figures and stories that recur in the period—Scipio Africanus the Elder, Julius Caesar, Cato the Younger, and the emperors Nero and Titus—I have tried to provide a structure around which I can also look at other subjects and more general themes and trends.

———————

Although early opera is not the rarity it used to be on the modern opera stage, the baroque pieces that do appear these days are generally presented as established works such as "Handel's" *Giulio Cesare* or "Mozart's" *La clemenza di Tito*, with no sense of the variety of settings by different composers that those librettos underwent in their day, and, for perfectly sensible reasons, not often performed with purely baroque production values. For those who would like it, therefore, there follows a brief sketch of how a libretto became a performed opera in the early modern period and the ramifications of that process for analysis of the subject.

The earliest operas were established works with their own identities. Monteverdi's and Cavalli's operas remained known as theirs, for example, even when they were revived in different venues, although music by other composers might be added. In the decades after opera became a commercial venture, however, what circulated from one operatic center to the next was most often a libretto that was then set and reset by different composers. Initially, either through a commission from a court or in negotiation with the manager of an opera house, a writer produced a libretto adapted from source texts according to the demands of the genre and performance context. The composer then interpreted the libretto in ways that included cuts, repetitions, and additions to the original text. The libretto text was printed up, sometimes very carelessly, for sale to the audience. These performance librettos indicated by means of inverted commas placed at line beginnings (called *virgolette*) which passages had been cut from performance but allowed the audience to know what the librettist had originally produced.

As often as not, a libretto saw revivals. In such cases, further changes were usually made. Arias were altered or replaced, recitative was cut, and generally the book was adapted to suit local need, the demands of sponsors, or evolving musical taste. Mozart's *La clemenza di Tito* of 1791, for example, is Caterino Mazzolà's two-act adaptation of Pietro Metastasio's original text of 1734. Between Caldara's setting and Mozart's there had been at least thirty-five others, and five more followed Mozart's.[36]

In a revival, the music might be mostly that of the original composer but could also be cut or amplified by someone else; or, as was more often the case in the eighteenth century, entirely new music might be written.[37] Figure 2 shows one such adaptation: A printed libretto for the 1703 performance of Antonio Salvi's *Arminio* in Florence has handwritten marginal notes for a restaging in 1716, with additions pasted over the old text.[38] An opera might also be set as a *pasticcio;* that is, a score that was stitched together from previous settings of the text (or of other texts) by multiple composers. The London *Muzio Scevola* for which Handel composed reflected this practice, including, as it did, music by a different composer in each of its three acts. More often in a *pasticcio,* arias by different composers were combined ad libitum throughout the opera. Handel also created a *pasticcio* on Metastasio's *Il Catone in Utica* in 1732 that included music by Vivaldi, Hasse, Leo, Porpora, and Vinci.

Heroic male roles were sung in the soprano and alto range by male castratos. If a castrato was not available, a woman sang the role. Occasionally the reverse occurred as well, and a castrato sang a female role. Lower male ranges were assigned to subordinate roles, including mentor figures, dramatic heavies, and comic servants. As opera was secular entertainment rather than religious performance, women appeared in female roles, and the female lament became a popular musical turn that could be separated from an opera and enjoy a life of its own, as happened with Monteverdi's lament of Arianna. Recitative dialogue was punctuated by lyric passages, which by the 1650s developed into what we would

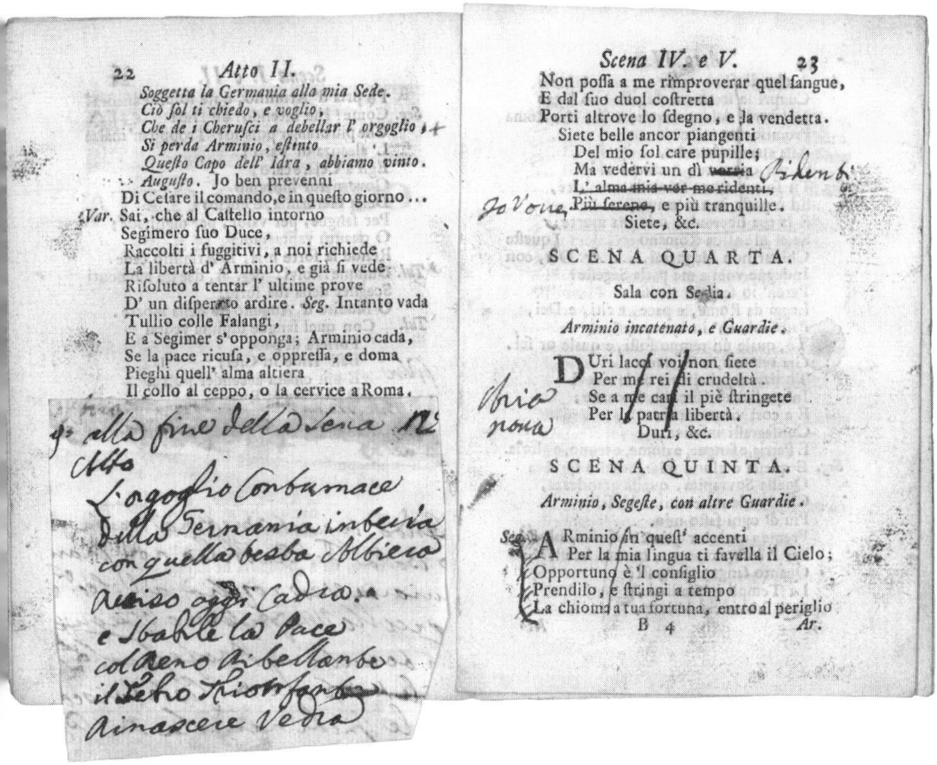
22 Atto II.
Soggetta la Germania alla mia Sede.
Ciò sol ti chiedo, e voglio,
Che de i Cherusci a debellar l' orgoglio
Si perda Arminio, estinto
Questo Capo dell' Idra, abbiamo vinto.
Augusto. Io ben prevenni
Di Cesare il comando, e in questo giorno...
Var. Sai, che al Castello intorno
Segimero suo Duce,
Raccolti i fuggitivi, a noi richiede
La libertà d' Arminio, e già si vede
Risoluto a tentar l' ultime prove
D' un disperato ardire. Seg. Intanto vada
Tullio colle Falangi,
E a Segimer s' opponga; Arminio cada,
Se la pace ricusa, e oppressa, e doma
Pieghi quell' alma altiera
Il collo al ceppo, o la cervice a Roma.

Scena IV. e V. 23
Non possa a me rimproverar quel sangue,
E dal suo duol costretta
Porti altrove lo sdegno, e la vendetta.
Siete belle ancor piangenti
Del mio sol care pupille;
Ma vedervi un dì vezzia
L' alma mia vor mo ridenti,
Più sereno, e più tranquille.
Siete, &c.
SCENA QUARTA.
Sala con Sedia.
Arminio incatenato, e Guardie.
DUri lacci voi non siete
Per me rei di crudeltà.
Se a me cari il piè stringete
Per la patria libertà.
Duri, &c.
SCENA QUINTA.
Arminio, Segeste, con altre Guardie.
Seg. ARminio in quest' accenti
Per la mia lingua ti favella il Cielo;
Opportuno è 'l consiglio
Prendilo, e stringi a tempo
La chioma a tua fortuna, entro al periglio
B 4 Ar.

Figure 2. Libretto of Antonio Salvi's Arminio. *Originally for Pratolino, 1703, edited by hand for a new production, Florence, 1716. Photo courtesy of The Newberry Library, Chicago.*

recognize as arias. By the end of the seventeenth century, aria structure was regularly in da capo, or A-B-A, form, in which the A section made a statement, the B section developed or contrasted with it, after which the A was restated, allowing the singer an opportunity to ornament further the A melody.

After some experimentation at the beginning of the seventeenth century, choruses were largely excluded, and there were very few duets or ensembles. A final *tutti* was sung by the opera's six or so characters, not by a separate chorus. This remained the practice until the middle of the eighteenth century, when slowly choruses began to appear again and librettists and composers began to include duets and ensembles of singers. (The French maintained their own style of opera, called *tragédie en musique* or *tragédie lyrique,* in which recitative and aria could hardly be differentiated, at least by the Italian ear. Choruses and ballets were always a feature of the French form, and French influence was partially responsible for bringing the chorus back to Italian opera.)

A libretto provided a more or less accurate guide to the performance. But particularly in the first half of the eighteenth century, a singer, in response to demands of individual ego or the audience, could import her or his own "baggage aria" into the performance, substituting or adding music with which that singer had previously made a hit but which was not part of the author's original production.[39] The evening at the opera also included dance, performed sometimes in the context of the opera, but increasingly as time went on between the acts of the opera. These entre'acte ballets had their own narrative lines—mythological, historical, or pastoral—that might or might not relate to the subject of the opera.

From the mid-sixteenth century on, theaters were built in an elongated horseshoe pattern, with audience boxes in vertical ranks around the walls and the lower-priced seats on the floor in the center. The orchestra, comprised largely of bowed and plucked strings and at least one keyboard, sat in full view in front of the stage. The stage was deeply recessed and gently raked toward the back to provide distance and perspective. Scenery consisted of progressively inset ranks of flats that were pushed in and out from the sides by elaborate stage machinery. In the seventeenth century there might also be machines descending from above to bring in supernatural beings. As time went on, both costumes and scenery became highly conventionalized and could be reused in different operas. This was the era before archaeological exactitude was expected in period pieces, but scenery tended to suggest appropriate venues such as palaces, formal gardens, or military encampments with a mix of early modern and ancient styles. Figure 3, the frontispiece to Matteo Noris's *Catone Uticense* (Venice 1701), which shows the mortally wounded Cato, illustrates typical costuming of the time.

The audience added yet another component to the performance. The house was not dark, and distractions were multiple. As John Rosselli has noted, "Whether in a pompous or a seedy house, at no time before the late nineteenth century was the audience chiefly concerned with the performance of an opera as a complete work of art. You were not necessarily expected to arrive on time, sit still, keep quiet, concentrate on the stage action, or stay to the end."[40] On opening nights in houses with royalty present, the audience could be relatively attentive throughout the opera. But as a general thing, while the message that was sent from the stage by the company might be uniform for the run of the opera, what was received was a much spottier thing. An operagoer might hear all of a given

Figure 3. Frontispiece for Matteo Noris, Catone Uticense, *Venice, 1701. Photo courtesy of The Newberry Library, Chicago.*

opera over the course of its run, but most likely as a result of multiple attendances in which different parts were heard on different nights.

Under these variable circumstances, what can it mean to analyze one of these early operas; for example, Cavalli's *Scipione affricano*? Here, if anywhere, postmodern reflections on the chimerical nature of text and intention seem to apply. Because of the fluid conditions of text, performance, and reception, what might be tentatively said about the original production in Venice in 1664 will probably not be true in a different opera theater in a different city with different musical tastes and a different political climate, or even for a revival back in Venice in 1678. Much can be learned by analyzing the permutations of a single text, as has been done in some cases.[41] In this spirit, I have tried everywhere to maintain an awareness of the history of these librettos, but in general I have privileged the earliest printed versions as a starting point for the discussion on the assumption that they are reasonable indicators of what was initially produced by the contributing forces of librettist, composer, and patron, and then received by the audience.

This essentially literary approach to a performance text is justified by the fact that the libretto, and not necessarily the music, was what circulated among the opera theaters over time. Furthermore, the libretto was treated as something to read on its own. It conventionally began with an address to the "Reader," suggesting the author hoped it would be judged on its own merits as a poetic production. Although librettists often dismissed their own efforts as the lowest form of poetic work, they nevertheless took the trouble to collect and publish them.[42] The double nature of the libretto as blueprint for performance and as independent literary work is vividly demonstrated in a letter, dated November 5, 1718, by Apostolo Zeno, poet laureate for the court in Vienna:

> This evening my *Ifigenia* goes on stage. You cannot imagine the conspiracy formed to destroy it. The scenery isn't finished; the costumes are either old or haven't been provided; the singers don't know their parts; the stage decor hasn't been executed according to my intentions; but with all this, and with as much of it as is able to succeed, two things console me very much: first, that my most August Patron [Emperor Charles VI] highly approved it, and second that my libretto has been read by the whole court and found great favor; as a result, if it does not create the effect it should on stage, the fault will not be mine. *

There are at least two lessons here. One is that the historical production of a play or opera may not have been, and in most instances probably was not, the ideal performance we might generate in the theater of our minds. But for the purposes of the analysis here, it is also worth noting that a libretto victimized by a poor production might nevertheless be seriously appreciated for its literary merit as a dramatic poem. That at least was Zeno's perception in 1718 for his *Ifigenia*, and it was apparently what Busenello, author of *L'incoronazione di Poppea*, had had in mind when he published revised versions of his librettos in 1656 in a volume titled *Le ore ociose*. Consequently, a literary approach to the text as a unified whole is not an anachronism, as long as care is taken to appreciate the performance contexts for which the text was produced.

Music is obviously the first of those contexts. Effective language for the musical stage is not the same as for spoken drama. The language of these librettos is highly declamatory and highly visual, meant to paint pictures that extend the visual range of the production and suggest musical ideas for the composers. In some instances there is a consistency of image that develops with the plot. This is especially notable in seventeenth-century librettos and those adapted from them that are still the heirs to baroque Marinism. The discussion will therefore often spring from a close reading of the language and imagery presented by the libretto and its relationship to that found in the ancient sources. That is where the verbal music lies, and it is in relation to that element that I will introduce musical examples, as they reinforce the argument being made about the text.

When not otherwise indicated, translations are my own. In translating the Italian librettos I have not tried to maintain the colometry. I have modernized the capitalization of the early modern texts but have maintained the original spellings, except very occasionally where an emendation will clarify the meaning. In London librettos, the Italian words were interpreted for the audience with an English translation on facing pages. In these cases I have quoted the English libretto text rather than translating the Italian, since that is how most of the audience would have received the opera's story and lyrics. Deviations of the English libretto text from the Italian that are significant for the analysis are noted in the discussion.

I have provided the original texts in Italian and Latin in the footnotes only when specific vocabulary is being analyzed or the relationship between words and music is at issue. Otherwise I have tried to make it clear where the original passage can be found. One exception: Longer passages from librettos and primary sources that have not been published in modern editions are provided in the appendix. Passsages appearing in the appendix are marked with an asterisk (*) at the end of the translation provided in the main text.

The names of historical figures that appear as characters in the Italian librettos naturally have Italian forms. Thus, for example, Scipio, Caesar, or Sulla in English are Scipione, Cesare, or Silla in English are Scipione, Cesare, or Silla in the librettos. In some cases the librettos themselves are not entirely consistent in choice of spelling, and in bilingual London librettos both English and Italian forms appear. All this makes discussion of history and opera together a challenge. In choosing of which form of a name to use, I have aimed for clarity as dictated by the immediate context of the discussion rather than a broad consistency.

2 The Coronation of Poppea

BUSENELLO/MONTEVERDI,
L'INCORONAZIONE DI POPPEA

L'incoronazione di Poppea condenses several years of Roman history into one eventful day, as the scheming Poppaea Sabina and her lover, the emperor Nero, rid themselves of an annoyingly moralistic Seneca, Poppae's lover Otho, and Nero's wife Octavia, after which Poppae is elevated to the position of empress. Its libretto is by Giovanni Francesco Busenello and the music by Claudio Monteverdi. It premiered in 1643 during carnival in Venice and was revived at least once during the seventeenth century, at Naples in 1651.[1] Busenello's libretto, striking for its imaginative combination of Tacitus's *Annals* with the Senecan-style tragedy *Octavia*, is usually identified as the first to be taken from a historiographical source. But its adaptation of a historical theme was not a creation *ex nihilo*.[2] Major elements of *Poppea* correspond to the preoccupations of the other operas of the day, both in Venice and elsewhere.

Most obviously, Roman literature had been a dominant source of subject matter since the beginning of operatic production in Florence, where it inspired the texts of *La Dafne* (1599), *Euridice* (1600), *Orfeo* (1607), and the first production of *Arianna* (1607–8).[3] Between 1636, when the first Venetian opera was performed at the Teatro San Cassiano, and 1642, the year before *Poppea* was produced, *drammi per musica* had included mythic material from Ovid, Catullus, and Vergil, with titles including *Andromeda, Gli amori di Apollo e di Dafne, Arianna, Didone,* and *Narciso ed Eco immortalati.*[4] The theme of the triumph of Love that dominates the action of *Poppea* had been very recently anticipated in two operas of 1642, *La virtù de' strali d'Amore* and *Amore innamorato.*

Tim Carter has pointed out that Giulio Rospigliosi in Rome had already begun to use historical material in the 1630s with operas on the lives of saints such as *Il Sant' Alessio, I Santi Didimo e Teodora,* and *Il Sant' Eustachio.*[5] Specifically Roman themes that verged on history began to appear in Venice around the same time Monteverdi's *Poppea* premiered. Giulio Strozzi explored the mythic connections among Troy, Rome, and the imperial inheritance of Venice in an emerging trilogy, *La finta pazza* (1641), *La finta savia* (1643), and *Romolo e Remo* (1645).[6] *La finta savia,* written and produced simultaneously with *Poppea,* included characters that appear in Livy's narratives of early Rome. The Cumaean sibyl and Procas appear, as do Amulius and Numitor of Alba Longa, immediate forebears of Romulus and Remus, although what they perform has very little to do with the events in Livy. Monteverdi himself had composed *Le nozze d'Enea e Lavinia* based on material from the *Aeneid* for performance in 1641. Moreover, 1642 saw the appearance of two prose *novelle* on the subject of Agrippina by Federico Malipiero and Ferrante Pallavicino, indicating a lively contemporary interest in Julio-Claudian imperial history.[7]

The choice to write an opera on a genuinely historical subject was therefore a natural step. Nevertheless, the effect of showing historical rather than mythical or legendary Romans in an opera was a striking innovation for northern Italy, and the choice of Neronian history for this experiment, even given the precedents noted above, was not the most obvious one for a Venice otherwise occupied in celebrating its own mythic origins.[8] *Poppea* opened up new possibilities for operatic treatment of material that is the subject of this book. In particular, this opera is interesting as a synthesis of the pattern of Neoplatonic transcendence inherited from the court celebrations with the neo-Stoic moralism that would characterize the myth of the clement prince for later operas.

Robert Donington suggested that the Renaissance Neoplatonism that had been so much a part of sixteenth-century musical stage productions in Florence and elsewhere had disappeared in this opera.[9] Scholarship in the last generation has emphasized instead the importance of neo-Stoicism as the moral backbone of the opera. Ellen Rosand's examinations of the role of Seneca in the opera place his Stoic view at the center of the opera's meaning. Fenlon and Miller have argued for the triumph of Stoic *constantia,* which survives the death of Seneca in the person of Drusilla.[10]

Certainly the Stoic element is important, and I will have more to say about it in connection with the figure of Seneca. Not everyone has been convinced, however, that Stoic values triumph, and some may even feel that the opera has, to adapt Tim Carter's words, been treated with less levity than it deserves.[11] I want to argue that, contrary to Donington's assertion, a Platonic element remains insistently present, that the opera's structure still reflects the late Renaissance, Neoplatonic celebrations of the prince and princess as exemplified in the Florentine court celebrations, and that the opera presents an ironic triumph over Stoic reason and virtue that results from a perverse but ultimately logical combination of ideas inherited from Platonic philosophy. The Platonic idea of love as a vector for the realization of ultimate truth, represented as light, combines readily with the earthbound, narcissistic, and essentially Ovidian passions reconciled through the medium of Plato's own description of the earthly and heavenly Aphrodites in the speech of Pausanias from the *Symposium*. This double identity of Aphrodite (Venus, or Venere, as she appears in this opera) corresponds to Venice's own double identification with Mary, the heavenly Virgin, and Venus the sea-born goddess of eroticism. I preface discussion of the opera, therefore, by a survey of the individual Platonic and Ovidian elements that contribute to the final triumph of Amore in *L'incoronazione di Poppea*.[12]

The Platonic Elements

Representations of the sun and its light as a symbol of the divine, and of divine knowledge, figured importantly in late Renaissance court celebrations and erotic lyric. These images come ultimately from Platonic passages such as the "allegory of the cave" in book 7 of the *Republic* (514a–517a), where the philosopher is required to break free of his earthly chains and make his way past the fire that lights the illusions of this life to the outside. There he can contemplate the pure light of the sun, obliterate the individual self, and be absorbed into transcendental unity.[13] These metaphors, coupled with the ancient Neoplatonic notion of the world as a series of emanations from the godhead via a world spirit to the human soul and finally to life in general, resulted in an image of the light of knowledge penetrating through and giving life to the world. The Renaissance Christian Neoplatonist, inspired by this hybrid of ancient Neoplatonism and the Aristotelian world system, experienced a yearning to get back to the source, his flame attempting to return to the upper spheres of fire and light.[14]

This solar imagery also had a musical dimension, related to the images of the universe available in book 10 of Plato's *Republic* and Cicero's "Dream of Scipio" from the end of his own *Republic*. By these accounts, the universe is a series of concentric planetary spheres—including that of the sun—which, as they turn, create a universal harmony. In the late Renaissance, this combination of images became associated with the ruler: As the sun is the eye and the heart of the universe, so by analogy can the ruler—emperor, king, or grand duke—be the eye and the heart of the state; just as the sun is intimately involved in the harmony of the spheres, so the leader is in the harmony of the state.[15]

In sixteenth-century Florence, where opera was invented, the Medici had associated themselves with the stories and iconography surrounding Apollo because of his connection both with intellectual light and musical harmony.[16] In 1589, for example, Grand Duke Ferdinand had celebrated his wedding to Christine of Lorraine with the well-known set of Neoplatonic intermezzi performed along with Bargagli's comedy *La Pellegrina*. This program, like similar kinds of presentations throughout Renaissance and baroque Europe, through the use of Apolline solar imagery placed the grand duke at the center of state and universe. The wedding was part of the harmony of the universe, bringing security to Florence and ensuring continued prosperity through the couple's offspring.[17]

A second, more individualized application of the Neoplatonic metaphor of sun and light in the Renaissance appears in the literature on love, in both prose treatises and poetic expression. In these cases, the Neoplatonic impulse is related to the idea in Plato's *Symposium* (210a–211e) that love of earthly beauty can lead one to love of abstract beauty and thence to ultimate beauty or Good. Pietro Bembo in 1505 wrote the following in a courtly Neoplatonic treatise on love titled *Asolani*:

> But because the soul dwells for diverse years shut up in this prison of our members, so that as long as we remain children it beholds no light, and later, beset by the host of youthful lusts and losing itself among terrestrial loves, may forget things divine, the sun each day, and the stars each night, and the moon at diverse times appearing recall it after their fashion. For what is their appearing but an eternal voice that cries to us, "Oh fools that vainly dream! . . . Like Narcissus, you feed yourselves on vain desire, and perceive not that these are but the shadows of the true beauty that you forsake. . . . Behold us, goodly creatures that we are, and think how beautiful must be the one of whom we are but ministers.[18]

That is to say, love should properly be directed from earthly beauty to the real beauty of the upper world, which is in the physical world represented by the heavenly lights. Ovid provides a counterexample to the Platonic ideal: Narcissus's self-absorbed passion for his own reflection, focusing attention downward to vain and empty earthly beauty (*Metamorphoses* 3.339–510).

The connection between light, knowledge, and love in the Platonic system is, furthermore, partly the result of the physical nature of sight. According to Plato's *Timaeus*, sight was given to humans by the gods because it is the most intellectual of the senses. It allows humans to contemplate the movements of the sun, stars, and heaven and thus to form ideas about time and number, and it leads most directly to knowledge of the nature of the All (*tes tou pantos phuseos*; 47a–b). Physiologically, sight is an attraction and mingling of different kinds of fire, our own fire of sight stimulated and attracted by natural fire or light:

> So whenever the stream of vision is surrounded by mid-day light, it flows out [from the eyes] like unto like, and coalescing therewith it forms one kindred substance along the path of the eyes' vision, wheresoever the fire which streams from within collides with an obstructing object without. And this substance having become similar in its properties because of its similar nature, distributes the motions of every object it touches, or whereby it is touched, throughout all the body, even unto the Soul, and brings about that sensation which we now term "seeing."[19]

This passage defines the Platonic theory of vision and, preserved in Calcidius's Latin translation of the beginning of *Timaeus*, was one of the few works of Plato to survive antiquity into the Middle Ages in Europe. Any subsequent discussion of sight and its relation to light that involves this combined intromission-extramission theory—that is, the theory that vision is effected by light flowing *from* the eye mixing with light flowing toward it from outside—is descendant from *Timaeus*.[20] Here is one link between Platonic idealism and earthly desire, because the theory results in the poetic conceit that makes love an active force streaming from the eye of the beloved. But earthly desire can also lead to enlightenment from the light of the beloved's eyes and face in the same way that one perceives the truth by contemplating the light of heavenly bodies.

An elaborately developed instance of this ideal love is of course Dante's Beatrice, who is associated with emanations of divine light focused through her beautiful eyes and ultimately leads Dante to heaven. For example, in *Purgatorio* (C. 31.133–38), Dante first sees Beatrice in the garden at the top of the mount of Purgatory, as the three theological Graces dance and sing for her:

> "Turn, Beatrice, oh turn the eyes of grace,"
> was their refrain, "upon the faithful one
> who comes so far to look upon your face.

Grant us this favor of your grace: reveal
your mouth to him, and let his eyes behold
the Second Beauty, which your veil conceals."

"O splendor of the eternal living light!" exclaims Dante the pilgrim as
he looks on Beatrice's face.[21] It is that face and eyes that accustom him
to increasing levels of brightness as he mounts through the spheres of
heaven to a final revelation of the ineffable light of God in the last canto
of *Paradiso* and his vision of a divine love that moves the very cosmos.

In poetry, Platonic notions of sight and ideas about perception of
truth are thus fused with a fascination with eyes of the beloved inherited
from the traditions of courtly love (and ultimately from Ovidian erotic
poetry)[22] to create an idea of the transporting power of the beloved. This
Neoplatonic imagery of sun and light, as applied to both civic and personal relationships, is a significant thematic element in *L'incoronazione
di Poppea* and betrays the opera's debt to the older tradition of Renaissance court celebrations of the prince as sun, while at the same time
expressing the individual passions of the protagonists. It leads naturally
to the comic and cosmic resolution of the union of the sun-king and his
queen in combination with another Platonic idea, the concept of the
heavenly and earthly Venuses or Aphrodites in the *Symposium.*

The *Symposium* consists of a series of accounts concerning the nature of Love, climaxing with Socrates's description of Love as a vector
to the Good. These separate stories about love subsequently developed
individual traditions of their own that could be used without reference
to the dialogue as a whole. Early in the dialogue (180c–185c), the inter-
locutor Pausanias suggests that Love is not a continuum that leads from
physical to spiritual but that there are two kinds of love that are entirely
separate from each other, which he characterizes as the Heavenly (*Ou-
rania*) and Common (*Pandemos*) Aphrodites, each with a corresponding
Eros:

> Does anyone doubt that [Aphrodite] is double? Surely there is the elder,
> of no mother born, but daughter of Heaven, whence we name her Heav-
> enly [*Ourania*], while the younger is the child of Zeus and Dione, and
> we call her Popular [*Pandemos*]. It follows then that of the two Loves
> also the one ought to be called Popular, as fellow worker with the one
> of those goddesses, and the other Heavenly.[23]

The Common Eros is concerned only with indiscriminate physical gratification, and includes physical love of both men and women. Heavenly
Love is concerned only with love between men as a means of expressing
love of Virtue.

Early modern interpretations eliminated the homoerotic aspects of Pausanias's story but still used the description of the two Loves to differentiate realms of erotic and spiritual activity. Common Love was characterized also as Earthly or Impure. Use of the passage in the seventeenth century may be exemplified in Giovanni Pietro Bellori's 1672 analysis of Annibale Carracci's procession of Bacchus and Ariadne on the Farnese ceiling. Bellori describes the painting as an allegory of the quarrel and reconciliation of heavenly love and common (*vulgare*) or earthly (*terrena*) love:

> The painter wished to represent with various symbols the strife and harmony between Heavenly and Common Love, a Platonic division. On the one side he painted Heavenly Love fighting and pulling the hair of Common Love, symbolizing philosophy and the most holy law taking the palm from vice and holding it high. Therefore in the center of the light glows a wreath of immortal laurel showing that victory over irrational appetites elevates man to Heaven. On the other side he symbolized Divine Love taking the torch from Impure Love in order to extinguish it, but Impure Love defends himself and shields it by his side in back. The other two putti embracing are Heavenly and Earthly Love and emotions united with reason, of which virtue and human welfare consist.[24]

Bellori's analysis is probably fanciful as an expression of Carracci's conception of the painting, but the point for us is that within a generation of the composition of *Poppea*, a mythic story about the triumph of divine love could be interpreted as the struggle and ultimate reconciliation of Pausanias's two forms of love. Plato had left their contradictions unresolved. It was in the mood of the baroque to find resolution, and the concept of the two Venuses is the means by which the Ovidian and Platonic loves become reconciled at the conclusion of *Poppea*.

Ovid and the Campaign of Love

The Ovidian metaphor of love as military campaign, which is vital to *Poppea*, found its way into Latin literature through comedy. Plautus and his contemporaries associated love with war, as young men in love competed with amorous soldiers for women and slaves lay metaphorical sieges against old masters to get money to pay for the young men's passions.[25] Latin elegiac poetry picked up the metaphor, and Ovid crystallized the tradition with his *Amores* 1.9.[26] Selections from the first thirty lines are relevant here:

Every lover is a soldier, and Cupid has a camp of his own; Atticus, believe me, every lover is a soldier. . . . Both keep watch through the night; on the ground each takes his rest—the one guards his mistress's door, the other his captain's. . . . The one is sent to scout the dangerous foe; the other keeps his eyes upon his rival as on the enemy. The one besieges mighty towns, the other the threshold of an unyielding mistress; the lover breaks in doors, the soldier, gates. . . . Naturally lovers profit from the husbands' slumbers, and bestir their own weapons while the enemy lies asleep. To pass through companies of guards and bands of sentinels is ever the task both of soldier and of wretched lover. Mars is doubtful, and Venus, too, not sure; the vanquished rise again, and they fall, who you would say could never be brought low.[27]

The first words, "Every lover is a soldier" ("Militat omnis amans"), juxtapose phenomena that ought to be mutually exclusive and, ironically, are not. In the same line Cupid is noted as an active participant in the campaign. Lines 7–8 and 19–22 note the necessity of watching before the door of a lover, a vigil that in its full dramatic form becomes the *paraclausithyron,* or lover's song, before the closed door.[28] Lines 25–28 equate crossing a guarded border and the attack on a sleeping enemy with sneaking in and meeting the beloved while her husband sleeps. Finally, lines 29–30 emphasize the uncertain nature of the whole enterprise.

The connection of Monteverdi's music to Ovidian elegy was direct. His eighth book of madrigals, published in 1638, was titled *Madrigali guerrieri et amorosi* (*Madrigals of War and Love*) and treated love as a matter of campaign and battle. Among these pieces is a setting of Ottavio Rinuccini's adaptation of *Amores* 1.9, which he titled "Ogni amante è guerrier" ("Every lover is a warrior"). The book 8 collection also includes the 1624 "Il combattimento di Tancredi e Clorinda," in which the Christian knight Tancredi fights with and kills the warrior princess Clorinda, unaware that this is also the woman with whom he has fallen in love (see chapter 1).[29] In order to signify the noise and excitement of battle, and by extension the emotional upheaval of love, Monteverdi invented a set of musical techniques for his madrigal texts called the *stile concitato,* or agitated style. This consisted of runs, vigorous series of staccato notes, pizzicato in the strings, and, most distinctively, a series of rapid repetitions on one or two notes, which Monteverdi claimed reproduced the ancient pyrrhic meter. Musical example 1 shows the sixteenth-note repetitions underlining the urgency of battle that resolve into pizzicato, which represents blows from the swords.[30]

Given this background, it was natural and perhaps unavoidable that Poppea's quest for erotic fulfillment and power against considerable odds

Example 1

Monteverdi's Combattimento

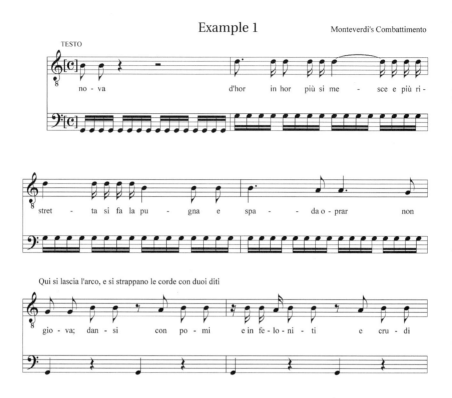

should include aspects of an Ovidian campaign for love. The means by which this earthbound pursuit of love in the opera is reconciled with the language of Platonic idealism to defeat Senecan Stoic virtue is the subject of the rest of the chapter.

L'incoronazione di Poppea

Poppea begins with a prologue in which the allegorical figures of Fortuna and Virtù quarrel over which of them dominates human life. Fortuna declares that Virtù is neglected and useless. Virtù claims that she is the only means to get to Olympus, "the one true ladder to reach highest goals." The debate is interrupted by the boy-god Amore, who says that both goddesses are helpless before him, that he will defeat them both that very day in a contest and put Poppae on the throne. The opera is therefore defined from the start as a contest based on a theoretical discussion of the sources and goals of human behavior. As in Ovid's

Amores 1.9, Amore is to be an active combatant in the campaign of human desire, but here he will even defeat the vagaries of Fortuna rather
than be subject to them. Beyond this, the figures in the prologue have
discernible relations to the classical schools of philosophy: Virtù is
the central goal of Stoicism,[31] represented in the action principally by
Seneca, the Stoic philosopher; Amore, the champion of Poppea, may
represent either a Neoplatonic vector for translation to upper realms
or an earthbound pleasure, as Nerone and several of the servant characters describe him.[32]

The conflicts on earth that are driven by the contest among the deities take the form of a series of interconnected rivalries. Poppea is trying
to take Nerone and the position of empress away from Nerone's lawful,
and initially virtuous, wife Ottavia; Ottone and Nerone are rivals for
Poppea's love; and Ottone divides his interest between Poppea and an
ahistorical attendant of Poppea named Drusilla, who loves him and begs
for his attention.[33] Seneca opposes on ethical grounds Nerone's proposal
to divorce Ottavia and marry Poppea; Nerone forces Seneca to commit
suicide after Poppea has convinced him that Seneca is trying to suborn
him. After the death of Seneca, a desperate Ottavia forces Ottone to attempt to murder Poppea. The ludicrous failure of the plot results in the
banishment of both Ottavia and Ottone. The result of it all is the removal
of the obstacles to the love of Poppea and Nerone and the final unification of the lovers. The dramatic structure is thus fundamentally comic,
however reprehensible the characters and their means of achieving it, and
however much it is overlaid by elements inherited from historiography
and (pseudo-)Senecan tragedy.

Amid the complexities, however, the philosopher Seneca defines
a moral baseline for the opera and for an assessment of the use of the
metaphors of light and their relationship with the action. Naturally
enough, Seneca takes a Stoic approach, but the imagery he uses is that
which we have identified as Platonic. Warned by the goddess Minerva
in I.viii that he will die that very day, he rejoices in a spirit of Stoic
constancy but adds, "After the shadowy days have run their course,
death is the dawn of an infinite day."[34] Just before Seneca's death in act
II, Mercury appears to assure the philosopher that he is heaven-bound
toward the spheres of light: "Happily, therefore; happily ready yourself for the celestial journey, for the sublime passage. I shall show you
the road that leads to the starry Pole." Thus when Nerone's freedman
(Liberto) comes in II.ii to tell Seneca that he must kill himself, Seneca
makes a cheerful reply, and the freedman observes, "As the days depend

upon the sun for their portion of light, so will the writings of others take their light from your writings."

His final scene is a debate on the nature of death with his friends and family, who attempt to convince him not to die.[35] They have learned nothing from him about constancy in the face of death and urge an Epicurean view that the day's light and the pleasures of life end with death, rather than Seneca's vision of an "infinite day":

> This life is too sweet, this sky too bright; every bitterness, every poison, is at last only a slight hindrance. If I lie down for an easy sleep, I get up again in the morning; but a marble tomb never returns what it receives. No, I have no wish to die: don't you die, Seneca, no.

Against such short-sightedness Seneca remains constant, and, as has been noted, his and the deities' position set a standard against which the behavior of the rest of the characters may be judged.[36] Nevertheless, the philosopher's infinite day only comes with his death offstage at the beginning of the second act. His bass vocal range associates him with Monteverdi's previous dramatic figures from the underworld such as Charonte in *Orfeo* and Plutone in *Il ballo delle ingrate*. For the purposes of this opera, he is associated with age and death, and his disappearance is a defeat. In the prologue, Fortuna had observed to Virtù, "Any devotee of yours, who opposes me, is like a painted fire that neither warms nor shines; a color stays hidden/buried for lack of light" ("resta un color sepolto in penuria di luce"). Fortuna's is a morally deficient view—Seneca's teachings will ultimately outlive everyone on stage—but for the life of this drama, it is not Seneca's songs that give warmth, and he does indeed remain buried as that life goes on.[37] Since the structure of the opera is comic, moralizing old age cannot triumph: Seneca stands in a long line of sensible father figures who must somehow be circumvented or removed; his point of view is structurally unsuitable to bear the light and heat of love.[38]

Instead, the images of sunlight and vision that produce warmth are connected with the lovers. That association is made already as the opera begins, with the anticipation of dawn. Ottone approaches Poppea's house and says,

> And so I return here, like a line to the center, like flame to its [fiery] sphere, like a stream to the sea; and though no light appears to me, ah! I know well that the sun is within!
> . . . Open your window, Poppea! With your beautiful face, which holds my fate, my love, anticipate and announce the day! Arise and chase away the darkness and the clouds from the sky with the blessed opening of your eyelids!

Nerone will speak of her later in similar terms, calling her his "Sun" (II.vi), observing that the only proper tribute to her eyes is stunned silence (I.x), and so the opening establishes Poppea as the beloved object in a manner that is consistent throughout the opera. In the meantime, Ottone discovers two guards sleeping outside the house and concludes correctly that their presence means Nerone is enjoying Poppea's favors within. Ottone leaves and they awaken to observe that the first rays of light are dawning.

The mortal campaign of love begins simultaneously with the introduction of the images of light. The guards, wakened by Ottone's laments, give yet a third view of events and of the opera's themes, this time from the perspective of comic servants (I.ii):

> 1.Soldier: The first rays of dawn are appearing.
> 2.Soldier: Get up, wake up at once!
> 1.S.: I haven't slept at all tonight.
> 2.S.: Up! Wake up at once, let's keep to our watch.
> 1.S.: Be damned to Love, Poppea, Nero, Rome, and the army. I cannot gratify my laziness for just an hour, or a day.
> 2.S. Our empress bathes herself in tears, while Nero scorns her for Poppea. Armenia is in rebellion, and he doesn't give it a thought; Pannonia takes up arms and he laughs; thus, as far as I see, the empire goes from bad to worse.

This exchange is a variation on the themes we noted in *Amores* 1.9. Ottone defines his own situation (I.xi): "The doors stand open for Nero, and Ottone is left outside." It is his *paraclausithyron*, as he is closed out and complaining before the door, "keeping an eye on his rival the way a soldier does." But the military half of the metaphor is explicated by real soldiers, who, though they are not the lovers, must nevertheless share Ottone's duty of lying on the cold ground outside the beloved's door. Their agitated music turns into an insistent quarter-note marching rhythm adapted from the *stile concitato* as they discuss military matters (I.ii, mm. 45–46); they point out that Nerone's affair has caused the emperor to neglect real battles in Pannonia and Armenia while he fights love's campaign in Rome. A schism is thus established between Nerone's duties as emperor and his personal interest in Poppea by the contrast between the real and elegiac battles. That schism is emphasized by the word order of the first soldier's curse on all the members of the drama, "A curse on Love, Poppea, Nero and Rome and the Army" ("Sia maledetto Amor, Poppea, Nerone e Roma e la milizia"), in which he brackets the names of Poppea, Nerone, and Rome with the two elements of the elegiac metaphor, *Amor* and *milizia*.

With the dawning of the day appear Poppea and Nerone, but now it is Nerone and not Poppea who is the sun. Poppea says, "Do not go, my lord, oh, do not go. The dawn has scarcely appeared, and you who are my sun incarnate, my tangible light, and the loving day of my life, will you leave me so suddenly?" The opening scenes thus encapsulate the complex of images we have been observing: Poppea is Ottone's sun, the source of light and the place for flame to return. While she sleeps it is dark; when she opens her eyes, light streams forth and the day dawns. Nerone, for his part, is Poppea's sun made flesh, the emanation of true light one can touch ("l'incarnato sole"; "palpabile luce"). He would be the sun-king in a civic conception of the role as conceived in the Renaissance pageants, but his soldiers have already made clear in the previous scene that he has abrogated civic responsibility in favor of his private passions, neglecting armed campaigns against the enemy for Ovidian campaigns of love. Poppea's makes a similar point in the next scene, as the nurse Arnalta undertakes to warn her that playing with royalty is dangerous. Poppea defends her ambitions and speaks of Love's battle. "No, no, I fear no trouble," she says, and the *concitato* marching rhythm returns, this time to underscore her assertion that "Love fights for me, and so does Fortune" ("per me guerregia Amor e la Fortuna"; I.iv, mm. 33–42).[39]

In act II the military metaphor becomes actualized, and something like a real armed conflict occurs. Ottavia, deprived of any external support by Seneca's suicide at the beginning of the act, resorts to blackmail and violence and forces Ottone to attempt to murder Poppea. Ottone comes to Poppea's garden disguised in the clothes of his admirer Drusilla and finds Poppea asleep (II.xii). It is another variation on the elegiac motifs—this time the *exclusus amator* sneaks in, but it is the beloved, not her husband, who is asleep, and Ottone's intent is a malicious and absurd inversion of Tancredi's attack on Clorinda in Monteverdi's "Il combattimento" (chapter 1). Ottone moves to strike Poppea with the words, "Love, farewell, adieu!" But he is, in the event, restrained by love, the god Amore himself, who has arrived (as he explains in the previous scene) to save Poppea "from others' rebellious weapons" ("Ti salverà dagl' armi altrui rubelle"):

> *Ottone.* . . . Poppea, I am killing you: Love, farewell, adieu!
> *Amore.* Madman! Villain! Enemy of my divine power! Do you presume so far? I should strike you with lightening! [*sic*] But you do not deserve to die by divine hands. Go, unhurt by these sharp arrows; I won't deprive the executioner of his tribute.
> *Poppea.* Drusilla! In this way you come, with a bared weapon in your hand, while I'm sleeping alone in the garden?

Arnalta. Hurry, help! Servants, ladies! Follow Drusilla, quick, quick, get the monster! Don't let her escape, after her, after her!
Amore. I have defended Poppea! Now I want to make her empress!

The action of this scene continues the allegory of the prologue: Love literally prevents Ottone from killing Poppea. The nurse Arnalta awakes and calls for reinforcements in marching eighth notes that turn into the sixteenths of the original *stile concitato* as her excitement builds to the climax on "after her!" ("dalli, dalli, dalli!"). Amore then celebrates his victory: Love is indeed "fighting for" Poppea as she said—and "defending" her against the rebellious *exclusus amator,* as it turns out. The insurrections that troubled Armenia and Pannonia in the soldier's complaint now have been transferred to Poppea's household.

Nerone, the lover-warrior, also employs the *stile concitato* to fight as Amore's surrogate on earth.[40] In each case his musical agitation has coincided with a confrontation with one of the obstacles to his union with Poppea. He first uses it with Seneca (I.ix, mm. 107–10) in an argument about morals and power and his intent to divorce Ottone. After Amore foils Ottone's attempt at murder, Nerone expresses his fury against Drusilla, whom he believes guilty of the plot against Poppea, with agitated eighth notes in triple time (III.iii, mm. 34–42). He finally employs it to announce his repudiation of Ottavia, as he condemns her to the mercy of the elements (III.iv, mm. 129ff., esp. 146–47).

Example 2

Monteverdi's Poppea

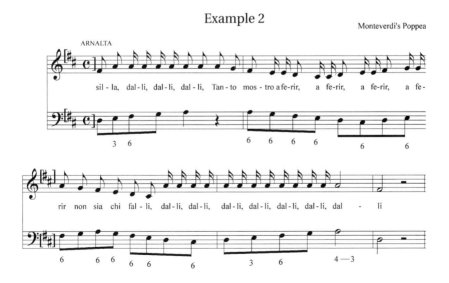

The success or failure of the campaigning lovers is marked by the Platonic images of light and sight. Ottone, rejected by Poppea, concludes (II. viii), "Despise me, hate me as you will, I would be Clytie [the heliotrope] to the sun of your eyes. I will love without hope and in spite of destiny find my delight in hopeless love. I shall cherish the torment born of your lovely face: I shall be damned, yes, but in Paradise!" Ottone can only yearn for the light: He is the heliotrope, which turns to the sun but can neither reach it nor return its heat.[41] It is a feminized image that anticipates his unsuccessful transvestite attempt to murder Poppea. He is not even a genuine blocking figure in the dramatic structure like Seneca, only a passive recipient of the pleasure or displeasure of those around him.[42]

Nerone and Poppea, on the other hand, are reciprocal suns that ultimately unite as one. Before the coronation (III.v), they sing a rapturous duet in which each asserts, "My heart is no longer in my breast: you have stolen it away . . . with the bright clear sky of your eyes: ["de' tuoi begli occhi il lucido sereno"]. . . . If I have lost myself in you, I shall find myself in you, and lose myself in you again, my darling, for I shall find myself lost in you forever." They are the combining lights of the Platonic conception in *Timaeus*: "So whenever the stream of vision is surrounded by mid-day light, it flows out, like unto like. . . . And this substance having become similar in its properties because of its similar nature, distributes the motions of every object it touches, or whereby it is touched, throughout all the body, even unto the Soul, and brings about that sensation which we now term 'seeing.'" Thus the Neoplatonic merging of self into a higher reality, expressed through the image of light, celebrates the comic triumph of the lovers.[43] It is the opposite of Ottone's agonized and unsuccessful self-injunction, "Come back to yourself" ("Torna in te stesso"; I.xii. Their reciprocal and now unified light becomes blinding at the end, as Poppea ascends her throne. Poppea says to Nero, "My mind, bewildered by the unaccustomed light/knowledge [*lume*] is almost at a loss, my Lord, for ways to thank you." Nerone replies, "To fit into your eyes, the sun grew smaller; to nestle on your breast, the dawn left the sky; and to make you queen of women and goddesses, Jove distilled the stars into your lovely face and achieved perfection."

Above it all, however, and controlling it all, hovers the figure of Amore. As we have seen, he reappears in II.xiii for the first time since the prologue to defend the sleeping Poppea from Ottone. Before Ottone enters he declares, "Sleep, Poppea, earthly goddess, Love will save you from others' rebellious weapons, Love who moves the sun and other stars." ("Dormi, Poppea, terrena dea: / ti salverà dagl' armi altrui rubelle. / Amor, che move il sole e l'altre stelle.") These are a very loaded three lines. As we have seen, the epithet "earthly goddess" (*terrena dea*) suggests the Platonic proposition that there are two Venuses, earthly and heavenly. Amore's declaration, "Love will save you from others' rebellious weapons," connects with the Ovidian military theme, the rebellious arms of Pannonia now explicitly changed to those of the battle for love. And most arrestingly, the line "Love who moves the sun and other stars" is not simply one more application of the dominant metaphor of light but an exact quotation of the final line of Dante's *Paradiso* (c. 33.145). Poppea, with her eyes that sparkle with the light of love, is to be seen as an analogue to Dante's Beatrice, and so, at some level, the brightly shining coronation scene, which is blessed by the appearance of Venere and Amore, is to be compared to the final revelation of God and light in Dante's *Divina Commedia*. This comparison of Poppea and Nerone to Beatrice and Dante cannot possibly be serious. Yet so thorough a success must, however cynically and ironically, signal victory over Virtù and the stolid Stoicism of Seneca. Ottavia, too, is gone; Ottone is happily paired with Drusilla and then exiled. The sordid historical deaths of both Poppea and Nerone remain in the unmentioned future.[44] The comic structure is complete, in both dramatic and Dantean senses. Whether we like it or not, Nerone and Poppea have, by their own account at least, returned through the spheres to final light and transfiguration.

But the exaltation is not really of the spirit to heaven—that was the destination of Seneca, the devotee of Virtue. Instead it is to the position of empress and glorification by Amore and Venere, who, like the gods in the Renaissance court pageants, descend to give their blessings. Musically, military *stile concitato* gives way to the fanfare of court ritual: A trumpet figure in the strings ushers Poppea to her coronation and into her new realm (III.viii, mm. 126–29).[45] Amore (and the music) transferred the battle from the military to the domestic front, and with the final victory of Amore and the coronation of Poppea, the schism between the battles of Love and those of the state observed by the guards at the beginning has apparently been closed.

In an article subtitled "How *guerrieri* Are Monteverdi's *madrigali guerrieri*?" Robert Holzer suggests that Monteverdi, like Ovid and other Roman elegiac love poets, talks about war only to reject it. He suggests that Monteverdi used the *stile concitato*, as he consolidated that style in the book 8 madrigals, only to back away from writing about war at all.[46] *L'incoronazione di Poppea* appears to be very much in that same spirit: Nero's refusal to worry about real wars on the empire's borders is consonant with Monteverdi's and Busenello's refusal on a poetic and musical level to use warlike material—stories of empire and music in pyrrhic meter—to speak of real wars. Instead of that, they assert the victory of Love and the defeat of Virtue and Fortune; the state and the lovers celebrate that victory together.[47]

And yet, it is difficult not to become lost in the triumph of eroticism at the end of the opera, however we may feel that its celebrants are awful people and their means and goals utterly reprehensible. They have lovely words and beautiful music to sing. The other voices—the sepulchral bass of Seneca, the mezzo of Ottone, and the competing soprano Ottavia—have been banished from the scene, and we are left at last with the two soprano voices rising to a welcoming heaven. For this is Poppea's embodiment as the Platonic *terrena dea* and the triumph of the Platonic, in however ironic a mode. Amore, Amorini, and Venere descend to proclaim that Poppea is the earthly Venus. Amore sings, "Mother, mother, by your leave, you are Poppea in heaven, and this woman is Venus on earth." Nerone and Poppea, protégés of a transcendent Amore, are virtually apotheosized into the Platonic realm of light before our eyes, and their drama ends not in the Aristotelian night of a single dramatic day but in blazing noon. It is not far from Donington's "sacred marriage" (above, note 11), a fact that must finally intensify the irony. We may very well concur with the First Soldier's exclamation, "A curse on Love, Poppea, Nero and Rome and the Army."

An old scholarly debate about which character is the hero of the opera has variously identified Nerone, Seneca, or Ottone. Perhaps out of moral distaste, Poppea was largely left out of the discussion. But if we must chose a hero in an opera titled *The Coronation of Poppea,* in which the prologue makes the coronation the goal of the plot and the *scena ultima* celebrates the achievement of that goal, that hero should surely be Poppea herself. Characters who disappear in the second act or are banished from the stage before the end cannot be regarded the heroes of what is structurally a comedy.

The carnivalesque mockery of the opera is all the greater for the fact that Poppea, triumphant and identified with the Platonic heavenly and earthly Venuses, also matches the mythicized self-representation of Venice in the early modern period. Venice counted itself protected by the Virgin Mary, the Queen of Heaven, and identified itself with Venus, born from the sea, whose planet was in ascendancy on March 25, the traditional founding date of the city.[48] Together the two images reflected the divine and the licentious aspects of the Venetian image for the Venetians themselves and for their foreign visitors. If Seneca and Virtue are victims of this opera, their persecutors, blessed by Venere and Amore, are to be associated not only with a corrupted Tacitean Rome but also even more with the *Serenissima Repubblica* herself. Seen from this perspective, *L'incoronazione di Poppea* is a wickedly funny reply in a dialogue with Giulio Strozzi's *La finta pazza* and *La finta savia*, which glorified the connections between ancient Rome and contemporary Venice.

Stoicism as an Emerging Theme

My conclusion thus differs from that of Fenlon and Miller, who suggest that "the European intellectual movement of Tacitism and Senecan Neostoicism provides the general conceptual framework for *Poppea*."[49] Nevertheless, Seneca and his Stoic views of life and death are forces to be reckoned with, despite their very thorough defeat by the combined forces of a libertine Amore, comic structure, and festival celebration. The criticisms leveled at him by the other characters have sometimes been taken seriously by critics of the opera and, after all, reflect an ambivalent attitude toward Seneca's life in the ancient sources, which record accusations of greed, toadying, personal aggrandizement, and hypocrisy.[50] In this opera, however, Seneca himself is entirely self-consistent. He tells Ottavia to thank fortune for the blows that will prove her virtue (I.vi); this is cold comfort, but it is advice he follows in his own case. He is calm and even happy in the face of death, reminding his *famigliari* not to forget the precepts he has taught them (II.iii). If he is mocked or ignored by many of the characters, that does not make him wrong, or a failure. It is the lot of the prophet not to be believed or honored. At crucial moments, his virtue and its reward in heaven are asserted by Minerva and Mercury, who stand in moral authority above the abstract deities of the prologue and Amore. Mercurio says Seneca is the true friend of heaven and his virtues capable of making him a god. ("The sovereign virtue in which you abound makes gods of mortals"; II.i.)

Monteverdi's Seneca is a Stoic *sapiens*, a saintly wise man of the sort that Cicero, in his widely read *On Duties*, declared was most estimable but for the most part not possible for the human race to imitate in their day-to-day lives (Cicero, *De Officiis* 3.13–18). His choice for virtue in the opera is the analogue to Hercules's choice at the crossroads, also described in *On Duties* (chapter 1). Seneca, therefore, departs to heaven, leaving the rest of the cast to make whatever compromises they can with reality.

As we observed, the Liberto tells Seneca that "the writings of others will take their light from your writings. Die happily." This is part of Seneca's private triumph, since what the Liberto says is perfectly true: The importance and pervasive influence of his works for medieval and early modern Europe are witnessed by the very fact that he appears in this opera to be mocked as well as praised. More narrowly it is also true for the genre of opera as it developed for the next century and a half. The Stoic notions of constancy, clemency, and friendship, here raised only to be defeated, become the moral basis for eighteenth-century serious opera. This, I believe, is the most deeply rooted contribution of *Romanitas* in early opera, since it is expressed even in operas that have nothing to do with the Romans themselves. Histories of opera explain that the reform of opera occurred when the Arcadians met French neoclassical tragedy.[51] This is true, but the impulses central to that reform were already latent in the earliest Venetian operas, and the librettos of Zeno and then Metastasio capitalized on what was already present in opera texts as much as they imported new ideas of dramaturgy from France. The moralities in the Stoic-romantic tragedies that Racine perfected were simultaneously and independently being explored in Italy on the opera stage.

The Stoic elements of this drama would not always be so evident in the extravaganzas produced in the next few decades, however, but they remain present, sometimes only as a counterexample embedded in the otherwise expansive romantic free-for-alls. The figure of Seneca occasionally appears as a sensible adviser in the Nero operas produced throughout the century to the 1690s. In Cavalli's *Scipione affricano*, as we will see in the next chapter, Cato the Elder appears as a similar adviser figure.

3 *Scipio in Africa*

MINATO/CAVALLI, *SCIPIONE AFFRICANO*

Nicolò Minato's *Scipione affricano* was first performed in 1665 to music by Fancesco Cavalli in Venice at the Teatro SS. Giovanni e Paolo.[1] It was an immediate success. Revivals of the libretto with Cavalli's music took place in Ancona (1666), Naples (1667), Ferrara (1669), Florence (1669), and Bologna (1670). It found its way to Rome in 1671, where it was dedicated to Queen Christine of Sweden and augmented with music by Stradella. Later productions took place in Perugia (1677, titled *Il trionfo della continenza*) and Venice (1678, with music added by Viviani). This second Venetian production gave a significant boost to the career of the castrato Giovanni Francesco Grossi, whose performance as the Numidian prince Siface was such a success that he subsequently took Siface as his stage name.[2] There was a German version of the opera in 1690 and a production in Milan in 1692.[3]

The libretto is dedicated to Lorenzo Onofrio Colonna, "Prencipe Romano, Grande di Spagna di Prima Classe, Gran Contestabile del Regno di Napoli, ecc." Colonna and his wife Maria Mancini Colonna were active patrons of the arts whose connections with both Minato and Cavalli were close during the 1660s and 1670s. In the next season, in 1666, three of four operas produced in Venice were dedicated to the Colonna circle.[4] Lorenzo Colonna, from the important Roman Colonna family, had strong connections to the Spanish Habsburgs, who were at that time in control of Naples and its holdings in southern Italy and Sicily. Five years earlier, in 1660, Lorenzo Colonna went to Madrid to thank Philip IV for his appointments as a grand constable of the Kingdom of Naples and the Habsburg honor (*dignità*) of the order of the Toson d'Oro, or Golden Fleece.[5] The subject of *Scipione affricano*, therefore, suits its dedicatee admirably, since it features Scipio, himself a *prencipe Romano*, whom the Habsburgs counted among their ancestors and who in the course of his early campaigns had had significant dealings with Spanish nobility.[6]

Scipio, the Spanish Maiden, and the African Queens

The military exploits of Publius Cornelius Scipio Africanus the Elder (236–183 B.C.E.), which culminated in North Africa with his defeat of Hannibal in 203 B.C.E., achieved mythic proportions that persisted well into the modern era. When Scipio's career began, however, he was neither "Africanus" nor "the Elder."[7] At the age of eighteen he was said to have made a dramatic rescue of his father from Hannibal's troops on the battlefield at the Ticinus River (218 B.C.E.). Eight years later he was sent to Spain, where he led a brilliant campaign, capturing the Carthaginians' central depot of New Carthage (modern Cartagena) in a surprise move and then decisively defeated the Carthaginian forces at Ilipa.

It was during the Spanish campaign that an episode known as the "Continence of Scipio" was said to have taken place. After the capture of New Carthage, Scipio's soldiers presented him with a beautiful young Celtiberian noblewoman found among the captives. Scipio was attracted: The historian Polybius (10.19) notes that he was *philogynes*, "fond of women." He nevertheless refused to treat her as captured booty and returned her to the local prince named Allucius, to whom she was betrothed, providing the ransom money brought by her father as a dowry. Livy (26.50) reports that the grateful young man forthwith "filled the ears of his people with the well-deserved praises of Scipio: a most godlike young man had come, who carried all before him not only by arms but also with generosity and kindly actions."

Minato's libretto is set seven years later, in 203 B.C.E., when the Roman army under Scipio in North Africa successfully defeated Hannibal at Zama and won the war. In the process of the African campaign, Masinissa, a local prince of the Numidian people allied with Rome, had conquered a rival king named Syphax. Syphax had been a Roman ally but was turned to support the Carthaginian cause when he married the beautiful and dynamic Sophonisba, daughter of the Carthaginian general Hasdrubal. Masinissa marched on Syphax's capital city and was met by Sophonisba. Livy tells us that her impassioned supplication to Masinissa that he not hand her over to the Romans began to sound more like seduction than pleas. Masinissa lost his head, for "as the Numidian race is very inclined to erotic passion, the victor was captured by love for his captive" ("amore captivae victor captus").[8] Masinissa fulfilled Sophonisba's wishes by marrying her at once, thereby preventing the Romans from taking her captive. Scipio, concerned about what he had heard from the captured Syphax about Sophonisba's charms and her ability to rally her fellow Africans against the Romans, and less than sympathetic because of his own continent behavior in Spain, took Masinissa aside and somewhat ponderously shamed him for his precipitate passion (30.14.3). Sophonisba, says Scipio, belonged as spoil to the Roman people.

The remorseful Masinissa returned to his quarters and sent a cup of poison to Sophonisba, indicating that although he could not save her, at least he could provide her with the means to prevent her from becoming the Romans' captive. Her reply to the messenger was short and biting (30.15.7–8): "I accept your wedding gift, not without gratitude, if a husband could give his wife no greater gift. But tell him this: I would have died better if I had not married at my own funeral." Then, says Livy, "[w]ith as much fierce courage as that with which she spoke, she took and fearlessly drank down the cup, showing not a sign of consternation."

Sophonisba dies by suicide, with all the ambiguous pleasure that act provokes: sorrow at the death of a beautiful and noble queen, along with the (male) satisfaction at having a (female) threat removed.[9] This esthetic pleasure was exploited in the early modern period in spoken drama in treatments by, among others, Giangiorgio Trissino (1515), John Marston (1606), Jean de Mairet (1634), Pierre Corneille (1663), and Nathaniel Lee (1675).[10] Trissino and Mairet are perhaps most significant because they were the first neoclassical tragedies written in Italian and French. The story also generated a series of historical paintings on the death of Sophonisba.[11] In Rutilio Manetti's painting (fig. 4), Sophonisba stands center with the goblet of poison raised; the grieving Masinissa turns aside on the right.

Livy's account of Sophonisba's story stands on its own as an affecting narrative, but his Sophonisba's combination of destructive threat and admirable courage is deliberately evocative of another African queen who had similarly threatened Rome and died courageously in the aftermath: Cleopatra VII of Egypt.[12] From 48 until 31 B.C.E., Cleopatra maintained Ptolemaic Egypt as a kingdom separate from the Roman empire, in part through sexual alliance and political union with Julius Caesar and then Marc Antony. When in 31 B.C.E. Cleopatra and Antony failed to defeat the forces of Octavian, Cleopatra, fearful that she, like her sister Arsinoë before her, would be led in chains in a Roman triumphal procession, committed suicide by means of her famous asp.

Figure 4. Rutilio Manetti, Masinissa e Sofonisba, *before 1625. Photo courtesy of Scala, Art Resource, New York.*

The story of Cleopatra's struggle for political survival quickly became legendary. Her dramatic death generated a strong immediate reaction from Horace in his *Ode* 1.37, in which he managed simultaneously to condemn and admire the queen. For him she was "a mad queen / with her contaminated flock of men / diseased by vice . . . preparing the ruin of the Capitol and the destruction / of [Roman] power." But when it came to the end, she behaved as nobly as a Roman:

> Daring to gaze with face serene upon her ruined palace,
> and brave enough to take deadly serpents
> in her hand, and let her body
> drink their black poison,
> fiercer she was in the death she chose, as though
> she did not wish to cease to be a queen, taken to Rome
> on the galleys of savage Liburnians,
> to be a humbled woman in a proud triumph.[13]

Cleopatra's proud desire for death rather than humiliation in a Roman triumphal procession remained a subject for art and literature, her anxiety and revulsion finding vivid expression, for example, in Shakespeare's *Antony and Cleopatra* (V.ii.55–62):

> *Cleopatra*: Shall they hoist me up
> And show me to the shouting varletry
> Of censuring Rome? Rather a ditch in Egypt
> Be gentle grave unto me! Rather on Nilus' mud
> Lay me stark nak'd and let the waterflies
> Blow me into abhorring! Rather make
> My country's high pyramides my gibbet
> And hang me up in chains![14]

In Minato's libretto, as we will see, it is particularly the fear of capture and public humiliation that drives the formal laments of both Sophonisba and Syphax and is transformed into a governing metaphor, once again through the agency of Ovid, for the erotic complications that involve Scipio in his own battle for self-control. Related to Sophonisba and Cleopatra is another African queen, Vergil's Carthaginian Dido from *Aeneid* 4. A fictional analogue to Cleopatra, she is a threat to the future of Rome because her sexual attraction keeps Aeneas from his duty and because she is the ancestress of Hannibal; her life ends in suicide and a curse against Aeneas and his descendants.[15] All three of these women—Sophonisba, Cleopatra, and Dido—as they are constructed in ancient literature, participate in a Roman stereotype of the North African femme fatale, dangerous to susceptible Roman males or their allies but admirable for the heroic way in which each goes to her well-deserved demise.

For early modern Europe, Cleopatra and Dido stood as strong, parallel figures whose cases might be alluded to or even merely hinted at to add poignancy, exotic color, or menace to a dramatic depiction of Sophonisba. The parallel is exploited, for example, in two spoken tragedies on the Sophonisba story, both formative for their respective national dramas: Giangiorgio Trissino's *Sofonisba* (1515) and Jean de Mairet's *Sophonisbe* (1634).[16]

The sources and background for *Scipione affricano* are therefore quite different from those of *Poppea*, consisting of Livy's essentially positive portrait of Roman destiny in his *Ab Urbe Condita* and, as I believe, resonances of Vergil's *Aeneid* in the presentation of both the hero Scipione and of the unfortunate Sofonisba. As in *Poppea*, there is a Stoic atmosphere, inherited from the serious source material, that plays off against comic and Ovidian erotic plotlines. This time, however, the Stoicism takes a more positive role in the conclusion in a way that was to become standard in the next century.

Scipione affricano takes place during fictionalized public demonstrations of Rome's victory over Carthage, although Hannibal never appears and is not mentioned. Scenes of public spectacle frame the action: It opens with gladiatorial combat celebrating the victory, set as a ballet, followed by a pact of truce between Scipione and Asdrubale (Hasdrubal). A scene of prophecy of the greatness of Rome closes the second act, and the *scena ultima* is preceded by the burning of the Carthaginian navy at Scipione's orders.

Two erotic plots are played out within the frame of these public events. Minato makes the relationship of Siface (Syphax) with Sofonisba the romantic backbone of the opera. Siface, captured by the Romans and imprisoned in a tower, observes that his beloved Sofonisba is being kept from the Romans by Massanissa [*sic*], who has fallen in love with her. The furious Siface makes a dramatic escape from the tower using his bedclothes as a parachute. He spends the rest of the opera disguised as a slave while attempting to rescue Sofonisba from the clutches of Massanissa. Massanissa, for his part, engages in several subterfuges in order to keep Sofonisba out of the hands of Scipione, who demands her as a prize of war. At the end, Siface exposes Massanissa's duplicity to Scipione, recovers Sofonisba, and is rewarded for bravery with the return of both his wife and his kingdom.

Minato provided a counterpoint to the more serious Siface-Sofonisba plot by transferring the Continence of Scipio story from Spain to the shores of North Africa and turning it into a comedy of disguise. Ericlea, a beautiful Carthaginian captive, catches Scipione's eye, but she informs him that she is already engaged to a Spanish nobleman named Lucejo, whom she has never met. Lucejo arrives on the scene disguised as a servant named Eurillo, while his brother, Polinio, pretends to be Lucejo. Ericlea of course falls in love with the real Lucejo and, until she discovers the ruse, is much tormented by the fact that she has fallen in love with a servant. She becomes involved in the Sofonisba plot when letters are mixed up, and she mistakenly believes that Scipione wants her to take poison meant for Sofonisba. In the end, the facts come out, and the *scena ultima* includes the union of Ericlea and Lucejo in the manner of the Continence narrative.

Vergil, Ovid, and the Triumph of Love

Livy's elegant phrase "Amore captivae victor captus," which reflects the concerns of the love poetry of Livy's own day, also summarizes the organizing concerns of Minato's libretto. As in *Poppea*, love in the time of war transforms into a metaphorical battle for love. A significant difference here is that Scipione struggles for self-control in a way that never troubles Nerone but is more reminiscent of Ottone's self-injunction, "Come back to yourself." The following discussion examines further poetic background for this erotic battle and its expression through images of chains and captivity.

The metaphorical link that Monteverdi's *Poppea* exploits between love and war, if natural enough, is not automatic. Vergil, the greatest poet of Roman imperial aspirations, had begun his *Aeneid* with an announcement of his subject that had everything to do with fate, duty, and hardship and nothing to do with love (*Aeneid* 1.1–7):

> Arms I sing, and a man [*Arma virumque cano*], who first came, Fate's fugitive, from the shores of Troy to Italy and the Lavinian coast—that man, tossed about on land and sea by the gods' violence, because of the unforgetting anger of fierce Juno; he endured much also in war, until he could found a city, bring his household goods to Latium, whence came the Latin race, our ancestors from Alba Longa, and the walls of high Rome.

By the end of the poem, Aeneas's love affair with Dido notwithstanding, nothing has changed. Before entering the final battle of the epic, Aeneas tells his son Ascanius (12.435–36), "My son, from me learn manly effort and hard work; good luck from others."[17] This duty to labor and suffering is societal as well as personal. We noted in chapter 1 Anchises's summation of the Roman "arts," to "impose the custom of peace, spare the humbled and beat down the haughty" (*Aeneid* 6.851–53). Such injunctions bring responsibility for conquest and rule but have no brief for enjoyment of the spoils.

The strong sense of Stoic duty in the *Aeneid*, as well as its preoccupation with the Augustan virtues of courage, clemency, piety, and justice, had a lasting influence on the presentation of the ideals of power by those who held imperial authority throughout the early modern period; those Vergilian ideals are thus a regular concern of the characters in early operas written with an intent to celebrate aristocratic and imperial sponsors. The figure of Scipio was no exception to this; already Vergil's contemporaries had suggested the parallels between Scipio and Aeneas. P. G. Walsh has observed, "Livy's Stoic outlook sees Scipio in the same way as Vergil depicts Aeneas—as a man of fate destined to lead Rome to enhanced greatness."[18] The impulse persists to present Scipio as a Stoic hero even as Minato introduced him to the operatic stage in a carnivalesque version of his story.

By contrast, the younger poet Ovid had to look over his shoulder at Vergil, as did every Latin poet of his and subsequent generations. He began his collection of elegiac love poetry titled *Amores* with a conscious echo of the *Aeneid*'s first line, claiming that he, too, had tried to write epic poetry. But Cupid himself prevented it (1.1–4):

> Arms and violent wars with a heavy beat [*Arma gravi numero violentaque bella parabam*]: I was all ready to produce it, with the matter suited to the medium. The second line was of equal length to the first—but, as the story goes, Cupid laughed and stole a foot.[19]

The god of love reduced Ovid's intended epic hexameters to elegiac couplets, and so Ovid's genre must change, too. Epic war and elegiac love are not compatible, it appears, and one must choose between them.[20] But though Ovid writes elegy, he nevertheless imagines himself in the same poem as the victim of a weapon common to love and war, the bow of Cupid (21–24):

> I'd made my complaint, when straightaway the god chooses darts from his open quiver made for my destruction. Powerfully he bent the curved bow on his knee and said, "Poet, receive the stuff that you're to sing!"

By the ninth poem of *Amores* 1, as we saw in chapter 2, the disjunction between the two genres and activities becomes illusory. "Every lover is a soldier," Ovid asserts: Though a serious soldier in the Augustan mold may not be a lover, a serious lover is a soldier, his campaign every bit as arduous, the consequences nearly as dire, and Love himself is armed with a dangerous weapon.

The Ovidian poetic language of love and war applied to the events of *Scipione affricano* takes a different turn than it had in *Poppea*. Carthage has been defeated and the battle is over for everyone but the gladiators who dance their combat in the first scene. This has important repercussions for the direction and spirit of the drama. With the war lost and won, there is no danger of failure or death to the Roman side, no serious challenge to Scipione's power or possibility of Carthaginian success. Death, should it come to any of the participants, would be the death of a captive or subject, not a hero's death on the battlefield for a cause deeply felt. With the events in the public sphere all but settled and largely the object of celebratory spectacle, the drama is freed to explore the private relations between captors and captives, and in particular their erotic attractions and repulsions. Or, to put it a different way, Minato and Cavalli were adapting Scipio Africanus's life to the genre of opera, which demanded musical exposure of private, and particularly romantic, feelings as well as a festive conclusion; in doing so, they chose to eliminate the actual danger of battle and concentrated instead on the results of victory and defeat.

Thus much of the libretto's poetic language, reflecting the events of the plot, is of victory, capture, and defeat rather than the active campaign of *Poppea*. The dominant imagery continues to have its source in Ovidian elegy, with the metaphor of love as war reaching its logical conclusion. In *Amores* 1.2, Ovid imagines himself a captive in the triumphal procession of a victorious Amor (lines 19–22, 27–34, 49–52):

> All right, I yield! Cupid, I am your new prize; I stretch my conquered hands out to your governance. No need for war—I ask for forgiveness and peace. Disarmed and conquered by your arms, I'm no source of praise for you. . . . Boys and girls will be led, captives all. This procession will be a glorious triumph for you. I myself, a recent prize, will wear my fresh wound, and bear my chains with the mind of a new captive. Sanity herself will be led, her hands tied behind her back, and Chastity, too, and whatever else stands in the way of Cupid's army. Everyone will fear you; the mob, stretching its arms out to you will shout "Io triumphe!" at the top of their lungs. . . . And so, though I can be part of the sacred triumph, victorious one, don't waste your force on me. Look at the happy arms of your brother Caesar—*he* protects his captives with the hand that conquered them.

As participant in an erotic fantasy, the Roman Ovid gleefully submits to the humiliation that the foreign queens Sophonisba and Cleopatra had feared for themselves in the real world of defeat and conquest. When Love is the conquering warrior, his victims become the spoils, captives bound by chains in the triumphal procession, objects of curiosity to the celebratory mob. Admitting his defeat by Amor-Cupido, Ovid only asks that the god have mercy in the same way that Augustus Caesar is supposed to have had mercy on his own real captives of war. This is an entertaining inversion of the Augustan program spelled out by Anchises's injunction to spare the humble. In Minato's libretto, Ovid's joyous inversion of Vergilian and Stoic virtues of clemency and self-restraint informs the language and visual representation of the plot's dilemmas.

Chains, Poison, and the Archer God: The Images of Captivity

In *Scipione affricano*, as in Livy's narrative, the phrase "*Amore captivae victor captus*" applies to Masinissa, but unlike in Livy, it describes Scipione as well. Furthermore, the opera dwells on the plights of captive lovers and the possible erotic relationships between victor and vanquished. For the North Africans, the issues of defeat, captivity, and humiliation are very real, causing loss of liberty and separation of lovers. For Scipione, the victorious Roman, the issue is metaphorical, his struggle philosophical, and his notions of chains and love derived ultimately from poetic imagery rather than reality. These permutations of Livy's and Ovid's theme of "*Amore captus*" serve to evoke the expectations of a racial inclination to lust and deceit in Minato's North Africans, only to overturn those expectations in every case but Massanissa's. For Scipione, the Ovidian themes serve as a dangerous challenge to his struggle to fulfill a Vergilian ideal of a Roman hero.

The opera, like the *Aeneid*, opens with an insistence on the preeminence of Rome through the wishes of an active Fate. The chorus of the *Popolo* sings, "Long live Scipione! . . . The Latins' Fate has conquered, and Destiny sides with Roman triumphs!"[21] Scipione replies, "The victories of the Tiber—Fate demands them, Fortune requires them. He who girds himself for battle for the Roman Empire does nothing other than reach for the gifts of Destiny."[22] This begins a constant drumbeat on the theme of *destino, sorte,* and *fortuna* throughout the play, for if Scipione's and Rome's fate is positive, that of its captives is not and is the subject of constant regret and lament by all the defeated Africans, for it has led them to bondage.

The point is strikingly made in the recitative at the beginning of I.iii, following the gladiatorial ballet, as Ericlea's entry makes visual some of the central issues of the opera:

> *Ericlea lifting her chained hands toward some soldiers. Scipione, Catone, Soldiers, Captains, People [of Carthage].*
> Ericlea. Let me be, fools. Give me those chains. Let no one else presume to take me to the great Scipio. *She goes before Scipio.* Unconquered general of Rome, victor over the fiercest kingdoms, you have subdued Carthage. I too am your subject amidst the general ruin. But let others with unsteady wills yield to force; I yield to nobility. In accepting my chains, I disdain to grant the honor of my imprisonment to those men. I claim the prize of voluntary servitude. Here are my chains, here my foot, here my spirit.
> Scipione. *(aside)* What an alluring siren! *(aloud)* Let the chains be cast off; rise. Let your noble soul not see a discourteous heart in my breast.

Ericlea's chains make a strong visual statement about the predicament of the North Africans, but her pride and her unwillingness to endure humiliation is equally powerful. She will yield of her own accord, but not, like others, to physical compulsion; her submission to Scipione's nobility ("*merto*") is symbolized by the control she takes of her chains. Scipione is smitten, and the removal of Ericlea's chains, a signifier of his respect for the nobility of his female captive, also connotes his attraction to her. It is an important moment, for it lays the foundation for the crisis in act III, when Sofonisba's chains and poison, transferred accidentally to Ericlea, generate an impassioned scene between Ericlea and Scipione.

The anguish at defeat and capture, and the fear of public humiliation, also drives the laments of Siface and Sofonisba. Siface sings as a captive in his tower in I.iv/v:[23]

> *Siface*: [*aria*] Tell me, Heaven, if it is the same destiny that made me King, and, unlucky and cruel, has now bound my feet in chains. [*recit.*] Unfortunate Siface! In a few moments I lost my kindom, wife and liberty; only so much of the world remains as—oh God!—the amount a short chain can measure.[24]

Cavalli's music emphasizes the image of the chain by repeating the phrase "unlucky and cruel Destiny now has bound my feet in chains" ("infausto e crudo [Destin] adesso mi legò tra ferri 'l piè"). Sofonisba, for her part, faces a double threat: fear of chains and humiliating triumph and unwelcome passion on the part of Massanissa. Her anxiety about being exhibited as a prisoner of war sounds a note familiar from the stories of Cleopatra and Sophonisba:

> My lost kingdom doesn't trouble me and an unconquered heart knows well how to forget. But that the Tiber should see me adorn Africanus's triumph, and the Roman mob point me out as their wretched slave: this is enormous grief, infinite pain.

But even more important to her than her liberty is her fidelity to Siface. She declares to Massanissa, who has rescued her from the Romans but has fallen in love with her, "Restrain these indecent endearments, Massanissa, which are worse for me than any chains."

Nominal freedom from Roman chains is therefore only the means to another form of captivity, both for Sofonisba while under the protection of Massanissa and for Ericlea under the protection of Scipione. True liberty includes freedom of association as well as movement. Ericlea pleads with Scipione, "Oh, if you have left me the freedom of my body, with your noble victory, leave me also the liberty of my soul" (III.xviii). Freedom for her can only come if the soul that she had publicly yielded to Scipione in the first scenes is rendered back again.

The male victors Massanissa and Scipione, on the other hand, believe themselves to be taken captive by an armed and bellicose Amore. Massanissa in II.xiv reflects unhappily on the rout of his reason by the armed god: "With the sharpest arrow of gold you pierce the toughest soul, whence its resolve is put to flight and destroyed."[25] Massanissa's predicament is what one might expect from the ancient sources. What has changed is that Massanissa's passion is a secondary reflection of Scipione's, and there is an irony in the Roman's own immediate susceptibility to behavior usually attributed to the racial stereotype of the North African. In I.iii, Scipione's attraction to Ericlea is instantaneous, as signified by his command to remove Ericlea's chains, and in his agitated mind their roles are reversed. He complains in an aria that he has been the victim of arrows sharper than the Scythian's and, having avoided the ravages of Mars, is made prisoner by Cupid (I.xiii/xiv):

> Two pretty little eyes shoot darts sharper than Scythian arrows.
>   The blindfolded god takes more prisoners with hair that's curled than Mars does with his battle ranks.[26]

His aria is set in a rapid 4/4 and extends the military images of the arrow (saetta) and battle ranks (schiere) with two-bar ornaments, then it repeats the final lines of the two stanzas to emphasize the greater dangers of beautiful eyes and hair. The instrumental ritornello suggests Scipione's agitation as the two violin parts sometimes play in unison and sometimes pursue one another, answering quarter and eighth notes with sixteenth-note runs. The emotional effect is heightened by the fact that this is the first aria in the opera with such rapid forward motion.

By the end of the scene, Scipione admits defeat to the god's weapons and surrenders. In the recitative that concludes the scene, he effectively reverses the conditions of victory and defeat, as he apostrophizes the absent Ericlea: "I'll give you the spoils, I'll give you soldiers, arms, and peoples as you will. All that I have, you can dispose. Ask what you want, O lovely one. I'll give you my heart. (To himself) But where is the madness of the archer boy leading me?" Another lyrical outburst by Scipione reinforces the point a few scenes later (I.xvii):

> If the god of war did not know how to triumph over me, I will be prisoner of a naked archer.
>   If the passion of a fierce god did not harm me, a lusty infant will be able to make me a lover.[27]

The final positions of "prisoner" (prigioniero) and "lover" (amante) in their two verses link these two conditions. Cavalli's score climaxes on the final words of each verse, "prigioniero" and "amante," then descends again with a quick ornament to a four-count hold on the final syllable. In contrast to the conquered Sofonisba, who had preferred sexual self-control to her freedom, Scipione appears to give up his self-control in favor of being a prisoner. His transition from Vergilian to Ovidian sensibility seems complete, and it becomes embarrassing to the point where his adviser Catone must scold him, employing the dominant military imagery (III.xi): "And so, should the unbeaten conqueror of proud Africa have fallen, pierced through with the lightening [*sic*] bolt of two eyes? Should the conquered, in wicked fashion, have carried chains on their feet while triumphing over your heart?"

The themes of captivity and freedom, with the attendant images of chaining and humiliation, finally reach fulfillment in act III, as the drama comes to the famous moment when Sofonisba is given the choice between captivity and death. Here is where Minato's invention in combining the two stories is particularly brilliant, for the crucial moment goes awry, as once again stage props become important visual signifiers of personal dilemmas.

In III.iv Scipione and Ericlea sing a duet at cross purposes.[28] For Ericlea the sharp arrows of love are sweet, now that she knows that the "servant" she loves is really her betrothed Lucejo. For Scipione, Love's arrows are fierce and a source of torment, since he feels honor-bound not to act upon his passion for Ericlea. Scipione expresses his feelings in military terms: He is defeated, cast to earth by her beauty and her two eyes, which have done what no army could. She describes herself as a *serva* and *vinta*, unworthy of his attention but destined for another, and asks to be given to Lucejo. Scipione is unable do it in person, and he tells her in agonized accompanied recitative to return and learn his decision from a letter.

Unaware of the ironic similarity of his own emotional state with that of Massanissa, Scipione reverts to his Livian model. In the following scene (III.v), he turns on Massanissa, in businesslike recitative condemns his treachery in withholding Sofonisba for himself, and demands she be handed over. Massanissa weeps but subsequently is unable to tell Sofonisba what her fate is and asks *her* to return for a letter. Accordingly, in III.viii both Scipione and Massanissa leave letters of instruction for their respective ladies. Massanissa's letter is accompanied by chains and a cup of poison, physical objects that once again make visual the verbal images that have accumulated since the first scene.

The historic narrative is being followed pretty closely at this point, but in III.ix things go awry. In the manner of comedy more than of tragedy, the letters get mixed up and Ericlea, finding the letter, chains, and poison of Massanissa, believes they are the message left for her by Scipione:

But what deadly scenery do I find here, oh Heavens? A vessel, chains and a letter. Ah, perhaps these are the writings of Scipione? [She reads.] "Either with these chains in bitter fate bind yourself as a prisoner, or drink down death with this poison." Wretched me, what is this I hear? Do you take back your gifts so cruelly, wicked Roman? Do you imitate the example of the blind, inexorable Goddess, luring the unhappy to you and then tormenting them? This is the freedom, this the husband for which you have saved me?[29]

This is the familiar scene in a drama or painting about Sofonisba, in which Massanissa presents the heroine with the choice between death or captivity and humiliation, and the dramatic moment when any of the "African Queens" choose death. Cavalli sets it to an emotionally powerful accompanied recitative, which begins in halting phrases that reflect Ericlea's initial puzzlement. Her phrases gather length and momentum as perplexity turns to outrage, her voice rising to a militant *stile concitato* at the top of her range, climaxing on, "This is the freedom, this the husband for which you have saved me?" (Example 3). The chains of which she was relieved in I.iii have apparently been returned to her; summoning servants to carry the chains and poison, the signifiers of the choice she apparently must make, she marches off to confront Scipione.

This crucial scene transfers the role traditionally played by Sofonisba to Ericlea. In III.xii she very nearly fulfills Sofonisba's role by drinking the poison rather than giving in to what she believes to be Scipione's tyrannical behavior. But she is prevented at the last second by Scipione, who recognizes the mistake and Massanissa's handwriting on the letter. She is saved from meeting the historical Sofonisba's fate and set on the path to the realization of a different tableau, that of Scipio's continence (fig. 1).

The result is that the secondary plot involving Ericlea, the disguised Lucejo, and his brother Polinio becomes entwined with the more serious elements of the plot and leads the opera to its happy ending. The transformation of Ericlea into the African Queen gives her the apparently dangerous erotic qualities of that type. The dangers she poses are real for Scipione but comic in her interactions with Lucejo. Lucejo's and Polinio's comic disguises also play into expectations of the proud and passionate Other, which in the drama means Roman expectations of Iberians, and in the performance context translates to Italian expectations of stage Spaniards. Because from this point the opera privileges Ericlea's role, it is her part of the story that takes over as the central plot, and the Ovidian and comic war of love is won by the non-Romans. The couples are correctly matched, and even the pathetic Massanissa is forgiven. The last word,

Example 3

Cavalli's Scipione

given to Ericlea, stresses the Ovidian rather than the Vergilian element in the story: "Oh, you who bear a heart alight with the loving passion, have hope, yes have hope: eh, Love's pains don't last; there's grief at the start, but joy in the end."[30] With the political issues settled and the captives freed, Ericlea has the liberty, as Lucejo did earlier, to consider the laws of love and happiness. The music correspondingly emphasizes the text's juxtaposition of "duole" and "gioie," lingering for three measures in meditative dotted rhythm over "grief" but ending grandly with seven measures of runs and syncopated elongations on the word "joy."

Scipione, vincitore di se stesso

When Scipione discovers the mix-up of letters and saves Ericlea from suicide, the meaning of the poison and chains changes once more. Scipione declares that the duplicitous Massanissa must either bring Sofonisba captive and in the chains or drink the poison himself (III.xiii). The action points to Scipione's growing control over himself in respect to Ericlea, and his own return to a Vergilian sensibility, but with that self-control he once again asserts his power over those around him, and his actions bring about dialogues that reflect the kind of Senecan and Stoic attitudes toward authority and tyranny that we observed in *Poppea*. The issue of tyranny is very much in Scipione's mind, but unlike Monteverdi's Nerone, Scipione struggles throughout the opera to avoid behaving tyrannically. To the conquered Cathaginians (II.i) he is concerned to impose conditions of peace that are the result of Roman thought, not that of a tyrant ("pensieri di Roman, non di tiranno"). He represents the ideal rather than its violation, and his characterization points forward to the reform operas at the turn of the century.

The relation of his character to the problem of tyranny, however, is the same as his relation to the chains and arrows of love. Scipione, in his own view, suffers from metaphorical tyranny just as he had suffered from metaphorical conquest. His personal tyrants are Duty and Love. He calls the letter he writes releasing Ericlea to Lucejo a "foglio tiranno" (III. viii) and addresses his love for Ericlea thus (III.xi): "Tyrant of my heart, you have stolen away my happiness, and the same barbarous tyrant has denied my desire."

For the conquered Africans, however, his occasional lapses into authoritarian behavior have serious consequences involving real chains and arrows, as when he discovers that Massanissa has been hiding Sofonisba and actualizes a dominant metaphor by threatening to have him shot full of arrows (II.iv). He is only just prevented from doing so by the disguised Siface, who acts with the intention of being able to take more violent vengeance later. Siface takes the high road, insisting in words that sound like Senecan philosophy on good governance that Massanissa must not be executed rashly. He is supported by the surprised Catone: "The slave [i.e., the disguised Siface] spoke wisely, Sir. And perhaps Heaven led him to such a defense, which often reveals its will by humble means." Scipione, unlike Nerone in *Poppea*, accepts correction—"Reason moves the careful man"—and instead gives Massanissa a day to find and turn over Sofonisba.

As noted in chapter 1, Scipio Africanus had since antiquity had a typological affinity with Alexander the Great, so it is perhaps not accidental that there is an operatic precedent for Scipione's difficulties in governing himself in this opera in Francesco Sbarra's 1651 *Alessandro, il vincitor di se stesso*. In Sbarra's libretto, Alessandro's dilemma, like Scipione's, is cast as a transfer of the political concept of tyranny to the personal sphere and expressed in an exchange with the philosopher Aristotle. Alessandro is in love with the beautiful Persian princess Campaspe, but she is elsewhere attached. Alessandro agonizes to Aristotle about his realization that it is best to let Campaspe go:[31]

> *Alexander.* My dear friend, must I take away my life?
> *Aristotle.* No, your death.
> *Alex.* And must I pass so cruel a sentence against myself?
> *Arist.* It's better so.
> *Alex.* That I be so strict with myself?
> *Arist.* No: merciful.
> *Alex.* That I seek my own injury?
> *Arist.* Your own good.
> *Alex.* And I who conquered others will be a rude tyrant to myself?
> *Arist.* Your feelings are the tyrants.*

In exerting self-control, Alessandro, in his own view, becomes tyrant over himself and has to be corrected by his adviser.

Minato revisits this debate on the responsibilities of the ruler to govern his passions, with Catone once again as Scipione's philosophical adviser (III.xi):[32]

> *Scipione.* Oh, don't make my grief worse.
> *Catone.* You are not cured if you still feel grief.
> *Scip.* Short moments do not have such power.
> *Cat.* Virtue is not the product of a short moment's effort.
> *Scip.* Time and Virtue are against lovers.
> *Cat.* And a prudent soul creates its own time?
> *Scip.* And so a merciful Heaven offers me this.
> *Cat.* But prudence in love is often imprudent.

These lines, like the dialogue in *Alessandro vincitor,* are in tragic-style stichomythia; that is, alternating lines of dialogue inherited from Greek tragedy through Senecan drama.[33] The subject of Virtue is one of the central issues in Stoicism, and Scipione's conclusion that he himself is the subject of tyranny a familiar topic in the play. If he is not finally a Nero, he, like Sbarra's Alessandro, has to struggle all the same against his feelings in the face of his responsibilities. He must even be corrected by others, and the danger is that, as a result of being tyrannized by his own perceptions, Scipione will in reaction visit real tyranny on others.

In the case of the more serious strand of the story, this means his threats against the life of the pathetic Massanissa, and most of all, the life, safety, and dignity of Siface and Sofonisba. The ramifications of their capture have already been explored, and for them Scipione embodies the Vergilian dictum "spare the humbled and beat down the proud." But in the case of Ericlea, the situation is different. She participates in the type of the dangerous African Queen and in this role poses a threat to Scipione's good behavior, but she also serves as the ingenue role in the comic plot. As such, she potentially draws Scipione into the comedy as well, turning him from a respectable authority figure to a comic heavy, the blocking figure who nearly prevents the young lovers—in this case Ericlea and Lucejo—from uniting, and so must be humiliated and driven away. This would seem to confirm Skippon's assertion that Venetian operas were comedies (chapter 1; he made his observation partly in reference to this opera), and a move appropriate enough for the Venetian carnival context, but hardly an attractive position for a cultural icon. In the event, Cavalli and Minato chose to separate Scipione and Ericlea, returning Scipione to Stoic solitude and virtue while relegating Ericlea to the comic elements of the plot. This occurs explicitly in III.xviii. Having summoned Ericlea to him, Scipione makes it clear in what now appears an almost sadistic exchange that he could take her as his share of the spoils if he chose:

> *Scipione.* You know that you were the spoils of our arms?
> *Ericlea.* Yes.
> *Scip.* You know that the victor lays down the law for the conquered?
> *Eri.* It's true.
> *Scip.* Then how do you see your position?
> *Eri.* I have imagined I would receive your consent.
> *Scip.* And if I am not quick about it?
> *Eri.* I'll try pleas.
> *Scip.* And if I resist?
> *Eri.* I will accuse Destiny of cruelty.
> *Scip.* And me?
> *Eri.* Of loving too much.
> *Scip.* And if I don't change my mind?
> *Eri.* I will argue in vain.
> *Scip.* Then you are conquered.
> *Eri.* Yes.
> *Scip.* And I am content. Do as you wish.

Scipione is using the philosophical elenchus to regain control by reducing Ericlea to the point of admitting that she, not he, is the conquered one and at his disposal. Having won that point, he can relinquish her to Lucejo without loss of face. In using this method he has apparently learned from *il filosofo* Catone and has himself become something of a philosopher. He frees himself from the Ovidian captivity of which he had complained, and in doing so he returns to the Stoic ideal, opting for the virtues of justice and clemency. Like Hercules, he chooses virtue rather than pleasure. After receiving everyone else's surrender, he then conquers himself, a victory that comprises the last words he utters in the final scene: "Now join your right hands, and let the world see that a province conquered, a king suppressed, is a glorious trophy of war, but the greater victory is to conquer oneself [*vincer se stesso*]."

The comic elements, the Ovidian *amor*, and the sense of carnival are left to the non-Romans, who according to Roman as well as early modern prejudices are temperamentally more suited to them. Foreigner and female are returned to their rightful places according to the social worlds of the play and the audience. In a certain sense Scipione, the figure blocking the comic resolution, *is* chased away, retreating like Tiepolo's Scipio onto his throne and his duty, leaving the other players to express warmer sentiments. In the *scena ultima*, love is rewarded all around with the equivalent of a double wedding and the comic elements given their last say. One last laugh extracted from the confusion of Polinio and Lucejo:

> *Scipione.* Prince, give your hand to Ericlea.
> *Polinio.* Obediently.
> *Lucejo.* (*Coming forward*) Wait, Sir. *I* am Lucejo, and *this* is my
>   brother Polinio.

But it is Ericlea who gets the final word, asserting the moral of the piece. After Scipione's assertion of political power and self-control, the score moves to arioso style with Ericlea's coda, discussed above, that the course of love runs true. On the performative level, the aria provides an opportunity for some final fireworks by the prima donna, and in the original performance it gave the singer Massotti the last word. (Cavalli did not set a final chorus in Minato's libretto that repeated Ericlea's last words.) At the dramatic level, Ericlea's clichés on the course of love after Scipione's self-isolating statement of power and self-control brings focus back to the female element and the comic reestablishment of society. In a controlled environment, the female and foreign element is allowed the last emphatic word, striking an ideal balance. In the context of Venetian carnival the subordinate figure is momentarily—though illusorily—dominant. The female singer dominates the male-owned opera house in a patriarchal society. The character she plays, a defeated Carthaginian woman, gives the final and most important lesson of the evening, taking center stage like the Spanish maiden in Tiepolo's painting. The allurement and threat of what I have characterized as the African Queen is transferred to the character of the Spanish maiden: The character in the story is transformed from a passive object to an exotic threat to the dominant male.

Nevertheless, behind it all stands the Scipio of the historical and dramatic world, by whose will everything was and is allowed to happen. The final moment seems to refer deliberately to the similar self-conquest of Alessandro in Sbarra and Cesti's opera of ten years earlier, drawing Scipione back into the sphere of traditional heroes that the early modern period had identified as Stoic. Sbarra's Alessandro, after refusing to impose his will, had announced in his final words, "But what is just must be observed, . . . I want to conquer myself [*Voglio vincer me stesso*]. My valor demands I have an unconquered heart, as I have an unconquered sword." Scipione echoes Alessandro's words with his own final statement of self-conquest, quoted above, thus associating himself with the heroic cluster that included Alexander, Hercules, and Aeneas. As with Alessandro, military and personal conquests are equated, and the public and private spheres are united in the person of the conqueror. The focus on Scipio's choice is even more pointedly a central issue in the 1678 Venetian libretto, which ends not with Ericlea's aria but with Scipione's final assertion of political and moral advantage. This focus will be blurred in interesting ways in Zeno's *Scipione nelle Spagne* (chapter 5), but here the prince's clemency replaces the royal marriage as the act that expresses the health and stability of the state. The final transcendence to realms of light, already obviously suspect in *Poppea*, becomes instead a transcendent act by an enlightened ruler—Seneca's philosophy does indeed survive—a prince upon whom we can depend, unlike Nero, to respect and protect our families, needs, and property.

4 Otho in Arcadia

GRIMANI/HANDEL, *AGRIPPINA*;
LALLI/VIVALDI, *OTTONE IN VILLA*

> But [Eurydice], while in headlong flight from you by the
> river, though she was on the point of death, did not see
> the enormous water snake at her feet, guarding the banks
> in the high grass.
> —Vergil, *Georgics* 4.457–59
>
> Q. So it has a happy ending?
> A. It has a very happy ending.
> Q. Almost none of these stories have completely happy
>   endings.
> —Mary Zimmerman, *Metamorphoses*

Two works that helped launch operatic careers in the early
eighteenth century, Handel's *Agrippina* (Venice, 1709–10) and Vivaldi's
Ottone in villa (Vicenza, 1713), returned for their subject matter to the
debauched and dangerous world of the late Julio-Claudian emperors. These
are also transitional operas, since they both combine elements of the
older, seventeenth-century librettos with ideas from the Arcadian literary reforms that began to affect the production of opera beginning in the
1690s and resulted in the *opera seria* of Zeno and Metastasio (chapter 1).
The libretto for *Agrippina*, usually ascribed to Cardinal Vincenzo Grimani,
is enacted in the same morally compromised world as *L'incoronazione
di Poppea*.[1] It is a tightly constructed comic drama that depicts the accession of Nero as heir to the imperial throne through the machinations
of his ambitious mother Agrippina. Domenico Lalli's *Ottone in villa* is

a perverse pastoral-style drama adapted from Francesco Maria Piccioli's satiric libretto *Messalina* (1678). Lalli substituted Emperor Otho for the duped and cuckolded Emperor Claudius of *Messalina* and, influenced by the Arcadian reforms, condensed Piccioli's sprawling libretto into a more modern structure.[2]

The figure common to both these operas is Ottone, a character derived from the historical Marcus Salvius Otho, who had already played the part of the rejected lover in Monteverdi's *L'incoronazione di Poppea.* In his early years the historical Otho seems to have been as dissolute a personality as any in the Neronian age, "corrupted even since childhood by luxury and love of pleasure as few Romans were," says Plutarch.[3] A partner in Nero's youthful debaucheries, Otho arranged to marry Poppaea Sabina so that Nero could have access to her while he was still married to Octavia, daughter of the emperor Claudius. Nero finally sent Otho away to govern Lusitania (roughly speaking, modern Portugal) when he found that Otho's genuine passion for Poppaea was interfering with his own pleasure. Separated from the temptations of Rome, Otho governed Lusitania competently. He was briefly elevated to the position of Roman emperor in the turbulent year 69 C.E., during which time he behaved with reasonable decorum and made efforts to reestablish order in Rome between the fractious praetorian guard and the ruling classes. He lasted only three months as emperor; he committed a dignified suicide in April 69 after his troops were defeated near Cremona by those of the insurgent Vitellius, the father of the fictional Vitellia who is the prima donna of Metastasio's libretto *La clemenza di Tito.* But to a certain extent it was the end of his life that left an impression. Montaigne, in "Of Sleep," commends Otho's ability to sleep soundly while contemplating his own defeat and suicide. In this respect, the "death of that emperor has about it many things like that of the great Cato."[4]

It is this more positive impression that Otho left at the end of his life that produced the operatic Ottone, who otherwise appears to be only tangentially related to the young Otho who was the friend of Nero. Beginning already with *L'incoronazione di Poppea*, the character Ottone takes on the role of a sheep among the wolves. His historical role as the rejected husband of Poppea suits him for a dramatic role as the unfortunate cuckold. His subsequent good behavior and his violent but dignified death together seem to have suggested his suitability as moral innocent to librettists needing a foil for the bad behavior of their principals. Otho is, in some respects, the least classical of the characters in *Poppea* and *Agrippina*, embodying in those operas a chivalrous knight, an odd man out, whose nobler actions might be thought to draw momentary distinction between the heroic "us" (Venice) and the villainous "them" (Rome, Spain, or France). At the same time he is undeniably a somewhat pathetic fall guy. Consequently, in *Ottone in villa* he slips naturally into the role played by the emperor Claudius in Piccioli's *Messalina* and Handel's *Agrippina*: a foolish *pantalone*, the comic *senex* who must be hoodwinked and put aside by the younger lovers in the plot.

Central to my discussion here is the identification of the character of Ottone with pastoral settings and themes. By the seventeenth century, "pastoral," in the sense I want to employ it, had become such a common mode of literary thought that its emotional qualities might be invoked in a wide variety of contexts. It was a generalized and fluid concept, signifying human interaction in an idealized natural landscape where the values are opposed to the supposed corruption of the city and court and most often involve amorous pursuits "divorced from duty and society."[5] The landscapes in which this takes place range on a continuum from formal garden within a palace to the natural wilds of a forest. At any given moment the point of reference may be drawn from a wide range of such locales, including the classical landscapes of Theocritus and Vergil, biblical Eden, or the varying Renaissance transformations of these. In its advanced state, the pastoral could even include elements that are by nature antipastoral.[6]

The pastoral may inform the whole spirit of a piece or may be evoked for temporary effect, creating what Poggioli calls a "pastoral oasis" in a larger work. Such an oasis occurs in *Agrippina*; the action takes place in the imperial court among historical figures, but the idealized tranquility of the natural landscape is suggested by scenes in the palace garden. The characters in *Ottone in villa*, in contrast, and despite the historicity of some of their names, take on the generic characteristics of the shepherds and shepherdesses of pastoral drama and retreat into an actual pastoral landscape around the country villa of the title.

But despite their idealized character, danger lurks in these pleasant settings. Death in the garden is a theme ubiquitous from the very beginnings of literature: A snake steals Gilgamesh's herb of immortality as he bathes in a pool in the wilds of Mesopotamia and reappears in the garden of Eden in the Hebrew tradition; in the *Odyssey*, Circe, Polyphemus, and the Lotus Eaters operate in idyllic surroundings; and Persephone is ravished from a flower-filled pasture by Death himself in the Homeric *Hymn to Demeter*. She is one of many young women in classical literature caught picking flowers in a *locus amoenus*, a pleasant locale, who are violated by a god or hero.[7] Death in the rural landscape is suggested repeatedly in Vergil's *Eclogues* and *Georgics*, as the example of Eurydice's flight from Aristaeus in the chapter's epigraph suggests. The theme was picked up by Vergil's heirs; perhaps the most famous early modern expressions of the contradiction between the ideal life of Arcadia and the reality of death are in two Poussin paintings titled *Et in Arcadia ego,* which depict a tomb discovered in a lush, wild landscape.

Death, or the threat of death, similarly invades the pastoral dramas of Tasso and Guarini, which had such an influence on the development of early opera. This is observable also in Shakespeare's late experiments with romance and tragicomedy in the *Winter's Tale* and *Cymbeline.* In both the latter cases, the inhabitants of a court torn by conflict arrive in a pastoral landscape, face death, and emerge to a world miraculously restored.[8] These pastoral oases, invested with danger and death by virtue of their relations with uncontrolled nature, also become surrogates of the underworld to which the hero must descend and return to achieve victory and the happy ending. Just as opera exploits the elegiac oxymoron that equates love and war in order to describe dramatic conflict, so too it exploits the tradition inherited from both Vergil and Genesis that paradise contains the seeds of its own destruction.

Robert Harbison observed that "plumbing the underworld" might be "a way of probing the psyche" in the earlier seventeenth-century operas.[9] That is equally true, as we will see, of Ottone's confrontations with the pastoral oasis. The danger latent in the idealized landscape, particularly in relation to second-act complications that result in tragedy or near-tragedy, are also the points at which Ottone (and others) find a combination of solitude and crisis conducive to baring their souls. Already in Monteverdi's *Poppea,* two gardens frame the second act. The first four scenes of the act take place in Seneca's garden, where, alone in contemplation, he receives the news of his impending death from Mercury; the act ends (scenes x–xii) in Poppea's garden, where Ottone's attempt on Poppea's life is thwarted by the god Amore. In both cases the idyllic retreat, superficially a haven for its inhabitants, is invaded by the threat of death. This second-act move to a garden is observable, too, in *Agrippina,* where a pleasant retreat becomes the center of conspiracy, deceit, and, nearly, physical violence. In *Ottone in villa* the characters make a second-act retreat from the formal gardens of the villa to a more purely pastoral landscape in acts II and III, where emotional violence leads once again to the threat of death.

In the context of these landscapes, Ottone, the passionate but scorned lover, embodies an intersection of heroic, chivalric, and pastoral characters who are as fluid in effect as the pastoral landscapes they inhabit. In chapter 2 we saw him characterized as the lover-soldier of Ovidian elegy, the actor of a *paraclausithyron* scene.[10] In *Agrippina* he is genuinely a soldier whose devotion to Poppea characterizes him as a chivalric knight errant of the kind that in medieval epic is apt to wander into a pastoral oasis that is a momentary break from the business of war and dragons.[11] In *Ottone in villa* he has become emperor, but in a similar way he rejects duty and worldly values for an amorous retreat into a pastoral landscape. Here he is closest to the historical Otho both because of his lascivious nature, which reflects his earlier life, and the trusting generosity with which he treats others that characterized his brief time as emperor.

Before discussing this intersection of Roman imperial history with the pastoral tradition in *Agrippina* and *Ottone in villa*, it will be useful to return to Otho's role in *Poppea*, where he first appears in a garden. This will help characterize the nature of the pastoral oasis in these operas. In addition, I believe Busenello's text may have contributed to Grimani's treatment of Ottone and Poppea as he wrote *Agrippina*.

Ottone and the Garden in L'incoronazione di Poppea

The second act of *Poppea* is bracketed by garden scenes that are not precisely pastoral either in setting or in musical treatment but share the pastoral preoccupation with the retreat from the troubles of civilization that is nevertheless invaded by the threat of death. The act opens in Seneca's garden, which is, as Fenlon and Miller have shown, a neo-Stoic retreat in the manner of that recommended in Lipsius's *De Constantia*. It is a place of natural beauty that is conducive to quiet contemplation and peace of mind, a suitable place for Seneca to assert the value of his teachings and bid farewell to life and friends.[12] There Mercury visits him on the orders of Minerva to announce Seneca's imminent ascension to "the starry pole." As such, it constitutes an opposition to the opera's second garden, the pleasure garden of Poppea, which is the setting for the last scenes of the act (II.x–xii). There the residing deities are Amore, whom Poppea invokes as her patron, and Poppea herself, whom Amore declares to be an earthly goddess. In this garden Poppea feels safe to discuss her ambitions with her nurse and to fall asleep.

Into this garden comes the serpent in the person of Ottone: "Here I am, transformed not from Ottone into Drusilla, no, but from a man into a serpent, the like of whose poison and mad fury the world has never seen and never will." Ottone's transformation traces its origins from Ovid's *Metamorphoses*, through the vicious serpents encountered by Cato in Lucan's *Pharsalia*, book 9, to Dante's *Inferno* (C. 25.94–102), where he boasts that his description of sinners metamorphosing into serpents outdoes both the ancient poets. Ottone here is not a biblical serpent in Eden, presenting a surrogate Eve with temptation. Rather, he is a danger lurking in a natural setting, like Eurydice's snake in the *Georgics* or the serpent killed by Cadmus in *Metamorphoses*, book 3. He continues in an even more grotesque fashion, suitable to the more excessive passages from Senecan tragedy and Lucan's epic, as he describes his heart as wandering about his "trembling guts" in an attempt to escape being an accomplice to the deed Ottone is about to perform.

The moment is at once comically grotesque and emotionally excruciating. Ottone in women's clothing can be funny, depending on how the scene is presented. He is also pathetic, as he has borrowed clothing from a woman he does not really love—at this point in the opera, anyway—to perpetrate murder against the woman he does love. The murder is of course prevented by Amor himself, who threatens Ottone the serpent with death in his turn. Love conquers, the garden is made safe, and Poppea will be made empress.

Thus this first opera on Julio-Claudian history explores two kinds of natural retreats, the contemplative garden that leads to genuine paradise and the garden of delights, a place for sensual relaxation and contemplation of the pleasures of this world. The character of Ottone, known historically for his devotion to sensual pleasure, can have nothing to do with Seneca's philosophical retreat. But neither do the historical Ottone's comparatively responsible actions at the end of his life put him precisely in harmony with the abandoned sensuality of the garden of delights. So in *Poppea* he can be introduced as a deadly threat to the latter, metaphorically as the serpent and in fact as a would-be assassin. In *Agrippina* and *Ottone in villa* he will show a similar ambivalent relationship with the garden, susceptible to its pleasures but nervously aware of its dangers.

Agrippina

Adaptation of an earlier libretto would have been one option for Vincenzo Grimani in his desire to write a Nero opera for the Venetian stage. Since *Poppea* in 1643 there had been at least five operas on the last Julio-Claudian emperors, including Piccioli's *Messalina* and Matteo Noris's *Nerone fatto Cesare* (1693), both of which appear to have contributed poetic elements to *Agrippina*.[13] But for the most part, the author seems to have created *Agrippina* from scratch. The result has sometimes been thought of as a throwback to the previous generation of libretto production, with its mix of comic and serious material, its relatively large number of characters, and its plethora of arias. But it is also tightly constructed, the more extravagant elements from the seventeenth century being reigned in and the plot developed from a carefully balanced set of characters and events.[14]

The opera tells a story about Agrippina's efforts to get her husband, the emperor Claudius, to adopt Nero, her son by a previous marriage, as his heir and successor. Grimani remarks in his *Argomento* that Agrippina's entire purpose in life was to bring her son Nero to the throne. Although she had been warned by an astrologer that her son would be emperor but also a matricide, she responded, "Then let him kill me, provided he's the emperor" ("Me quidem occidat dum imperet"). The Latin quotation is adapted from Tacitus's *Annals* (14.9). Tacitus confirms in other passages that Agrippina was ambitious, unscrupulous, and single-minded in her aim to make her son Nero emperor; she was willing enough to make use of her beauty to get what she wanted but was not distracted by her passions, as was Claudius's previous wife, Messalina, whose adulterous affairs finally resulted in her execution. Handel, for his part, having recently set the cantata "Agrippina condotta a morire" while in Rome, was well aware that Nero had his mother killed.[15] Consequently, these darker underpinnings to the story give *Agrippina* an edge like that of *Poppea*. But with its elaborate and often farcical intrigues and erotic complications, the text of *Agrippina* often reads like a comedy by Wycherly or Congreve.[16]

The opera opens with the news of Claudio's death in a shipwreck while returning from the conquest of Britain. Agrippina advises her adoring son Nerone to win the people's vote for his accession and enlists the help of Claudio's two freedmen, Pallante and Narciso, with insincere promises of sexual and political favors. Just as Nerone is about to be declared emperor, Claudio's servant Lesbo enters to announce that Claudio is alive after all, saved from the storm and wreck by Ottone. In gratitude, Claudio has declared that Ottone will be his successor. There is general dismay, expressed as asides, among those who expected Nero to succeed. Lesbo retreats to announce Claudio's arrival to the beautiful Poppea, whom Claudio desires and wants to visit in secret prior to his official arrival in Rome.

Ottone arrives, happy in his success and imminent elevation, but makes it clear that his one true concern is his love for Poppea. Because Poppea is also being pursued by Nerone, she is in a difficult situation. Agrippina promises to help Ottone in his suit to Poppea but instead undermines his position by convincing Poppea that Ottone has agreed to give her up to Claudio in exchange for his being declared heir. Poppea receives Claudio in her chamber and, by prior agreement with Agrippina, pretends to love him, telling him that Ottone has forbidden her to see him. Claudio is furious and agrees to reject him as his heir. Agrippina arrives to rescue her from Claudio's attentions and further provokes her anger against Ottone.

In act II Agrippina's stratagems begin to unravel. Pallante and Narciso realize that they have been used by Agrippina, but like everyone else in the cast, they are angry with Ottone, who has usurped their hopes of power. Claudio makes a triumphant entry to a hypocritical welcome by the rest of the court. When Ottone tries to claim his reward as successor, he is rejected without explanation, first by Claudio and then by everyone else on stage. He is left to sing a perplexed and wounded lament.

In II.vi the scene changes to a garden, which will be the scene for the rest of the act. Poppea reflects on her inclination to find Ottone innocent after all. She sees Ottone coming and pretends to be asleep. Ottone enters, reflecting on the beauty of the garden; Poppea, after pretending to cry out against him in her sleep, "awakes" and charges him with trading her for power, an accusation he denies. He offers her his sword to kill him if she believes otherwise. They reconcile. Poppea, realizing that she too has been deceived by Agrippina, determines to take retributive action, and from this point the opera is a contest of strategy between the two women. Poppea, assuring Ottone of her love, arranges to meet both Nerone and Claudio in her bedchamber as a means toward her own ends.

Agrippina now arrives in the garden, expressing her fears of failure and worse.[17] She attempts to induce Pallante and Narciso to kill Ottone and then one another. She then meets Claudio, who is urgently anxious to meet Poppea, and convinces him to declare Nerone heir. In his haste he agrees. She closes the act in a better frame of mind, declaring that every wind blows her ship safely to port.

In act III Poppea is ascendant. In a farcical series of scenes, she hides Ottone and Nerone in separate closets in her bedroom, receives Claudio, and then exposes Nerone to him, revealing that Agrippina had tried to make him emperor in Claudio's absence. She also declares that Claudio had misheard her before, and it was Nerone, not Ottone, who had demanded that she not see Claudio. She then sends them both away, thereby simultaneously compromising Nerone's chances of becoming emperor and proving her love to the hidden Ottone. Nerone runs to Agrippina for protection and declares that, like clouds fleeing before the wind, he is abandoning his affection for Poppea. His fire is spent.

The scene changes to a hall in the imperial palace. Narciso and Pallante resolve to save themselves by revealing everything they know to Claudio. The cornered Agrippina very nearly comes to a bad end, only averted by her own quick thinking and Claudio's gullibility. Confronted by Claudio, she boldly declares that she had thought Claudio dead and put Nerone on the throne to protect the family and empire. She calls Narciso and Pallante as witnesses that this is true. Claudio, stymied, forgives her and admits his love for her. In the *scena ultima* he decrees that Nerone shall marry Poppea and that Ottone is to become the next emperor. There is general consternation, as he has got things wrong way around. But Ottone refuses the crown and asks for Poppea; Poppea declares, "Let Nero have the scepter, rule, and power; I shall be no one's but Ottone's." Agrippina has won. Claudio summons the goddess Juno *pronuba* (Juno as patroness of marriage) to bless the union of Ottone and Poppea, and the opera ends in apparent joy and a ballet by Juno's divine attendants.

The overt maneuvering for power in *Agrippina* has encouraged political interpretation of the opera. Its probable author, Grimani, was a highly political man who was exiled from Venice in 1690 for supporting the Austrian Habsburgs against the pro-French inclinations of Venice and her allies. He spent many years representing Vienna in the courts of Italy and Savoy and at the Papal court in Rome. He became Austrian viceroy in Naples and sided with the Habsburgs in the War of the Spanish Succession. Reinhard Strohm suggested specifically that Grimani intended the foolish and deceived Claudio, whose exit aria in III.viii asserts that he is "di Roma il Giove," to represent Pope Clement XI, whom Grimani opposed in various ways.[18] But it is equally true that the Habsburg house had long attached to itself the imagery and nomenclature of imperial Rome. The repeated references to Agrippina and Claudio as Augusta and Augusto, and to the "laurel crown of the Caesars" (*"Cesareo allor"*) that Agrippina identifies in I.i as the desirable end of her designs, might even more easily connect with the modes of self-reference of the court in Vienna than that of the Vatican.[19] It is therefore difficult to identify precise political references in this opera.[20] The reference to Jupiter seems to me to point instead to an element inherited from Ovidian versions of Greek myth and developed through the verbal and musical imagery. While the mythological interpretation does not preclude a political reading, given the limitations of what we know, the mythological and literary approach can more readily be discussed.

There is a cosmological dimension to the opposition of Claudio and Agrippina and its effects on the characters surrounding them. This mythic element gives a structure and atmosphere to the political and erotic maneuverings, for which Ottone's participation as a pastoral figure and a chivalric lover serves as a foil. The enraged Claudio declares in III.viii that he is Rome's Jupiter; true to this role, he is able in the final scene to summon Juno herself to bless the wedding of Poppea and Ottone. Behind the actions of Claudio and Agrippina stands the paradigmatic story of an Ovidian intrusion of quarreling gods into the human realm, a disruption of Arcadia by divine presence. The paradigms for Claudio's pursuit of Poppea and of Agrippina's countermoves are to be found in the stories of Jupiter's pursuit of Io or Semele or Pluto's abduction of Proserpina, with the resulting angry reactions of the goddesses Juno and Ceres.[21] Often enough this irruption of divine violence occurs in a wild or pastoral landscape full of flowers, a *locus amoenus* sentimentally attached by the civilized pastoral tradition to tranquility but more fundamentally the place for the sometimes violent, generative sexuality of the sky with the earth (see note 7). The opera also underscores this cosmic story with a persistent link to the principal elements of nature: earth, air, fire, and water, with particular emphasis on the last. Even the most powerful human characters in the opera are of course subject to the elements rather than their masters. But in the end they survive the elements, and nature and human design are in concord: Wind and water are tamed, fires are put out, and the earth is pacified.

In this regard there seem to be connections between *Agrippina* and two earlier librettos. The first, Piccioli's *Messalina,* has several elements in common with *Agrippina,* including Claudio as the ruling figure and an imperial wife dominating the court's intrigues who is finally able to hide her own misbehavior. More specifically, *Agrippina*'s final scene is suggested by Piccioli's. Messalina herself opens the spectacular finale of *Messalina* with a reinvention of the world, a cosmogony loosely adapted from ideas in Lucretius and Ovid:[22]

> After the Omnipotent differentiated the atoms wandering in the primal chaos, and gave them form and name; as nature weak from the leisure of peace grows slow and sluggish, and almost sorted out the whole: air, warmth, land and wave, formed already of non-discordant stuff, in the mixture of life work in concert with one another.
>
> Nature, contrary to herself, now divides her powers, Water, Fire, Earth and Air, and look! Discord sets a challenge. [*A peacock appears aloft.*] Now, from the kingdom of Juno, the winged herald descends to maintain command of the air.

The peacock breaks open and Air comes out on an armed horse. There then emerges in sequence from a mountain in the background the earth mother Cybele's lion, a dragon, and a sea monster. Each of the animals breaks apart to show, respectively, Earth, Fire, and Water. They quarrel but are put to rest by Peace, who appears ex machina. This allegorical ending presented by Messalina represents the resolution of the antagonisms of the play, suggesting that the powerful figures of this fantastical drama are nevertheless akin to the forces of nature. The appearance of the peacock, Juno's bird, and the mention of Juno's kingdom in a Julio-Claudian context provide a precedent for the actual appearance of Giunone in *Agrippina*. The literal appearance of the elements in this allegorical finale may have suggested to Grimani a more thoroughgoing use of the four elements as images for the interplay of power in the action of *Agrippina*.

The dominant elements in *Agrippina* are water and wind, principally expressed in terms of a storm battering a ship on the sea. This is a common enough image that fascinated artists of all kinds in the baroque—Shakespeare's *The Tempest* (1611), genre paintings, or Vivaldi's multiple concertos titled *La tempesta di mare* provide examples.[23] For Grimani there may be a second operatic precedent in Matteo Noris's 1693 *Nerone fatto Cesare*, which features several of the same characters as *Agrippina*: Pallante, Nerone, and Agrippina. Pallante opens Noris's opera by likening himself to a pilot putting into port from a stormy sea as he approaches the house of his beloved; the fourth scene features a thunderstorm on stage to accompany Nerone's violence, after which various characters liken their efforts to sea voyages, their troubles to storms, and their rescue to a following calm. The imagery is pertinent to the action but not systematically developed as it is in *Agrippina*.

In *Agrippina* the nautical imagery begins with a literal storm at sea, the report by letter in I.i of a shipwreck caused by a storm in which Claudio is supposed to have died: "Into the great danger of the storm-tossed sea, the Roman Eagle has been sucked down. And Claudius your consort has died in the general cataclysm."[24] A storm on the sea involves already two of the natural elements, wind and water; by extension it can easily encompass the other two with the inclusion of the fire of lightning and the safe haven of the land. Consequently, the recurring references to Claudio's near disaster in the ocean generate metaphors of storm, wind, and rescue on land. Agrippina suggests the loss of Claudio is the result of a jealous quarrel between sea and land: "The faithless sea, jealous that there exists on the earth such a treasure, has taken him from us" (I.ix).[25] Her own troubles are like those of a sailor on a stormy sea (I.vi), and her successes blown by gentle favoring winds (II.xx). After his exposure to Claudio, Nerone rejects Poppea, as clouds fleeing before the wind and extinguishes the fire of his love (III.xi). Ottone overcame the violent sea to save Claudio (I.ix) but cries out in accompanied recitative against the thunderbolt that falls on him once he is back at court: "What unexpected thunderbolt is this? Ah, ungrateful Caesar, faithless, friends, and unjust Heavens!" (II.v).[26]

But in the end, with the appearance of Juno *pronuba* there is a resolution of all the elements in concord with the earthly powers, who appear to have mastered the elements themselves. The water of the Tiber
sparkles; light shines from the laurel crown, stars, and fire of the wedding
torches; and heaven and earth rejoice:

> *Chorus*: May the happy Tiber ruffle its wave in the light of the new
> triumph, and may the god of Love, filled with joy, feast on the
> bank.
> *Juno*. Juno descends from heaven to scatter lilies on the happy grafting
> of Otho and Poppea; and in the exalted marriage chamber I will
> happily provide subjects for Claudius, and children for high Rome.
> [aria] The rays of stars light the torches for you; they shine more beau-
> tifully because of so much good faith.[27]

The Ovidian quarrel between king and queen of the gods that stands behind the main action of the opera has apparently been resolved, as signified by the general concord of the elements. Whether this resolution is
genuine in the actual absence of "so much good faith" will be the subject
of the conclusion of this section, but let us turn first to Ottone's role in
weathering the storm. For this purpose the most important scenes are
II.ii–vii, during which Ottone finds himself an outcast from the court,
and appears in the palace garden where he confronts and reconciles with
Poppea. Like Seneca's death scenes at the beginning of act II in *Poppea*,
Ottone's scenes here occur at the center of the drama and propose a moral
baseline from which the other characters may be judged. Like Seneca's
scenes, too, they take place in a garden, a site that brings to them multiple layers of meaning, and invest Ottone with qualities inherited from
pastoral, chivalric, biblical, and neo-Stoic sources, all of which may be
elements of the pastoral mode in the baroque.

All this adds a genuine element of pathos that, in a heavier opera,
could make Ottone into a tragic figure. The serious elements of Ottone's
role are painted in with deft strokes. In his first scene he speaks words
appropriate to a dutiful and victorious Roman:

> To your laments, I return, O Augusta, amidst mishaps that have fortu-
> nate outcome. The sea, filled with the conquered Britains, carries the
> grand triumph; but envious still, it tries among the squalls to deprive
> Rome of her conquest.

Later he echoes Anchises's famous injunction to Aeneas in the underworld (chapter 1) to beat down Rome's proud enemies: "parcere subjectis
et debellare superbos." Ottone can claim to have fulfilled this injunction

and so to be worthy of the position of emperor (II.ii): "I would like to have enough courage and bravery to see the kingdoms in Latium happy, and to beat down her enemies [*debellare nemici*]."

He nevertheless rejects power if it does not include union with his beloved Poppea and his moving lament after his rejection by the imperial court summarizes his position: "I lose a throne, and indeed I scorn it; but that love, that I value so much, ah, it is torture to lose it, and it unmans my spirit." His character as heroic warrior and savior of the emperor who nevertheless prefers love to power puts a different emphasis on his character than had *Poppea*. I argued that in Monteverdi's *Poppea* Ottone was a lover who took on the metaphorical role of warrior inherited from Ovid through the madrigal texts. His primary occupation in *Agrippina* as a successful soldier who is nevertheless in love, positions him as a chivalric knight errant from Romance rather than the Ovidian lover-warrior. His choice to devalue power and prefer love also has resonances of pastoral rejection of worldly concerns. By II.vii, at the center of the drama, he has been established as the one virtuous, innocent, and sympathetic character on the stage, a suitable figure to stray into a pastoral oasis.

Like his namesake in Monteverdi's *Poppea*, Ottone enters the garden in II.vii to find Poppea asleep. Before he sees her, however, he remarks on the beauty of the surroundings: "Pleasant streams, that slip murmuring in the bosom of the grass." The element of water appears once again, accompanied by Handel's music in a pastoral mode. But the words sound a note of caution, for the phrase "that slip . . . in the bosom of the grass" ("serpeggiate nel seno all'erbe") also implies a snake in the grass, a serpent in paradise. The point is illustrated in Handel's music by the sinuous sixteenth notes that extend the final syllable of *serpeggiate* and suggest the serpentine quality of the flowing and murmuring stream (Example 4). The pastoral vision breaks off abruptly as Ottone notices Poppea pretending to sleep peacefully among the flowers. The combination of image and word is extraordinarily dense at this moment, for Poppea asleep in this *locus amoenus* recollects generations of mythic molested maidens caught by gods while wandering among woods and flowers. But immediately the roles are reversed from those in myth; Ottone is the potential victim and Poppea the bearer of danger. Indeed, this role is conferred upon her by Ottone himself. He offers Poppea his sword and the chance to kill him if she thinks him guilty of unfaithfulness:

> *Ottone.* Listen: take my sword, which I give to your right hand, and if you find me guilty, then I am content for you to kill me.

Poppea takes the sword, and turns the point against Ottone.
Poppea. Then speak. But mind you, you have already prescribed the
    punishment for the crime if you are a traitor. You will fall a blood-
    less victim in the arena.

Death has entered the garden, although only for a brief moment. Agrippina is found to be the source of the misunderstanding, and Ottone can
finish the scene with an exit aria to a vigorous walking bass line that
asserts his innocence once again.

It should be emphasized, however, that Ottone's pathos also makes
him a straight man for the comedy and satire that plays out around him.
The more serious minidrama that began with Ottone's entry in I.xi and
ends with this exit does not linger once he and Poppea have reconciled.
There was already comedy in his early scenes (I.xi–xiii) resulting from
the contrast between his own oblivious joy in his proposed elevation
as imperial successor and the suppressed frustration of everyone else
on stage who greets the news he brings of Claudios's safety. After his

Example 4

Haendel Agrippina

exit in II.vii he becomes another player in the bedroom farce staged by Poppea in III.i–x to humiliate Nerone and rid herself of Claudio. In the *scena ultima* he has little to do except react to his good fortune. Ottone is, however, from beginning to end, the only genuinely sincere and honest character on stage. Even Poppea, whose affection for him seems genuine enough in the context of this opera, spends much of her time in manipulating others, including Ottone himself. Her deceptions are nearly the equal of Agrippina's, and the historical record ultimately belies her constancy to Ottone.

We have observed already that the *scena ultima* is described as a calming of the storm, a concord of the elements and renewed peace between the rulers of the imperial Roman world of the stage, and that this conclusion has resonances of resolved quarrels between the king and queen of the gods. Claudios, the self-proclaimed Jupiter, can even summon the real Juno to bless the nuptials of Poppea and Ottone. The sometime-pastoral lovers are successfully united, and the finale is a celebration of their union on a cosmic scale, harking once again to the late Renaissance origins of the genre in court celebrations of dynastic marriages and festivals. Of course, everything in the historical record militates against this ending. Agrippina was supposed to have poisoned Claudius, Nero pursued Poppea, exiled Ottone, and killed both Agrippina and Poppea herself. Nero's reputation had already been neatly summarized, for example, by Giulio Cesare Corradi in the preface to his 1679 *Il Nerone* for Venice:

> Nero, having ascended Rome's throne, made his people believe he was the Solon of those times. But Astraea's scales having fallen from his hand, soon he changed his name of "The Just" into "the Greatest Tyrant in the World." The despoiling of the people's material goods to clothe the arrogance of his whims was the least of all his offenses. Rapes, murders and acts of violence were the continual triumphs of that wicked soul.*

The question is whether we are meant to forget all this in the comic and cosmic resolution of *Agrippina*. It is possible that we are, since such an approach was attempted by Matteo Noris in his 1699 *Il ripudio d'Ottavia*, in which history is frozen to create a happy ending, practically in the middle of a Tacitean sentence. Nerone repents of his adultery, rejects Poppea, and reinstates Ottavia as empress, with no hint of irony and with the triumph of Virtù.[28] Conceivably, *Agrippina*, too, might have ended in a "frozen moment" of history, when Nerone could still be regarded as a Solon of his times, a neo-Stoic ruler in the bud who had rejected pleasure in favor of duty, leaving Poppea and Ottone as a happy couple.

This seems unlikely, and there are indications even in this joyous *scena ultima* that Grimani had dynamic rather than frozen history in mind. Scholars have already noted an apparent subversion by Handel's music of the overtly happy resolutions in the action, including the reconciliation of Ottone and Poppea.[29] A final look at what is implicit in the libretto may suggest a similar subversion in Grimani's text. The presiding deity in the *scena ultima* is Juno, invoked by Claudio as *pronuba Giuno*; that is to say, the queen of the gods as patroness of marriage. She seems most appropriate for the occasion, although she does not much appear in such contexts in opera, and for good reason. Juno in the ancient sources is also the jealous wife of Jupiter, visiting horror and destruction on the illegitimate children of Jupiter and the women who bear them. One need only note the example of Semele to observe this. Juno's role as *pronuba* here does nothing to soften her negative image; quite the opposite, for her most famous appearance in that avatar is in book 4 of the *Aeneid*, where she presides over the ill-fated union of Dido and Aeneas (4.165–68). A storm sent by the goddess ruins their hunting party: "Dido and the Trojan leader enter a cave together. First of all the Earth and Juno, patroness of weddings (*pronuba Juno*), give the signal. Fires flash and Aether, sharer in their union, and on the mountain peak the Nymphs cried out in triumph."

We have already briefly associated Ottone with Aeneas in his opening claim that he has beaten down Rome's enemies. His marriage blessed by Juno under these circumstances does not appear to be a stable or comforting thing. Coupled further with Agrippina's final words in the opera is a restatement of her famous claim that Nero may kill her as long as he rules: "Now that Nero reigns, I'll die content" ("Or che regna Neron, moro contenta"), which suggests "me quidem occidat dum imperet." This is no "completely happy ending," in Mary Zimmerman's words, but only a step on the road to disaster.[30] The snake is still alive, and death is still in paradise. The irony of the *scena ultima* is, all things considered, more comic than tragic, but the implications of Ottone's "Vaghe fonti serppegiate nel seno del erbe" may be read as emblematic for the entire opera.

Ottone in villa

Four years after the premiere of *Agrippina*, Ottone appeared yet again in a pastoral context, this time as emperor of Rome. The entirety of Vivaldi's *Ottone in villa* is set in "a Roman villa where Otho used to stay for his own pleasure." It is a pleasure garden of the type we observed in *Poppea*, verging into a pastoral wilderness. It is in no sense a place for philosophical contemplation. The music is mostly conventionally serious, but here and there Vivaldi underscored the rural setting of the piece with pastoral musical techniques.[31] The scenes develop in increasingly more remote retreats into the country: first a delightful place with leafy bowers, tree-lined avenues, fishponds, and vases of flowers, then a bathing rotunda near a cascade, then a sunken garden with a pool and a cave nearby, then a rural lodge, and, finally, a lonely path with leafy nooks. For an audience seeing the opera in Vicenza in 1713, the gardens of Ottone's Roman villa must surely also have evoked also the villas and gardens of the surrounding countryside, where the Venetian nobility retreated for its relaxation and pursuit of pleasure that was becoming increasingly self-indulgent in the eighteenth century.[32]

Although the opera presents events surrounding Otho that have no basis in fact, the depiction of the emperor's character is, perhaps accidentally, close to the historical man in certain respects. Despite Otho's responsible management of Lusitania and then the empire itself, he could not entirely escape his earlier reputation for dissolute effeminacy; he even capitalized on it to win favor from a populace that had also favored Nero and that saw the comparatively young Otho as an acceptable replacement. (He was thirty-seven in the year 69 C.E.) The characterization of Ottone in this opera as a man devoted to his passion and at the same time willing to believe the best of people and ignore their betrayals is not inconsistent with the character represented in the ancient sources.[33]

As already indicated, Lalli adapted his libretto from Piccioli's *Messalina*, but the original is much attenuated, and the characters altered, some of them beyond recognition.[34] In *Ottone in villa* the emperor Claudio from *Messalina* becomes the emperor Ottone. Messalina is turned into the invented character Cleonilla, a noble beauty loved by Ottone but not his empress. Gaius Silius, a real person, whom the historical Messalina married while still Claudius's empress, remains here as Caio Silio, but he is simply, according to the *Argomento*, "Rome's handsomest young man," in love with Cleonilla. Caio is in turn loved by Tullia, "a foreign woman" he previously wooed and rejected who appears on the scene disguised as the boy Ostilio. Cleonilla has fallen for "Ostilio" and spends the opera pursuing "him" while rejecting Caio. Tullia as Ostilio encourages Cleonilla's attentions as a means to get revenge on Caio for deserting her. Ottone's confidant Decio, a Roman of solemn convictions, has no real parallel in *Messalina*; he continually warns Ottone of Cleonilla's infidelities and Rome's dissatisfactions at their emperor's irresponsible absence from his duties as ruler. His fears for the emperor's position and even his life are indirect reminders of Otho's historical fate.

These interrelationships define the action. Cleonilla pursues Ostilio (Tullia). Tullia in her turn pursues Caio, who pursues Cleonilla. Ottone is tangential to this cycle of erotic attraction, himself passionate about Cleonilla but not desired in return by anyone. Eventually at the promptings of Decio, Ottone confronts Cleonilla, but like Claudio in *Agrippina*, he is prevented by her luck and duplicity from ever finding out the truth about her infidelities. The opera ends in a sudden flurry of activity. Cleonilla makes love to "Ostilio" while Caio watches from a hiding place. Caio emerges with the intent to stab "Ostilio," and the ruckus attracts the attention of Ottone and Decio, thereby bringing the entire cast onstage for the *scena ultima*. Caio denounces Ostilio for "his" apparent affair with Cleonilla. Ottone turns in fury on Cleonilla and sanctions Ostilio's death at Caio's hand, but murder is prevented when Ostilio reveals, by exposing her breasts, that "he" is really Tullia. Everyone is astounded. Ottone forgives them and begs Cleonilla's pardon for having mistaken her fidelity. Caio is to be married off to Tullia, and Cleonilla resolves in an aside to live a better life. There is a final celebration that joy has emerged from pain, as a sailor rejoices at the calm after the storm.

The libretto is well constructed, given both the limitations of the plot and the expansive excesses of the model on which it was based. As John Hill has pointed out, this opera, like *Agrippina*, shows the influence of the Arcadian reforms, reducing the plot complications and the numbers of characters and eliminating overtly comic roles while still looking back to the satirical and carnivalesque elements inherited from the seventeenth century.[35]

There is a significant difference between *Ottone in villa* and *Agrippina*, however. *Agrippina* is a comedy of court intrigue in which the governance of the world itself is at stake, and the mythic underpinning of the story is expressed as a struggle between the king and queen of the gods. Agrippina's exclusive concern was the elevation of her son to the position of emperor, not her own aggrandizement or physical gratification. The second-act garden was a putative retreat from the overt politics of the public spaces. But it turned out to contain all of the world's dangers—even the pleasant rivulets were snakelike—and to be a place where we caught momentary glimpses of the characters' inner processes. In *Ottone in villa*, there are only the villa gardens and the corresponding inner processes: they generate a sense of claustrophobia correlative with the tight circle of erotic attraction that moves the plot. The beautiful landscapes are the site of stifling self-indulgence rather than of power politics. The grand historical figures are reduced to pastoral ciphers, and those who would remind them of the outside world of responsibility are rejected. The most arresting reference to myth is not to cosmic struggle between the elements (even as it was briefly in the *Messalina*) but to the destructive self-absorption of the story of Echo and Narcissus. The story that served Pietro Bembo as a negative, anti-Platonic example of earthly delusion in *Asolani* (chapter 2) returns here as a metaphor for the actions of the central figures of the opera.

Cleonilla, in her opening recitative and aria (I.i) is seen gathering flowers. The image is pastoral; she may be like a shepherdess, but like Poppea in the garden in *Agrippina*, she presents the image of a nymph from Ovidian myth in danger of being pursued, raped, or carried off. It becomes immediately clear, however, that *she* is the ravishing deity of the place. She is of noble birth, she says, and as the emperor's lover holds highest honors. But what good is that, when "I have a heart and soul that only desires its liberty. I do not care about jewels and gold as long as I am free to pursue Love, who like a tyrant has made his home in me, and constantly forces me to make myself servant to every beautiful boy." She loved Caio's beauty, but now is beside herself with passion for Ostilio's white cheeks, eyes, brow, and lips. It is a remarkable passage, because it manages to overturn in a few lines nearly all the Roman standards of virtue: birth, honor, liberty, and female subordination in matters of sex and social standing. She is a woman of noble birth, and her heart yearns for liberty, but not as we defined it in the myth of liberty. Rather, it is freedom of self-indulgence, liberty as Ovid defined it to be a slave to the tyrant love and to every beautiful young boy that comes her way (chapter 3). Yet while she is a slave to her passions, she is also the aggressor, rejecting and pursuing the men in the opera as suits her designs and so in this respect is the dramatic equivalent to the other designing Roman women of earlier operas, Poppea, Agrippina, and of course Messalina, who is her immediate model.[36] She is, moreover, apparently omnivorous: The boy whose features she so passionately desires is really a woman, and in the *scena ultima* she will actually excuse the fact that she was caught making love to Ostilio on the grounds that she knew Ostilio was a woman.

Her attachment to promiscuity is shared by Caio, who, although he will plea his own constancy to Cleonilla as the opera progresses as an argument for her continued attentions, nevertheless rejects it as a general principle when it does not suit him (I.v):

A man who wants to pursue constancy either does not look for his own contentment, or betrays his own pleasure.

It isn't faithfulness but a silly habit to adore one object alone, because love becomes a torment if you don't vary your pleasures.

Hill points out that Vivaldi's music plays on the words of the first line, the violin line constantly pursuing the voice in canon.[37] In the ritornello, the bass similarly echoes the violins, and the whole aria might be thought to anticipate the important echo scene (II.iii) in which Caio will reveal his true feelings.

The cycle of passions and unrequited love in an idealized setting is typical of the pastoral mode, where worldly power and goods are rejected in favor of personal desires.[38] Caio and Ottone share this rejection of the world with Cleonilla, but their expressions of it, at times in terms that are superficially idealistic, cover over impulses that are essentially selfish. They reject reminders of their responsibility to the outside world that come from Tullia and Decio. The most striking example is an extended scene at the center of the opera, fairly brief in text but given serious attention by Vivaldi with some of the most notable music in the opera. In II.iii Caio rejects warnings from Decio that his affair with Cleonilla constitutes unfaithfulness to his emperor. He then sits on a turf bench beside a pool in a sunken garden, not to rest but to commune with his grief. Tullia, hidden in a cave on the hill above, engages in a dialogue with him "as if she were an Echo," accusing him of betraying her. The first dozen lines of the scene give the idea. Italics (mine) emphasize echoed phrases:

> *Caio*. Parli Decio che vuol, che a me non cale
> Udir ciò ch' ei favella: io qui m'assido
> Non per cercar riposo,
> Ma sol per ragionar col mio dolore.
> *Tullia*. (Pena, smania, t'adira , o *traditore!*)
> *Caio*. Qual dal colle vicin voce rimbomba,
> E *traditor* mi chiama?
> *Tullia*. (Quella che abbandonata anche pur *t'ama*.)
> *Caio*. Chi *m'ama*, or dunque, un *traditor* m'apella?
> *Tullia*. (Chi tu ingrato *tradisti or ti favella*.)
> *Caio*. Or *ti favella;* e chi? Se a Tullia solo
> Fui mancator di fede?

> (*Caio*. Let Decio say what he will, I don't have to listen to what he
> says: I will sit down here, not to seek repose, but only to converse
> with my grief.
> *Tullia*. Suffer, rant and rage, o traitor.
> *Caio*. What voice echoes from the nearby hills and calls me traitor?
> *Tullia*. The one who, though abandoned, loves you still.
> *Caio*. Who loves me, but now names me traitor?
> *Tullia*. The one you betrayed, ungrateful one, speaks to you.

Caio. Now speaks to you? But who? If I have only lacked faith
  with Tullia.)

This scene, with its quiet pool in a remote setting, is an obvious heir
to the Echo and Narcissus episode in Ovid's *Metamorphoses* (3.339–510).
There the handsome Narcissus has rejected the advances of the nymph
Echo, who unfortunately can only repeat his final words. At a grassy site
with a pool so peaceful that it transcends the pastoral, Narcissus catches
sight of himself (3.407–17):

> There was a deep pool with shining silver waves, of which no shepherd
> partook, nor goats fed on the mountain, nor cattle; no bird, nor beast,
> nor drooping tree-branch disturbed it. Watered by the nearby pond, grass
> grew around. The forest never let the sun heat the place. Here the boy
> Narcissus, weary from the hunt and the heat, took his ease, attracted by
> the spot's beauty and offer of a drink. And as he wants to slake his thirst,
> another thirst starts to grow: while he drinks, smitten by the reflection
> of beauty he sees, he loves a hope without a body, he thinks something
> that is water is solid.

Narcissus, like Echo, wastes away from love of himself and dies with her
voice repeating his farewells to his own image:

> quotiensque puer miserabilis "Eheu!"
>   dixerat, haec resonis iterabat vocibus "Eheu!" . . .
>   . . . dictoque vale, "Vale" inquit et Echo.
>
> (Every time the wretched boy said, "Alas!" this "Alas!" was
>   repeated in echoing sound. . . . And with his farewell said,
>   Echo, too, says, "Farewell!")

Whatever one may think of a protagonist with no more intelligence than a
parakeet with a mirror, one must acknowledge the considerable influence
this passage has had on subsequent literature and music; the echo scene
is an old technique in stage music and was quite common in Renaissance
pastoral drama.[39] In this scene in *Ottone in villa*, the ultimate debt to Ovid
is visually clear as Caio sits on a grassy bench beside a forest pool while
the voice of the unseen, rejected Tullia emerges from the cave.[40]

There is an important formal difference between this passage and
the Ovidian model, however. Despite the stage direction indicating that
Tullia is "like an Echo," the voice of Tullia in fact takes the initiative
in the recitative section, and the puzzled and increasingly anxious Caio
plays the echo, repeating her words until he admits that they are reflections of his own inner torment ("Ah, how voices are born from my
pain, and so I seem to hear what I do not hear"). Only in the aria, when

she has successfully worked Caio up into a maddened state, does Tullia actually echo his final syllables, and even then her reply, "Hear, hear" ("Senti, senti"), at the end of the A section generates his own repetition that begins the B section:

> Tullia. (Faccia la mia vendetta il tuo tormento.)
> Caio. L'ombre, l'aure, e ancora il rio
>   Eco fanno al dolor mio;
>   Se questi solo, oh Dio, qui son pre*senti.*
> Tullia. (*Senti, senti.*)
> Caio. *Senti, senti!* Ahi, quale orror,
>   Qual'affanno, qual timor
>   *Sento* in me!

> (Tullia. May my vengeance create your torment.
> Caio. Shadows, breezes, and even the stream echo to my grief, if it is
>   only these, oh God, that are here.
> Tullia. Hear, hear.
> Caio. Hear, hear! Ah, what terror, what sorrow, what fear I feel
>   inside me.)

The text never suggests that Caio actually looks into the pool, although it would be a natural move; instead, the voices act as mirrors of his inner torment, reflecting his anguish back and forth.[41]

For Caio, as for Narcissus, the reflection is a closed circle. The echoing voice does nothing to bring him out of his self-absorbed passion: There is no recognition or metamorphosis here. When Caio believes that his grief has given birth to the voices, we may think that the moment is not sterile and that he has connected with the world outside himself. But no self-knowledge of a deeper kind results, since he concludes with "Povera la mia fè! / Non mera per mercè / Tanti tormenti," to which Tullia replies, "Menti, menti." ("My poor constancy! It does not deserve such torments." "You lie, you lie.")[42] In I.x, Tullia-as-Ostilio had told the jealous Caio that she would not speak with him until she saw in him what she did not see at that moment; that is, his acknowledgment that he has wronged her. That moment has not arrived.

The self-absorption consistently expressed by Caio and Cleonilla, who are impervious to any notion of responsibility to others, is remarkable even in a pastoral context. This is perhaps due to its background in the outrageous misbehaviors of the imperial court in Rome as described by Tacitus. (Hill, thinking in generic terms, calls this self-centeredness "a deliberate mixture of the pastoral with the heroic.")[43] When we turn to the character of Ottone, it is evident that he shares their self-absorption, even if his gullibility and his naïve and monogamous devotion to Cleonilla make him seem less selfish and more like his hapless namesake in *Poppea* and *Agrippina*.

Unlike the characters of Monteverdi and Handel, however, Vivaldi's Ottone is not a subject, but the emperor and the opera's authority figure. In this role, he repeats the chivalrous sentiment that the character Ottone had expressed in *Agrippina*, that he does not care for power without the one he loves (III.i): "I scorn everything, both throne and power, so long as I am experiencing the satisfaction of enjoying my only love." But whereas in *Agrippina* words like these were a statement of self-sacrifice on the part of the single virtuous character on stage, in this aria they are consonant with the inward-looking self-indulgence endemic to all the main characters. It is a statement of self-interest parallel to that of Cleonilla in the opening scene and of Caio's rejection of *costanza* in I.v. This pursuit of erotic gratification is legitimate for the subordinate characters in *Scipione affricano*, but it is an occupation inappropriate for a general or emperor, whose duty should be first to their office and the general good. That distinction is made explicitly by Ottone's adviser Decio, who declares in an aria, "It is no fault to be a lover, but in a ruler, it becomes a defect, it becomes baseness. For a royal heart is no longer such, if it becomes a slave to a wicked love." The aria is a minuet; the dotted rhythms, inherited from the music of French court, give a heightened tone and perhaps a hint of irony to Decio's critique of royalty.[44] In criticizing the governing ethos of the opera, Decio reports Cleonilla's opening image of herself as a slave to love in order to point out that those in a position of power in fact have no such "liberty." As Tullia is Caio's reminder of a world outside the garden to which he had obligations, so the warnings of Decio suggest that Ottone's neglect of Rome is actually dangerous: He prefaces the preceding aria with the observation, "Indeed, I foresee the impending fall of Otho; He no longer listens to my faithful advice, nor sees his great peril: his unfaithful lady makes him stupid and blind."

Ottone in villa reveals its seventeenth-century source through the nature of its *lieto fine*. An *opera seria* such as the one we will observe in the next chapter would involve full revelation of the truth followed by forgiveness given by the emperor. This ending falls far short of that: Caio, catching Cleonilla and Ostilio (Tullia) in passionate embrace, denounces them to Ottone in a jealous rage, omitting to mention his own affair with the emperor's consort. Tullia, intent on reclaiming Caio, exonerates Cleonilla with her revelation that that she is no boy and makes no mention of Caio's guilt. Ottone thus remains ignorant of Caio's affair with

Cleonilla and Cleonilla's general unfaithfulness, and he even apologizes to her for doubting her fidelity. Decio's sour observation, "Oh, how base Rome's seat of power has become," remains a just judgment, one made in the spirit of the first soldier's curse in Monteverdi's *Poppea*. The deluded Ottone makes no move to deny his passion or return to Rome, and the historical record, about which Decio has been reminding us, tells us he will indeed be overthrown and dead within a short time. There are gestures of repentance in the *scena ultima*, but they are mostly of relief at not getting caught. There is not even an intrusion of the divine, as there was in *Agrippina*, to sanction the proceedings, however ironically. Death is not so much *in* the garden as it is the garden itself, and the decadence it represents. As in the Echo and Narcissus story, the site of perfect peace and beauty in the end can only produce echoes and reflections of love and self-knowledge, not the real thing. Everything remains reflection and echo, with nothing solid to take away at the end.

The language of betrayal contributes to the sense of instability that ultimately suggests how easily this whole world could collapse. The charge of "*traditore!*" between lovers is common enough in opera. Nearly everyone in *Agrippina* charges Ottone with *tradimento*, and there the charge is notable for its injustice. But the vocabulary of betrayal—*traditore, tradimento*, and forms of the verb *tradire*—is repeated with an urgency that is notable in *Ottone in villa*. It is used in recriminations that move around the cycle of erotic attraction, from Tullia to Caio to Cleonilla. For Decio, Cleonilla's betrayals take on a political dimension, but he is literally a voice crying in the wilderness. When others, even Tullia, use political language, it is a metaphor for personal feelings or behavior. Caio in the lovely aria "Leggi almeno, Tiranna infidele" ("At least read it, faithless Tyrant"; II.vi) combines the idea of tyranny with betrayal to express his anguish that she has rejected him for Ostilio. This apparently trivial opera in the pastoral mode, not the more overtly historicized *Agrippina*, anticipates themes that will come to the fore with new urgency in revolutionary Europe. Decio's verdict on the selfishness of the governing classes and the discontent of the governed might have been written by Beaumarchais or Alfieri. Its implied evocation of the Venetian nobility at play in their pleasure gardens, mindlessly unaware of approaching cataclysm, may have been intended only as mildly comic social satire. In hindsight, the opera is weirdly prophetic of the conditions of the late eighteenth century, when an ennervated, self-indulgent Venice found herself helpless before the invading powers of France and lost her independence altogether.

The very instability of Otho's character and of the historical time in which he lived make him a useful character in these operas that were written in the period of transition from seventeenth-century carnival opera to eighteenth-century *opera seria*. The historical Otho, both dissolute and noble, effeminate and aggressively masculine, is the natural inhabitant of the pastoral landscape, itself an ambivalent location embodying both idealized retreat from sin and the origin of that sin. He can be the serpent in the *locus amoenus* but is more often its victim in a world where the female characters themselves are dangerous rather than endangered. In this respect he stands in distinct contrast to Scipio Africanus, whose strict Stoicism came under fire in Cavalli's seventeenth-century *Scipione affricano* but who will right himself and become a model of stability in Zeno's *Scipione nelle Spagne*. In Ottone's world, a "completely happy ending" is all but impossible, and solutions can only be temporary. In this respect *Agrippina* and *Ottone in villa* represent a late efflorescence of a type of opera that is as fluid in its approach to Roman history as the pastoral garden and the character of Ottone are fluid in their representations of good and its opposites.

5 *Scipio in Spain*

ZENO, *SCIPIONE NELLE SPAGNE*

If contemporary political relevance is at best oblique in *Scipione affricano* and *Agrippina*, it is by contrast impossible to miss in Apostolo Zeno's *Scipione nelle Spagne,* written for production in the Catalan capital of Barcelona in 1710. The opera was performed during the War of Spanish Succession for the Austrian contender for the Spanish throne, Charles III (later Emperor Charles VI), and his queen, Elizabeth Christina, styled as "monarchi delle Spagne" on the title page to the libretto. According to Francesco Negri's *La vita di Apostolo Zeno,* the libretto of *Scipione nelle Spagne* was initially written at the request of the Marchese Giorgio Clerici, *capo del Senato* of Milan, and the plot chosen on purpose to please the Spaniards' sense of dignity ("di lusingare la gravità degli Spagnuoli").[1] In writing this first *dramma per musica* that explicitly told the story of the Continence of Scipio, Zeno adapted a prose drama by Giovanni Battista Boccabadati titled *Scipione, overo Le gare eroiche,* which had been performed for the marriage of Francesco d'Este and Margherita Farnese in 1693. Zeno's libretto is entirely the product of the Arcadian reforms in spirit as well as structure and the first example in this book of what came to be called *opera seria.* In its dignified presentation of imperial power (as opposed to the carnivalesque depictions we have seen so far), it is also our first example of the myth of the clement prince in its wholly positive form. Unlike the operas in the previous chapter, *Scipione nelle Spagne* is meant to have a completely happy ending.

Apostolo Zeno was the second Venetian librettist to be cultivated by the Habsburg court. Nicolò Minato, subsequent to celebrating the Spanish connections to Lorenzo Colonna with his *Scipione affricano,* had gone to Vienna to serve as the first *poeta cesareo* under Leopold I for nearly thirty years (1669–98). He was followed in that capacity by Donato Cupeda (1698–1705) and Silvio Stampiglia (1705–18), the former from Naples, the latter an Arcadian with connections to the Habsburgs through the Roman Colonna family and Giovanni Bononcini. Stampiglia was still in Vienna when Zeno wrote *Scipione nelle Spagne.* Zeno would follow as *poeta cesareo* from 1718 to 1729.

The music for the 1710 Barcelona production no longer exists but may have been by Antonio Caldara.[2] Following the Barcelona premiere, versions of Zeno's libretto were produced in Naples (1714, with a score by Alessandro Scarlatti), in Vienna (1722, Caldara), Venice (1724, Albinoni), Wolfenbüttel (1728, in German), Genoa (1728), Munich (1732), Florence (1739), and Milan (1740).[3] The official text of the libretto was published (Venice, 1744) in the *Poesie drammatiche* of Zeno, "formerly poet and historian of Emperor Charles VI and now of her most Serene Royal Majesty Maria Teresa, Queen of Hungary and Bohemia, etc." This opera may therefore fairly be regarded as an Austrian Habsburg piece, intended originally as an affirmation of Charles III's claim to Spain during the War of the Spanish Succession and performed subsequently in contexts that celebrated Habsburg history and power.

Charles VI, after he left Barcelona in 1711 for Vienna to become emperor, developed a thoroughgoing artistic and moral program, drawing on the iconography of his Spanish Habsburg predecessors, especially Charles V and Philip II. Charles V, for example, had led a fleet from Barcelona in 1535 to Tunis in North Africa, where he had defeated Turkish forces decisively, becoming "the hero of Christendom, the new Scipio, the conqueror of Carthage." He appeared on special medals as Carolus Imperator Augustus Africanus.[4] The Habsburg iconography included the complex blending of Judeo-Christian tradition with that of Greco-Roman antiquity; the emperor and his power and dignity were allied in various ways with Solomon and the Virgin Mary from the one tradition, and with Apollo, Hercules, Aeneas, and the emperor Augustus from the other.[5] An elaborate canon of virtues associated with the Habsburg house, which included justice and equality, clemency, and wisdom, went back to the time of Emperor Ferdinand II, whose text *Princeps in compendio* (1632) set out principles of Habsburg imperial governance based on neo-Stoic ideas.[6]

It is no surprise, then, that while still the claimant to the throne of Spain, Charles III should appeal to the young Scipio's exploits in the

Iberian peninsula. A consideration of *Scipione nelle Spagne*, performed the year before Charles left for Vienna, strongly suggests that the kind of program promulgated for Charles as emperor was already in his mind and that of his advisers while he was still in Barcelona. Habsburg virtues, particularly clemency and justice, are displayed by all the leading characters in this opera, both Spanish and Roman.[7] Zeno was already creating for Charles an ideal synthesis of artistic medium and Habsburg message, and the Stoic content that has been claimed for *L'incoronazione di Poppea* genuinely does structure this opera and those like it in the decades to come.

Scipione nelle Spagne *as Neo-Stoic Drama*

The action of *Scipione nelle Spagne* takes place at New Carthage just after the Roman siege and capture of the town and thus places it in the historical situation described in Polybius and Livy (chapter 2). The Romans are represented by Scipione the proconsul, by his tribune Marzio, and by another officer named Tribellio. Among the captives are Elvira, a native Spanish woman of the Illergetan people, and Sofonisba, daughter of the Carthaginian commander Mago. Mago himself does not appear. The other native Spaniards are Cardenio, prince of the Illergeti and brother of Elvira, and Luceio (Livy's Allucius), prince of the Celtiberi, an enemy of the Romans and engaged to Sofonisba. This is obviously not the historical Sophonisba, but the name raises deliberate associations of the kind described in chapter 3.

Before the action started, Sofonisba and Luceio were betrothed and in love, but their marriage was interrupted by the Roman siege and capture of New Carthage. Cardenio and Scipione, too, fall in love with Sofonisba. The Roman tribune Marzio conceives a passion for Elvira, who in her turn loves Luceio. The only reciprocal affection is between Sofonisba and Luceio, a fact that is responsible for many of the difficulties in the opera. But in addition to—and finally more important than—the romantic relationships, is the strong and immediate attraction Scipione develops to Luceio's nobility of character, and his concerted effort to win Luceio's admiration in return. Luceio, against his will, is slowly brought to recognize Scipione's own nobility. His commitment to Scipione's friendship generates a series of challenges to his honor that cause the principal tensions of the opera as they come into conflict with his private affections.

In act I Luceio, regarded as a dangerous enemy by the Romans, appears disguised in armor taken from a dead soldier, and claims to be a servant named Tersandro. He finds his beloved Sofonisba on the beach, where she has washed up after leaping in despair from a tower where she had been prisoner. Scipione arrives looking for Sofonisba and there meets "Tersandro." In the meantime, the Roman tribune Marzio has been pursuing Elvira aggressively, but she has bluntly rejected him. When Elvira's brother Cardenio defends her honor, Scipione and "Tersandro" appear to break up the fight. Scipione scolds Marzio, sends Elvira off to the city for protection, but has Cardenio put in chains as an enemy of Rome. "Tersandro" objects and Scipione then agrees that Cardenio may be released if "Tersandro" will swear friendship to him. He agrees to the bargain. Sofonisba, for her part, is politely pursued by Scipione but says she will only marry him when "Tersandro" says she should.

In act II the unfortunate consequences of Luceio's disguise and his oath to Scipione become clear: Scipione sends Luceio to woo Sofonisba for him, and Luceio, believing that his honor demands that he keep his oath to Scipione, does so, much to Sofonisba's hurt outrage. He forces her to accept Scipione by threatening to reveal his true identity to the Romans and so be killed by them. Elvira, in love with Luceio and believing he is now free, confesses her love to him. The tribune Marzio overhears and denounces her for loving what he believes to be a lowborn servant. To protect Elvira's honor, Luceio reveals his real identity to Marzio, and Marzio in angry triumph demands Luceio's death from Scipione.

Act III begins as Scipione offers Luceio the opportunity to escape with Sofonisba. Luceio almost agrees, but finally honoring his oath of friendship, he determines to leave Sofonisba to Scipione and go to his death. Marzio arrives to explain that if Scipione gives him Elvira, he will save Luceio. Scipione is outraged but has no alternative but to accept the offer. Luceio appears to go along with the decision but makes Marzio swear that if anything goes wrong, Marzio will give up any claim on Elvira forever.

Marzio brings Luceio, once again in disguise, to the Roman camp, asking them to spare "Tersandro." Luceio foils his plan and identifies himself to the Roman army, demanding that they kill him, and hence ensures Elvira's release from Marzio. With his speech he impresses upon the Romans both his own and Scipione's nobility, so instead of killing him they cry, "Viva, Scipione!" and turn on Marzio. In the *scena ultima*, Scipione forgives a remorseful Marzio and tries once again to unite Luceio with Sofonisba. Luceio insists that despite his love for her, Sofonisba by rights belongs to Scipione. It is finally given to Elvira to judge, and despite her own feelings for Luceio, she decides in favor of giving Sofonisba to him. The opera ends in general rejoicing at the victory of love and virtue.

Despite the heady complications caused by the characters' love, jealousy, and sense of honor in this libretto, it is more tightly organized than Minato's *Scipione affricano*, showing the effects of the Arcadian reforms in which Zeno was a leading figure.[8] There are places where it appears that Zeno was consulting Minato's libretto, but the sense of the miraculous and spectacular has largely disappeared. Sofonisba's leap from her tower into the sea may be a deliberate reference to Siface's famous parachuting scene in Minato, but it takes place discreetly offstage.[9] There are no intrusions by oracular sibyls or helpful deities, no burning ships, heroic plunges into the harbor, nor even a gladiatorial combat. Gone, too, are the overtly comic elements. There are no lower-class buffoons as there were in Monteverdi and Cavalli, and no secondary comic plot such as the one involving Luceio and Ericlea in *Scipione affricano*.[10] Instead, as was to become typical in Zeno's librettos, a central set of related moral issues are emphasized by the complications resulting from the characters' romantic interests.[11]

The anxiety about *honore* and *virtù* among the men, especially Luceio and Scipione, reflects a general continental European interest with what Gordon Braden has called the "drama of self-respect"; that is, a "mixture of conscience and egoism."[12] But in this opera it is meant to evoke a particularly Spanish concern with what the Marchese Clerici had called the "gravità degli Spagnuoli" when commissioning the libretto. In the case of the women, this means fear of physical violation, about which more will be said below. Issues of freedom and slavery arise, of course, but they are not the source of anxiety that they were in *Scipione affricano*. Elvira tells Scipione (I.ii), "Being your prisoner is not my misfortune; I fear that military license is contemplating new victories over my honor." Sofonisba confirms this, saying to Scipione (I.vii): "I do not count being your slave among my misfortunes." The central conflict is instead summed up in Sofonisba's complaint, "O cruel laws of love and of honor!" ("O d'amor, e d'onor leggi crudeli!"; II.vi). This conflict of love and honor is not finally resolved until the summation of the final chorus.

There were hints of similar concerns in *Scipione affricano*, too, particularly in the motivations and behavior of Siface, but overall in that drama these issues—the formalization of victory and defeat—were more overridingly public. The private passions were governed by public action but did not contribute directly to the movement of history. In *Scipione nelle Spagne*, by contrast, the principals' preoccupation with personal virtue and honor is what drives the public events of the opera, for the "public"—that is, the Roman army—is only brought in to second the passions of the central individuals.

In *Scipione nelle Spagne*, Luceio's oath to be Scipione's friend, sworn on Scipione's sword, is pivotal in producing the moral conundrums that challenge Luceio as he negotiates his position between Scipione, Sofonisba, and Elvira. At I.xvi Scipione has agreed that he will not imprison Cardenio if "Tersandro" swears to be his friend. Sofonisba witnesses the event and comments aside:

> *Scipione.* That burden that hangs at your side: first, yield it to me.
> *Luceio.* I understand. I'll happily succeed Cardenio in chains. Here is my sword, and know that only my virtue could take it from my side.
> *Sofonisba.* (Deadly virtue!)
> *Sci.* Swear to be my friend. That is my condition.
> *Sof.* (I breathe again.)
> *Luc.* (Bitter condition, that takes from me my hatred of my rival, in order to free another from him.)
> *Sci.* Does Scipio's friendship cause you so much pain?
> *Luc.* More than you think. But destiny requires it. I swear.
> *Sci.* Swear on this sword. Then accept it as a gift.
> *Luc.* Tersandro swears. And now I am your friend. And be this the pledge of my faith, that now I accept this illustrious blade, your gift, and I hang it at my side in service as your warrior.*

After Scipione's departure, Sofonisba wonders to Luceio how he can swear friendship with his rival for her love: "One who can love Scipio can also lose me without grief," she reasons. His answer is that *virtù* constrained his actions, but that he could not lose her without pain to himself.

This scene is an expression of another aspect of the Spanish heritage; that is, an intense concern over the niceties of ethical choices, expressed in casuistic argument.[13] In the dramas of Lope de Vega and Calderón, impossible moral conflicts are set up for the apparent theatrical pleasure of watching the characters squirm under the contrary demands of personal obligation and those of the heart. This fundamental dilemma is, of course, part of tragic and melodramatic theater from its very beginning, but the difference in Spanish-style drama is the joy taken in teasing out the fine points of a problem only to have it reappear and be argued all over again.[14] Luceio's uncompromising determination to do the honorable thing generates such crises in all three acts.

In Luceio's case, his sense of honor that will be the source of these conundrums is firmly connected with the tenets of Stoicism. Neo-Stoic thought had colored intellectual life in Zeno's Venice for much of the seventeenth century, as we have seen already, and it informed the moral dimension that Zeno and the Arcadian reformers were trying to instill in operatic texts.[15] This, too, is part of the Spanish texture of the opera. Seneca, a primary source for Stoic thought, was himself born in Spain, and so was a national hero in the early modern period. Moreover, Spanish Jesuits were active in promulgating Lipsius's fusion of pagan Stoic and Christian philosophy.[16]

Thus, when Elvira says in the *scena ultima*, "Thus far virtue competes with virtue between Luceio and Scipio," her statement identifies the quest for virtue, the central goal of Stoicism, as a fundamental issue of the opera. The Stoic preoccupations had come together definitively in the crucial scene at III.ii: Luceio has revealed his identity and is in danger of his life from Marzio and the troops. Scipione offers him the possibility of escape in an exchange that takes the form of philosophic dialogues familiar from earlier operas and derives from Senecan drama and philosophy (chapter 3). Marzio has roused the Roman troops to demand Luceio's death, a fate that Luceio himself believes his honor demands that he accept. Scipione disagrees:

> *Scipione.* Rome is not accustomed to punish an act of virtue.
> *Luceio.* Virtue that harms the public interest is betrayal.
> *Sci.* The Senate has given me sovereign authority.
> *Luc.* Here the power belongs to the military camp, not the senate.
> *Sci.* I am the camp's leader.
> *Luc.* A blind fire is free from laws, and consumes everything.
> *Sci.* Oh, make your escape! As a friend, I beg it of you.
> *Luc.* That word [friend] is sacred to me, wherever it doesn't
>   contradict duty.*

Two key Stoic concepts, virtue and duty, are fundamental to this argument, and both prevent Luceio from accepting Scipione's offer. When Scipione commands him to escape and take Sofonisba with him, Luceio objects that he has already ceded Sofonisba to Scipione. "Oh costanza!" remarks Scipione, and Luceio echoes with an agonized, "Oh dover!" Constancy, another important Stoic concept, joins duty as an operating cause of Luceio's actions. Then Scipione steps aside where he is visible to Sofonisba but not Luceio:

> *Luceio.* What proof of my faithfulness do you demand to my shame?
>   But I will obey you—let us go. Let Carthage be left behind. Let a
>   brave death be lost: Scipio asks it, Sofonisba desires it. My promise imposes it. Let us go. You have won.

*In the act of leaving, he sets out past the place where Scipio is, and
after seeing him, stops in thought.*
(Ah! What am I doing? Where am I going? Scipio is the judge of my
   cowardice.)
Sofonisba. Now what is stopping you?
Luc. to himself, while holding Sofonisba's hand. (Die. And die, too,
   with your Sofonisba's hatred. But do not fail your duty.) *He goes
   toward Scipione.*
Scipione. (He is once again uncertain.)
Sof. (Once again I am fearful.)
Luc. Alas, Sir, pardon me for my weakness. Too great a love almost
   made me betray my friendship. Here is Sofonisba. I have made
   her your wife. I leave her behind; and I go to my death. *

Because Luceio has sworn friendship with Scipione, it is his duty to fulfill
the requirements of that friendship. He is reminded of that obligation by
the very sight of his friend, whom he fears is judging him for his *viltà*. He
is behaving in accordance with the precepts of Seneca, who wrote (*Epistle*
11.8), "We must love some good man, and always keep him before our
eyes, in order to live as if he were looking on, and do all as though he
was seeing them." Luceio, like a Stoic sage, is able to face death rather
than disgrace, despite his passion for Sofonisba.[17] As he stands between
Sofonisba and Scipione, he makes his Herculean choice for virtue rather
than pleasure, yet another indication of the Stoic bent of the opera.

Luceio as Cato

This foregrounding of Luceio and his moral dilemmas is the most striking
aspect of Boccabadati's play *Scipione, overo Le gare eroiche* and, in consequence, of Zeno's adaptation. Scipione's passion for the Spanish maiden,
in this case transferred to the Carthaginian Sofonisba, becomes almost
beside the point. As required by the story, Scipione conquers himself in
the last scene. But since his suit to Sofonisba is always gentlemanly and
even hesitant, it is not a very interesting self-conquest, nor is it accompanied by a complex of erotic verbal imagery, as it had been in *Scipione
affricano*. Scipione does not even announce his own self-conquest; it is
Luceio who declares in the *scena ultima*, "I shall see the world subdued
by your valor, now that, despite so great a love, you have conquered
yourself."[18] Luceio's moral authority to make such a statement arises
from his own self-conquest, as again and again he fulfills his obligations
to Scipione, Cardenio, and Elvira. To his beloved Sofonisba, on the other
hand, he makes clear that his honor is more important than his affections,

and he is ready and willing to sacrifice them to fulfill his obligations of friendship to Scipione once he has sworn it.

The ancient referent for Luceio's behavior is Cato the Younger (95–46 B.C.E.), the great-grandson of the Cato who appeared in Minato's libretto, a staunch and uncompromising member of the pro-senatorial faction in the late Roman Republic, his resolve stiffened by his adherence to Stoic philosophy.[19] He joined Pompey's forces to oppose Julius Caesar, whom he regarded as a threat to the republican form of government, and after Pompey's defeat and death, led the senatorial resistance in North Africa. His suicide at Utica earned him the name Uticensis, and he became a symbol of resistance to imperial tyranny, as we have already observed in chapter 1. Because of Cato's saintlike virtues, Dante placed him at the shores of Purgatory to goad newly arrived souls on to their cleansing torments (Purgatorio C. 1). In the eighteenth century, Cato was a symbol of liberty against tyranny, as we will see in the next chapter, represented as the hero of Addison's tragedy Cato and Metastasio's opera Il Catone in Utica. Lewis Theobald in 1713 produced a summary of his life distilled from the ancient sources, meant as a guide for readers of Addison's play Cato. Theobald's quotation from Velleius Paterculus summarizes the value of Cato's life:

> He was a man (says Velleius Paterculus) that was the very picture of virtue, and in all his faculties more allied to the purity of the gods than the frailties of man; who never did a good action in ostentation of honesty, but because he could not recede from the sentiments of honour which were engrafted in his breast, and only thought such proceedings had reason on their side which were founded on justice.[20]

A famous but somewhat puzzling episode from Cato's life is especially pertinent for this opera. Cato's wife Marcia had borne him three children when his friend Hortensius asked him to divorce her so that he, Hortensius, could marry her and link his family with Cato's. According to Plutarch, Cato acceded to Hortensius's request because of their friendship (Cato 25.4–5). After Hortensius's death, he took Marcia back again into his home as his wife, apparently at her own request, just before he left for the wars against Caesar. The episode was famous but met with mixed reactions from subsequent interpreters.[21] Dante only glancingly alluded to the episode ("all she asked, I did") and chose to represent Cato as stoically resolute against the demands of passion even in death. When Vergil tells him that Marcia, who is in Limbo, prays constantly to her husband, Cato replies,

"Marcia was so pleasing in my eyes
there on the other side," he answered then
"that all she asked, I did. Now that she lies
beyond the evil river, no word or prayer
of hers may move me. Such was the Decree
pronounced upon us when I rose from there."[22]

This tradition of Cato and Marcia, taken together with the overt neo-Stoicism in *Scipione nelle Spagne,* especially in connection with Luceio, suggest that the Luceio's behavior is meant to call to mind the steadfast Stoic virtues of Cato. Luceio's choices are always made according to moral reasoning connected with his virtue and duty, to the exclusion of the demands of love. It is true that a similar situation occurs in *Scipione affricano,* when in II.xvii Siface finds himself obligated to plead Massanissa's suit to Sofonisba. The results are very different, however. Minato's Siface is disguised as a slave, and has no wish for his pleas to succeed, as indeed they do not. The unswerving insistence of Zeno's Luceio on giving his beloved Sofonisba up to his sworn friend Scipione, and his willingness to go to his death, pass understanding unless seen in the light of Cato's own devotion to friendship in preference to romantic love. On a dramaturgical level, the figure of moral adviser, so common in the seventeenth-century librettos, has been absorbed by one of the main characters.

Based on what we have said so far, one might conclude that the opera maintains a reasonably close relation to the spirit of the original Continence story in its narration of male alliances. In Livy and Polybius the Spanish maiden is nameless, essentially a commodity. The analysis above suggests that the women in *Scipione nelle Spagne* do not enjoy a much better position, acting as markers of the shifting contest for male superiority in a field of Spanish honor, Stoic virtue, and political dominance. The focus shifts from Scipione to Luceio, despite the celebration of Scipione's self-conquest at the end. What matters most is that Luceio has prevailed by his determined, Catonian insistence on his Stoic values and Spanish sense of honor. It is he who makes the Choice of Hercules, and the continence in the opera appears to be Luceio's far more than Scipione's.

Feminine Virtue and the Theme of Judgment

These conclusions must be provisional, however, for the women in this opera are neither nameless nor simple commodities, and there is one more philosophical turn to the plot before all is resolved. Practically speaking, the women's power comes from the fact that they are played by singers with requirements for arias. Moreover, the age of chivalry has intervened between the classical and the early modern worlds, and a certain gallantry is due to noble women, especially as the opera was being played partly in compliment to Queen Elizabeth Christina.[23] In addition, there is an issue of genre, which will be discussed at the end of this section. But Zeno is also clearly interested in these women as dramatic characters and made good use of professional and cultural demands.

The very names of the women are significant. Sofonisba was of course a name to conjure with, perhaps taken from Minato's libretto and suggesting potential danger for Romans as well as their susceptible native allies.[24] Elvira's name, on the other hand, sticks out from those of the historically based personae as aggressively modern and Spanish, an icon of her pride in her birth and position.[25] Her first words to Scipione make this clear: "I am a Spaniard: Heaven has given me noble spirits equal to my birth." To Marzio's offer of marriage she replies with incredulous indignation, "I, born to a throne, I, married to a lowly tribune?" As a Spaniard she is therefore as mindful of her honor as is Luceio; her proud words to Scipione are followed immediately by the statement that we have already quoted indicating that she is more concerned about the protection of her honor (onestà) from violation by Scipione's soldiers than she is about the loss of her freedom. The sentiment is anticipated by Sofonisba, who tells Luceio that she sought her own death by leaping from the tower partly because of Scipione's unwanted attentions (I.v/vi). In I.xii she asks Luceio to kill her out of a similar fear.

This concern about physical violation of the women is present in the ancient sources: Both Polybius and Livy report that after the sack of New Carthage the Carthaginian captive women approached him to plead for protection from violation.[26] The fear is not, however, a mere nod to historiographical accuracy and Spanish honor but is a motive for the opera's action that was based in reality. Fear of rape is a genuine anxiety for women caught in the path of any invading army, a fact vividly demonstrated by the upheavals of the seventeenth century, and still not very far away in the battlegrounds of 1710. Montaigne had reported an episode in France remarkably similar to Sofonisba's leap from her tower:

> During the disorders of our poor country, I was told that a girl, living near where I then was, had thrown herself out of a high window to avoid the violence of a knavish soldier quartered in her house. Not killed by the fall, she reasserted her purpose by trying to cut her throat with a knife. From this she was prevented, but only after wounding herself gravely. She herself confessed that the soldier had as yet pressed her only with

requests, solicitations and gifts; but she had been afraid, she said, that he would finally resort to force. And all this with such words, such expressions, not to mention the blood that testified to her virtue, as would have become another Lucrece.[27]

The similarity of the unfortunate woman's circumstances and their results to those of Sofonisba and Elvira is arresting and serves as an example of the reality behind the anxieties of Sofonisba and Elvira. At the other end of the social scale, Empress Maria Theresa could be caricatured in similar danger. A cartoon from 1742 shows the Austrian War of Succession as a group of men surrounding Maria Theresa and pulling her clothes off, exposing her leg and breasts and evidently intent on fully disrobing her.[28] The caption says, "The Queen of Hungary being undressed," but the implication of humiliation and sexual violation is clear. If the Queen of Hungary was not actually in the same danger of physical violation as Montaigne's peasant woman, she could still be depicted that way in a world of male politics. The native princesses of Zeno's libretto suffer a very real threat. In Sofonisba's case, it is a matter of avoiding marriage to an enemy she cannot love. Elvira's case is worse, because Marzio makes it clear that he will take by force what is not given willingly.

This sense of danger to Zeno's heroines is heightened by the powerful resonances of the name Sofonisba. The situation of a captive city taken by the Romans must call to mind the heritage of the African Queens described in chapter 3, who preferred death rather than submission to Roman domination. Therefore, the combination of gritty reality with the larger sense of legendary paradigm gives these women a dramatic force and power in this opera equal to that of the relationship between Luceio and Scipione.

That power of the female characters grows until ultimately, in the *lieto fine*, Elvira is granted the final disposition of judgment that amounts, really, to a Clemency of Elvira. The way for this culminating event is prepared by a series of briefer judgments that make clear where the source and nature of power of judgment lies. On the seashore in I.vi, as Scipione politely pursues his interest in the damp but otherwise unharmed Sofonisba, she replies to him that she will love Scipione when "Tersandro" tells her to do so. "You make him my judge, and I accept him," replies Scipione gallantly. ("Tu mio giudice il rendi, ed io l'accetto.") Sofonisba sets her condition in the complete confidence that Luceio-Tersandro would never give her to Scipione. But she is mistaken about that: Since Luceio subsequently swears friendship to Scipione, he will in turn come to insist in II.xiv that Sofonisba marry Scipione, a position he will staunchly maintain until the end of the *scena ultima*. In the meantime, Scipione has generously acceded to Sofonisba and accepted an apparently

low-born enemy soldier as his arbiter over the case, based on his perception of the man's nobility of spirit. In this way Scipione marks his own
humanity and his difference from the violent Marzio by indicating his
willingness to relinquish power to others who deserve it.

In I.xvi, however, Scipione's iron fist shows itself under the felt glove
of his gallantry. He has broken up the fight between Marzio and Elvira's
brother, Cardenio, but having reprimanded Marzio for insubordination
and sent Elvira away under protection, he turns to Cardenio, an enemy
of Rome, and subjects him to captivity and incarceration. "Tersandro"
objects, and Scipione is surprised that there should be a problem: "I am
now his judge; I must punish him if he offends us" ("Suo giudice or son
io; deggio punirlo / Se colpevole ci sia"). The moment is important, for
despite the fact that Scipione commutes Cardenio's sentence at "Tersandro's" request, the reality of his power is briefly exhibited and results
in the bargain by which Cardenio will be released if Luceio swears friendship to Scipione. Luceio's agreement to do so, as we have seen, creates
the principal dilemmas of the opera.

In III.ii, already quoted at length above, in connection with the Stoic
values of the opera, the theme of judgment, combined with Stoic ideas
about virtue, friendship, constancy, and duty, precipitates a crisis that
nearly turns the drama into tragedy. Luceio, about to escape with Sofonisba, is torn by a paroxysm of doubt, for he fears that his new friend,
famous for his own virtue, is judging Luceio's own behavior: "Oh, what
am I doing? Where am I going? Scipione is judge of my cowardice" ("Ahi!
che fo? dove vò? giudice è Scipio / Di mia viltà"). He returns Sofonisba
to Scipione and goes, as he thinks, to his death at the hands of Marzio
and the Roman troops.[29]

It is clear, then, who is the superior force both tactically and morally.
Despite Scipione's magnanimous willingness to defer to "Tersandro"
as judge in matters of love, when real questions of power arise, he is
the final authority by virtue of his position as conquering general. It is,
therefore, interesting to observe how the balance of power tips to Elvira
in the *scena ultima*.

First, a brief pair of scenes at III.v–vi unites Elvira and Sofonisba in
their mutual love for Luceio. In III.v Sofonisba refuses to hate Elvira, despite the fact that it was through her that Luceio revealed himself and is
in danger of dying at the Romans' hands. Elvira is then left in III.vi with a
solo scene and aria in which she resolves to love Luceio, with "love that
is wholly faith, wholly love, and constancy; without hope and without
jealousy." Her aria envisions her love in a Platonic-style flight above the
earth, kept aloft by Virtue.[30]

Raise yourself, Love, and go up; take passionate flight and debase yourself no more. In order that you not fall to earth from new deceits, Virtue
will support your flight.[31]

The pact between the women, followed by Elvira's solo, has the effect
of giving Elvira the last word between them and making her the active
agent. She then grows in authority over both Luceio and Scipione in
III.x–xi, claiming her right to decide her own fate: "In this decision, the
discretion is mine" ("In questa legge / l'arbitrio è mio").

In the final scenes, Luceio, in revealing himself and thwarting Mar-
zio's intentions, saves the day where Scipione apparently cannot, and fur-
thermore returns Scipione's power to him by inspiring the troops to shout
"Viva Scipione" (III.xvi). This action results in Scipione's act of *clemenza.*
He replies that the cry of "Viva" applies to the troops themselves and to
Rome, and then he forgives a penitent Marzio and bestows Sofonisba on
Luceio.

But all is not yet resolved in this contentious drama. Luceio rejects
the conventional *lieto fine* and refuses Scipione's gift:

> *Scipione.* But, Luceio, what reward can I return that is sufficient for
> your merits? I have nothing other than Sofonisba. I give her back
> to you.
> *Luceio.* Pardon me: Sofonisba is already betrothed to you.
> *Sci.* She should be yours.
> *Luc.* You have her pledge.
> *Sci.* You have her heart.
> *Luc.* Duty has made her yours.
> *Sci.* And Love, yours.
> *Sof.* (Rivalries [*Gare*], my constant trouble!)*

The resolution can therefore come from neither of the men. Instead it
is given to Elvira, whose soaring *virtù* makes her the ideal arbiter. The
moment is cast as the final and most important judgment, though not
perhaps without potential for humor as the men once again indulge in
legalistic hairsplitting:

> *Scipione.* In so illustrious a dispute our judge should now be Sofonisba.
> *Luceio.* She would be at once a judge and plaintiff. I would welcome
> Tribellio.
> *Sci.* He is a Roman. I choose Cardenio.
> *Luceio.* He is my countryman.
> *Sci.* I choose Elvira.
> *Luc.* I am content. . . .
> *Elvira.* Now ready yourself for a grand assault, oh my heart.
> *Sci. & Luc.* Beauty, . . .

Sci. On you depends . . .
Luc. On you awaits . . .
Sci. The peace of two hearts.
Luc. The sovereign judgment.
Sci. She is on fire for Luceio. I hope in vain.
Elv. Up to now virtue contends with virtue between Luceio and
Scipio, glory with glory. The honor is equal. Now only love de-
cides such heroic rivalries between you. He that united with an
immortal chain the hearts of Sofonisba and Luceio, let him also
bind together their right hands; let Spain applaud and let Hymen
be proud. *

Elvira pronounces the male competition for virtue a draw and bases
her final judgment on mutual love. It is she who really creates the *lieto
fine* through her own self-conquest and her Herculean choice for virtue
rather than pleasure.[32] To put it a different way, through Elvira, the erotic
values of opera prevail over masculine pride and military power to assert
a happy ending resulting in the marriage of the appropriate couple. The
question of how Sofonisba could finally love the recalcitrant Luceio after
all that has happened might push verisimilitude to the breaking point. If
I am right about the association of Luceio with the younger Cato, however, their love is not to be understood in Ovidian or comic terms, as
was that of Ericlea and Lucejo in *Scipione affricano.* It is more akin to
the devotion and reunification of Cato and Marcia, based on honor and
virtue rather than passion.

The Spanish and Stoic contests of virtue by the men are nevertheless bested by Elvira's love, which transcends issues of personal honor
and creates true harmony; it is perhaps a faint echo of the Platonic ideas
about the heavenly love described in chapter 2. The final chorus recognizes the victory of love as virtue:

Sof. & Luc. And now I find in love,
Scip. Elv. & Card. And I find in virtue,
Together. . . . My own peace. When love is virtue, one is always happy.
Armed with his own strength he will find delight either in his
own love or in his own honor. *

The apparently irreconcilable demands of love and honor, as expressed
in Sofonisba's agonized cry, "O d'amor, e d'onor leggi crudeli," have been
reconciled after all. Elvira has become the female figure of Justice, a Hispanic Astraea, returning to earth from her airborne flight of virtue, as
represented in her aria, to bring equality and justice to human endeav-
ors on earth. The connection is not fanciful. Already in 1711, the year
after this opera was first produced, when Charles became emperor, his

official antiquary, Carl Gustav Heraeus, was suggesting a complicated series of interconnections between Charles's accession and the return of the Augustan golden age as depicted by Vergil. That return was marked most famously in the fourth *Eclogue* by the return of Astraea (Justice) to earth after her offended departure in the early ages of men.[33] This opera anticipates the use of that imagery, probably connecting once again to imagery associated with Charles V. Ariosto, for example, had celebrated Charles as the bringer of the new golden age:

> By [Charles V] againe *Astraea* shall be brought,
> And be restored from her long exile,
> And vertues that have long been set at nought,
> Shall raigne and banish fraud deceit and guile.[34]

Justice was one of the principles in the Habsburg canon of virtues, one linked closely with the piety and godliness of the emperor.[35] Since in heaven Astraea was figured as the constellation Virgo, the virgin, she was also associated with the Virgin Mary, and so the figure of Astraea comprises both the Christian piety and worldly justice in Habsburg iconography.[36] The result is that in *Scipione nelle Spagne* Elvira becomes an analogue to the heavenly virgin come to earth to bring redemption and justice. Whereas Poppea was Venus on earth in an ironic mode, Elvira is a figure that appears to transcend even the role of Scipione to connect with the philosophical issues of the drama and refer subtly to the iconography of Habsburg self-presentation. The Spaniards' sense of dignity in Barcelona of 1710 was well served.

In an opera presented before the Habsburg claimant to the throne of Spain, then, the emphasis is not on the fact that the Spaniards are conquered peoples and Scipione the conqueror as much as on their qualities as equals who deserve one another. Scipione rules, to be sure, but he can be aided and at times corrected by his subjects who themselves demonstrate the Habsburg virtues: the steadfast honor of a Cato and a sense of Justice equal to that of Astraea herself. Ericlea was allowed a carnivalesque reversal of authority in order to pronounce the final words at the end of *Scipione affricano*. Elvira's reversal carries far greater moral weight, elevating her to an abstract version of the Justice and Clemency to which both Scipio and the Habsburgs claimed to aspire. Ironically, this abstraction of the female character to an almost allegorical figure of virtue is a tactic we will see used for very different purposes in republican, anti-imperial operas such as Metastasio's *Il Catone in Utica* and, in the wake of the French revolution, Salfi's *La congiura pisoniana*.[37]

Imperial Virtue and the Reform of Opera

As we noted at the beginning of the chapter, Charles VI instituted his iconographical program to promulgate his ideas about power and imperial government in earnest with his accession to the throne in 1711. But Charles had a liking for music and public show, and he was not shy of spending money on it that he could not really afford while prosecuting a war.[38] Part of this expense, during his time in Catalonia, was the introduction of Italian opera to the peninsula. If the analysis of *Scipione nelle Spagne* above is correct, the beginnings of the Viennese program were already taking shape in the art produced while Charles was still in Spain.[39]

The difference between Zeno's ideological and philosophical stance in *Scipione nelle Spagne* and Minato's in *Scipione affricano* is quite striking. *Scipione affricano* was an opera written by Italians for an Italian sponsor and Italian audiences. The flattering analogies that could be drawn between the operatic hero Scipione and the dedicatee Lorenzo Colonna, minimal as they were, were relatively natural and straightforward. Minato's Scipione represented a tradition of Italian nobility that stretched back to the Romans and might still express itself in the present day, either in Venice, which regarded itself as Rome's heir, or in Rome herself.

Something different was happening in *Scipione nelle Spagne*. Although the text and, probably, the music, were produced by Italian artists, the opera was created for an Austrian sponsor who was, in the habit of his family, appropriating the Roman myth for his own purposes.[40] In an Italian artistic project, the Italians themselves have been excluded entirely from the political picture painted by the opera, which celebrates the virtues of Austrians and their would-be subjects in Spain. This picture reflected exactly the European political realities. In the first decades of the eighteenth century, Spain itself, its power diminished but still important because of its holdings in southern Italy and the New World, became the object of dispute between the Sun King of France and the Holy Roman Emperor. Italy was certainly not a contender in the imperial game; it was the consolation prize for Charles, when France and the allied states agreed that as emperor he should not be allowed to possess Spain as well as Austria and so reconstruct the empire of Charles V.

Nevertheless, an imperialist project of a different kind was afoot in Italy. The reform of literature and drama associated with the Arcadians was gathering momentum. Zeno was an active organizer of the *Accademia degli Animati* in Venice. His letters from 1698 show that he was in continual communication with Crescembeni in Rome in an effort to link the *Animati* with the Arcadians and spread the membership and effects of the reform movement in Venice. He wrote to Crescembeni that he considered Arcadia "the most worthy promoter of literature and of good poetry."[41]

A principal vector of this movement was Italian music, the popularity of which allowed the reformed libretto to spread beyond the boundaries of Italy to all the capitals of Europe, except Paris, which had its own agenda and set of tastes. Vienna's experience of the Italian invasion and of the Arcadian reform was already long-standing when Zeno moved from Venice to become Charles's *poeta cesareo*.[42]

Elena Sala di Felice has demonstrated that Zeno's dramatic work shows a progression from librettos that cater overtly to the traditions of the public theater in Venice, to a reformed drama more attuned to the moral ideology of the court at Vienna and less dependent on public favor.[43] Despite Zeno's desires to impose a reform on operatic (and other) texts, to purge them of their baroque flourishes and comic elements, and turn them toward moral didacticism, he was initially obliged by the very nature of the public theater to include those elements in his opera texts.[44] The move from Venice to Vienna in 1718 made him less financially dependent on public favor and allowed him to write dramas much more in the manner he wished, matching his work to the personality of the court and of the emperor, whose "stern sense of duty never let him deviate from his high principles."[45] The project of proclaiming Habsburg virtue as justification for Habsburg power would suit exactly the artistic program that wished to reclaim art from what it regarded as vulgar public spectacle. The cultural imperialism of the Arcadian reformers accorded well with Charles's imperial aspirations and the emperor's own notions of government and ethics.

Scipione nelle Spagne, written for a young version of Charles's court sitting in Barcelona, its imperialist ambitions still not realized, was a first move in that direction and no doubt constituted a compelling argument that Zeno should once again be offered a position as *poeta cesareo* when Charles moved back to Vienna.[46] As we saw at the beginning of this chapter, Zeno's *Scipione* became one of the staples in the expression of Habsburg power and was produced multiple times in the Habsburg sphere of influence during Charles's reign. In these later productions, it no longer had relevance for the conquest of Spain, but it continued to be an effective part of the Habsburg program of self-representation due to its appeal to their canon of virtues.

The continuing relevance of the libretto is made clear enough by the epilogue, or *licenza*, that Zeno appended to the published version of the libretto in the *Poesie drammatiche* of 1744. In it, he compares both the virtues and conquests of Scipio to those of Charles and finds Charles superior, with the one regret that Charles had no Ennius to celebrate him in epic verse, as Scipio had. But then, Charles really has no need of an epic poet, because his name alone is sufficient to bear witness to his glory:

> May there come one through whom your great NAME may rise to heaven, as Scipio found in Ennius. Your honor lacks this one boast: a song worthy of Charles.
>   What heroic trumpet resounds to your NAME, CHARLES Augustus? Let others be silent. So great a name is a worthy trumpet for itself. Its own glory can praise it fully: and virtue recalls in it the trophies that, more than the laurel crown, grow as ornaments for your head.
>   *Chorus.* Your name Charles Augustus is your greatest honor.*

The compliment in this passage springs directly from the text of the opera and, ultimately, from the source in Livy. Livy's Allucius had declared of the young Scipio that "a godlike young warrior had come, who carried all before him not only by arms but with generosity and kindliness." Following this lead, Zeno's Luceio declares to the rebellious Roman troops (III.xvi), "And in him respect how much greatness the gods ever create in him. Sea, earth and heaven acclaim his name with a loud cry. Only his heart is greater than his renown."[47]

Now, declares Zeno in the licenza, Charles's own name is similarly broadcast throughout the world.[48] Under these circumstances, if Charles is like Scipio, then Zeno becomes both his Ennius and his Luceio, a subordinate who is nevertheless necessary to reflect the glory of the prince and, as a result, has a claim to honor and position of his own by virtue of his own accomplishments. The imperialist projects of both the emperor and his poet benefit and complement one another perfectly. The partnership of poet and powerful patron is as old as Homer, but Zeno might indeed have reflected on the applicability to his own case of Horace's tag from the *Epistles*: "Graecia capta ferum victorem cepit et artis intulit agresti Latio" ("Captive Greece captured its fierce victor and brought its arts to rude Latium").[49] As Greek literature had come to the service of the Roman empire, so Zeno's brand of Italian literature had been employed to glorify the Austrians. The parallel was all the more applicable, since the conquering Italian literature of the Arcadian reform sprang from a theoretical attachment to Aristotle's *Poetics* and Greek dramatic poetry.

Certainly Charles presented himself and his relation to art in similar terms: Heraeus in 1711 described a dramatic tableau that represented Charles as Augustus sitting between Vergil and Horace and emphasized the connection of power with literature, Charles with Augustus.[50] The Italian imperialist project had therefore succeeded brilliantly. Zeno, like Stampiglia just before him, and Metastasio who was to follow, was in a position aptly suited to experimenting with the new moral and intellectual forms of musical drama in a place where it would be viewed by educated audiences able to judge it, and where its impact was felt and disseminated across most of Europe. The Roman version of the myth of the clement prince, which was to receive its most concentrated and enduring expression in Metastasio's *La clemenza di Tito*, found its natural home with the Caesarean poets in Vienna.

6 The Problem of Caesar

HAYM/HANDEL, *GIULIO CESARE IN EGITTO;*

METASTASIO/VIVALDI, *IL CATONE IN UTICA*

Scipio and Nero have thus far exemplified extreme poles of virtue and vice in these operas. We have seen Otho occupying a middle ground, a role made possible in part by his mixed reputation, but his fleeting importance to Roman history makes him a dramatic convenience rather than a character of genuine historical interest. Gaius Julius Caesar, too, occupied a moral middle ground, but of a wholly different order of magnitude. Caesar's brilliant military successes and exercise of the virtue of clemency during the civil war with Pompey demonstrated nevertheless what an empty thing the Roman Republic was. His actions led to autocracy and the Julio-Claudian dynasty of emperors, of which Nero was the last unfortunate member. Caesar's conflicting attributes made him a significant problem for the Romans, and for those who inherited their tradition. Dramas of the early modern period were still exploring that problem, but one thing was certain: A dramatic version of Caesar could not step back, like the Scipios of Minato and Zeno, and allow the society around him to proceed on its own terms. The only way to get rid of him, in history or in drama, was to kill him.

A variety of approaches to Caesar's character is represented by the works in this chapter. The *Giulio Cesare in Egitto* of Nicolà Haym and G. F. Handel, and Pietro Metastasio's libretto for *Il Catone in Utica*, are based on the events of Julius Caesar's campaigns in North Africa during

the civil wars of the mid-first century B.C.E. *Giulio Cesare*, first performed in 1724 at the King's Theater in the Haymarket, is a reworking
of a libretto Giacomo Francesco Bussani wrote for Venice in 1676. *Catone in Utica* was one of Metastasio's early librettos, written for Rome
in 1728 and set by at least twenty-four composers in various adaptations throughout the rest of the eighteenth century. In the background
of both these librettos stands Joseph Addison's play *Cato*, first staged at
the Drury Lane Theater in London in 1713. Addison's *Cato*, although
a spoken drama, is important here because it defined the dramatic and
sociopolitical environment in which Handel was working and represents
a possible treatment of Julius Caesar in many respects opposed to that in
Handel's *Giulio Cesare*. It seems to have had a formative influence on
Metastasio as he wrote *Catone in Utica*, and even more on Vittorio Alfieri
in the later eighteenth century, whose patriotic and republican tragedies
in their turn inspired Italian librettos of the age of revolution.

The relevant historical background is as follows. The defeat of the
Carthaginians in the third and second centuries B.C.E. that we observed
in the Scipio operas, as well as victories against the Hellenistic kingdoms
in the east, had brought Rome a Mediterranean empire and the problems
that came with it. Roman authors of the first century B.C.E. described
a gradual decay of Scipionic virtue and republican liberty, which they
blamed on the influx of wealth and luxury from Rome's conquests and
which they felt was leading to the fall of Rome itself.[1] However that
may have been, it was certainly true that the ability of the aristocratic
senate to govern city and empire had come under increasing challenge
from wealthy and powerful individuals who used armies to get what they
wanted. The '80s B.C.E. saw a series of hideous civil wars between the
populist Marius and the conservative Sulla, the latter of whom inspired
several eighteenth-century operas on the theme of tyranny, including
Mozart's early *Lucio Silla* (chapter 9). The next generation of Romans,
which included Sulla's junior officer Gnaeus Pompey and his sometime
victim Julius Caesar, renewed the struggles.

The confrontation between Pompey and Caesar that began with Caesar's crossing of the Rubicon in 49 B.C.E. ended a year later at the battle
of Pharsalus in Greece with the rout of Pompey's troops and his flight to
Egypt. In Egypt, Pompey hoped to receive help from King Ptolemy XIII,
whose father Pompey once had helped to power. But the young Ptolemy
and his ministers had Pompey killed, decapitated, and his head presented
as a gift to Caesar to gain his favor when he arrived in Egypt. The scheme
backfired, and Caesar instead supported Ptolemy's sister Cleopatra VII in
her bid for the throne. After spending more time than planned in Egypt

with Cleopatra, Caesar made a lightning campaign to Pontus in Asia Minor, about which he famously said, "I came, I saw, I conquered." He then returned to Rome to consolidate his victories.

The republican challenge was not yet eradicated, however, and Caesar was forced to return to North Africa. In 46 he defeated republican troops under Metellus Scipio, Cato the Younger, and the Numidian king Juba at Thapsus in North Africa. We have already had cause to observe that because of Cato's Stoicism and staunch resistance to Caesar's authority, his life and death held as great a fascination for the early moderns as did Caesar's (chapters 1 and 5). Thus Cato's death in Utica is the second important event for this chapter, a political and ethical gesture that balanced Caesar's military conquests in North Africa. Nor did Cato's defeat end matters for Caesar. Pompey's sons Gnaeus and Sextus also raised troops in Spain, but they were defeated in a hard-fought battle at Munda in 46 B.C.E.. Caesar returned to Rome again in 44 B.C.E., and in February of that year he was finally declared dictator for life. A month later, shortly before departing again on campaign against Parthia, he was assassinated.

The ancient sources that the librettists mined for this period of Roman history provide a narrative filled with colorful incidents and characters, described from a wide variety of viewpoints. Caesar's autobiographical *Civil War* is of course uniformly positive toward its author and sidesteps the issue of his affair with Cleopatra altogether. Its sequel, the *War in Alexandria*, written by an anonymous Caesarean, is similarly uninformative on the subject of the romance. Later sources with different agendas were not so hesitant to relate the gossip. Caesar's sexual appetite was famous. Cassius Dio (42.34) said Caesar was *erotikotatos* ("extremely lustful") and apt to have sex with most any woman he came across. Suetonius reports an even more catholic taste ("every woman's man and every man's woman"; *Caesar* 52) but speaks of Cleopatra as the most famous of Caesar's affairs.

Lucan and Plutarch provided the most effective connected narrations of Caesar's exploits in Egypt, which continued to appeal to posterity. Lucan's epic poem *Pharsalia*, written during the reign of Nero, ultimately presents Pompey as a Stoic martyr while consistently putting Caesar in the worst possible light, "mitigated only by touches of grudging admiration for his demoniac energy."[2] Lucan concludes that the world had been reduced to a choice between Freedom and Caesar (*Pharsalia* 7.691–97). Plutarch's view is more even-handed; as with most of his subjects, he was willing to report Caesar's good qualities as well as his bad ones. The following analysis will take particular note of the varying uses of Lucan's and Plutarch's Caesar for political and esthetic purposes.

Approaches to Caesar: The Theatrical Background

In 1643, the year that saw the premiere of *L'incoronazione di Poppea*, Corneille put his *La mort de Pompée* on stage in Paris. The play dealt with Ptolemy XIII's plot against Pompey, and the aftermath, which included the meeting of Caesar and Cleopatra. While the operas in this chapter are not directly adapted from Corneille's play, the idea of bringing Cornelia, the widow of Pompey, onto the scene in Alexandria as an avenging spirit may originate with Corneille. (Historically, Cornelia fled Egypt directly after the murder of Pompey.) Corneille also treats the conflict between Caesar's duty to Rome and his passion for Cleopatra, a conflict that does appear on the opera stage.

G. F. Busenello, librettist of *L'incoronazione di Poppea*, had first experimented with the contradictions associated with Caesar in *La prosperità infelice di Giulio Cesare dittatore* (1646).[3] The libretto presents five episodes from Caesar's life in as many acts and deploys a huge cast that includes divinities (Time, Astraea, Fortune, Liberty, Neptune), comic servants, and choruses of Roman soldiers and people of Lesbos, as well as the relevant historical characters. It comprises the stretch of history between the battle of Pharsalus and the assassination of Caesar on the Ides of March and takes place in Greece, Lesbos, Egypt, and Rome. The contradictions of Caesar's life are expressed in the libretto's oxymoronic title and in Busenello's *Argomento*: "Whoever has read Plutarch's 'Life of Caesar' and has studied the ten books of Lucan's *Pharsalia* will come up with the plot of this drama on his own, in which Julius Caesar goes from victories over others to his own ruin and destruction." Busenello's Caesar is therefore a combination of bad and good qualities and is assassinated as a result of his own actions. Although the conspirators, along with Cornelia and Sextus, Pompey's widow and son, celebrate the dictator's death in the final chorus, it is not entirely a happy outcome for Rome, for we know that Caesar's death did not end the question. The *scena ultima*, a scene between Liberty and Neptune, foretells that Liberty, departed from Rome, will instead settle in the Republic of Venice.

Giacomo Bussani's 1676 *Giulio Cesare in Egitto* was set to music by Antonio Sartorio for Venice and concentrates on Caesar's time with Cleopatra in Alexandria. Since it is the basis for Haym and Handel's London opera, it will be discussed in more detail below.

On the English stage, Addison's *Cato*, which premiered in London in 1713, depicted the death of Cato at Utica. Caesar, who never actually appears onstage in the play, is the unseen enemy, vilified from the very first scene in black Lucanian terms as the destroyer of republican freedom. "I see / Th' insulting tyrant," says Cato's son Marcus, "prancing o'er the field / Strowed with Rome's citizens, and drenched in slaughter, / His horse hooves wet with Patrician blood" (I.i.17–20). The picture never gets more positive. Cato's rebuke in act II to Caesar's ambassador states the case: "Didst thou but view [Caesar] right, thou'dst see him / Black with murder, treason, sacrilege and crimes / That strike my soul with horror but to name them" (II.ii.51–53). These accusations of murder, treason, sacrilege, and so forth describe exactly the intentions of the characters who represent Caesar on stage. Sempronius (a figure probably modeled on the reprehensible Metellus Scipio) is a supposed partisan of Cato, but he instead looks to his advantage in the wake of Caesar's successes; he plots with the Numidian captain Syphax to betray Cato, take over Utica, and abduct and rape Cato's daughter, Marcia, who is in Utica with her father. Syphax (not a historical person; the name is taken from the Sofonisba story) has the job of using his North African wiles to win over to Caesar's side the young Juba, who has (anachronistically) just inherited the throne of Numidia from his father, the elder Juba having recently been killed at the battle of Thapsus. Caesar's image suffers on every front from those who are associated with his cause and remains to the end the source of evil.

Cato is clearly the hero and stands for republican liberty and Stoic virtue, reason and constancy. In a typical moment he asks the young Juba, "Dost thou love watchings, abstinence, and toil, / Laborious virtues all? Learn them from Cato: / Success and fortune must thou learn from Caesar." This is a variation on Aeneas's observation to Ascanius at *Aeneid* 12.435–36 (chapter 3); it situates Cato in the Roman tradition of Stoic duty and as far from an Ovidian sensibility as possible. The prologue of the play, written by Alexander Pope, indicates the opinion we are supposed to adopt toward the play's action:

> Our author shuns by vulgar springs to move
> The hero's glory or the virgin's love;
> In pitying love, we but our weakness show,
> And wild ambition well deserves its woe.
> Here tears shall flow from a more gen'rous cause,
> Such tears as patriots shed for dying laws.

Although we are clearly meant to admire Cato, it is hard in this play, as in any of the ancient sources, to love him much. As a counter to the Stoic sternness, Addison makes Cato sympathetic by association, just as he had blackened Caesar by association. Despite the protestations of Pope's prologue, Addison fabricates romantic complications that are not much different from those in Zeno's *Scipione nelle Spagne,* written three years previously. (Addison's contemporaries alleged the love element was to please the commons.) Both Cato's sons, Portius and Marcus, love Lucia, the daughter of the pro-Catonian senator Lucius. Unaware of Portius's own feelings for Lucia, Marcus sends his brother to plead with Lucia on his behalf, and although Lucia prefers Portius, neither of them is willing to hurt Marcus. The crisis is resolved in act IV when Marcus dies in battle against the villainous Syphax.

More important, however, is the love affair between young Juba and Cato's daughter Marcia. Their affair is conducted with strict Stoic reserve, but they finally confess their love in a histrionic scene that is in the spirit of contemporary opera. In act IV, Sempronius, with the help of Syphax, disguises himself as Juba to win entry to Marcia's apartments and take her. Juba finds Sempronius and kills him, but leaves to tell Cato what has happened. In the meantime, Marcia discovers the body and, fooled by the disguise, thinks it is Juba who is dead. Juba overhears her heartbroken laments, and so Marcia, "surprised in an unguarded hour," must admit her love, and Juba utters a very un-Catonian sentiment: "Let Caesar have the world, if Marcia's mine."

But Juba recovers himself when actually speaking with Cato, and declares, "I'd rather gain / Thy praise, O Cato! than Numidia's empire" (IV.iv.53–54). In the final scene, the dying Cato blesses the union, saying, "Juba loves thee Marcia. / A senator of Rome, while Rome surviv'd, / Would not have match'd his daughter with a king, / But Caesar's arms have thrown down all distinction; / Whoe'er is brave and virtuous is a Roman" (V.iv.87–91). In a single stroke the lovers are blessed, Cato becomes not only a Stoic martyr but also a loving father, and Caesar is vilified once more. Caesar has turned the world so topsy-turvy that a Numidian can now be a Roman.

The play evoked strong political reaction in the audience between Whigs, who were still working out the nature of the constitutional monarchy established by the Glorious Revolution of 1688, and the Tories, allied with Queen Anne and opposed to the Whig champion Lord Marlborough, whose exploits in the War of Spanish Succession they felt revealed a Caesarean ambition. Alexander Pope reported that the "numerous and violent claps of the Whig party on the one side of the theatre, were echoed back by the Tories on the other, while the author sweated behind the scenes with concern to find their applause proceeding more from the hand than the head."[4] The audience reaction was so mixed because Addison had done a good deal of fence-sitting to produce the final version of the play, adding speeches in defense of liberty against tyranny at the suggestion of his Whig friends, while meeting with the Tories Jonathan Swift and Lord Bolingbroke to be sure that the play would not unduly offend the government. The result was pandemonium in the house.

At issue in the audience's mind was whether the virtuous Cato was meant to represent Lord Marlborough, the current Whig champion, or whether the wicked Caesarians represented Lord Marlborough (that was the Tory view) because he had attempted to have himself made captain general for life. Both Queen Anne (Tory) and the imperious Sarah, Duchess of Marlborough (Whig) wanted the play dedicated to them. To avoid either offending the queen by dedicating it to the duchess, or turning it into a Tory play by dedicating it to the queen, he published the play without any dedication at all, leaving a continuing battle over its political meaning.[5]

Ironically, the last moments of the play actually argue against just the sort of factional rivalry that occurred at the theater. Over the body of Cato, Lucius pronounces the moral of the play:

> From hence, let fierce contending nations know
> What dire effects from civil discord flow.
> 'Tis this that shakes our country with alarms,
> And gives up Rome a prey to Roman arms,
> Produces fraud, and cruelty, and strife,
> And robs the guilty world of Cato's life.

This was deemed by a contemporary commentator to be the most important theme of the play, which has "the noble design of shewing us the fatal effects of faction, and domestic feuds, which are at so great and desperate a height in our days."[6]

As Pope's comment, quoted above, suggests, Addison had a broader agenda. In his mind the issues that the play addressed were esthetic and dramatic rather than strictly moral and political. George Berkeley wrote to Sir John Percival on April 16, 1713, that Addison's "aim is to reform the stage."[7] Addison's disdain for much of the operatic drama is clear, even as Handel was producing his first London operas: "If the Italians have a genius for music above the English, the English have a genius for other performances of a much higher nature, and capable of giving the mind a much nobler entertainment."[8] Pope's prologue to *Cato* remonstrates in the same vein:

> Our scene precariously subsists too long
> On French translation and Italian song.
> Dare to have sense yourselves; assert the stage,
> Be justly warm'd with your own native rage.

Such plays alone should please the British ear,
As Cato's self had not disdained to hear.[9]

A remark from Addison in the *Spectator* had explained what he thought tragedy should accomplish: "As a perfect tragedy is the noblest production of human nature, so it is capable of giving the mind one of the most delightful and most improving entertainments. A virtuous man (says Seneca) struggling with misfortunes, is such a spectacle as gods might look upon with pleasure: and such a pleasure it is which one meets with the representation of a well-written tragedy. Diversions of this kind wear out of our thoughts every thing that is mean and little. They cherish and cultivate that humanity which is the ornament of our nature."[10]

In this respect the play appears to have succeeded, despite somewhat awkward casting. In a subsequent letter, Berkeley reported to Percival, "Mr. Addison's play has taken wonderfully, they have acted it now almost a month, and would I believe act it a month longer were it not that Mrs. Oldfield [playing Marcia] cannot hold out any longer, having for several nights past, as I am informed, a midwife behind the scenes, which is surely very unbecoming the character of Cato's daughter. I hear likewise that the principal players are resolved for the future to reform the stage, and suffer nothing to be repeated there, which the most virtuous persons might not hear, being now convinced by experience that no play ever drew a greater concourse of people, than the most virtuous." Alexander Pope reported that "Cato was not so much the wonder of Rome itself, in his days, as he is of Britain in ours; . . . The town is so fond of [*Cato*], that the orange wenches and fruit women in the Park, offer the books at the side of the coaches, and the Prologue and Epilogue are cried about in the streets by the common hawkers." An admirer wrote to Addison, "I gave myself the pleasure of seeing *Cato* acted, & heartily wish all discourses from the pulpit were as instructive and edifying, as pathetick and affecting, as that which the audience was then entertain'd with from the stage."[11]

The play's moral and political messages resonated abroad as well as in England. It was translated and produced on the European mainland—in Italy alone there were six translations between 1713 and 1718.[12] There it helped inspire the republican plays of Vittorio Alfieri, who, as we will see in the final chapter, influenced in his turn opera librettos of the 1780s and 1790s. In America its lines became the stuff of revolutionary rhetoric, quoted and paraphrased by Benjamin Franklin, John Adams, George Washington (whose officers and their wives performed it at Valley Forge), Patrick

Henry, and Nathan Hale.[13] In England, after the accession of George I in 1714, the Whig majority dominated but continued to be anxious about the possibility of successful challenge from the Catholic Jacobites resident in France. Fear of Jacobite resurgence, generated in part by the Atterbury plot of 1722, resulted in a series of plays, which trumpeted what one journalist in 1731 could still regard as "wild notions of liberty and patriotism" that were descended directly from *Cato*.[14]

Giulio Cesare in Egitto

It was in this context, esthetic and political, that Handel's *Giulio Cesare in Egitto* was produced in London at the King's Theater in the Haymarket in 1724.[15] It, too, was a success in its own day, and it was a reliable revival piece during Handel's lifetime.[16] Unlike *Cato*, it has now gained a new popularity and is one of the most performed and familiar of Handel's operas. As J. Merrill Knapp observed forty years ago, the reasons for its success are not hard to find.[17] The opera is well constructed, has heroic and exotic characters that are well defined, and, most important, has lots of terrific music that is imaginatively deployed to reinforce both plot and character.

Nevertheless, Handel's and Haym's Caesar and Cleopatra are an embarrassment to the postmodern age. Whether we like it or not, overtly, at least, the opera celebrates imperialism, trades on racist stereotypes, and buries issues of incest (among the Ptolemies) and adultery (Caesar was married) to create an adventure story with a happy ending. And we don't like it or, anyway, those who produce *Giulio Cesare* don't like it. Often on the modern stage the imperialism is deconstructed and the characters are either treated cynically or trivialized, the productions keeping the opera at a Brechtian arm's length. In Munich, Caesar is entrapped by Cleopatra in a giantic, garish Venus flytrap in a scene that utterly overwhelms any deeper passion the two characters might be developing for each other. After Egypt goes up in flames in a nuclear holocaust, Caesar and Cleopatra win, but the final chorus, presenting them for the first time in ancient Roman costume, sets them in tableaux that dramatize the violent ends to their lives. The Houston Grand Opera production presented the whole thing as a 1930s Hollywood movie production, with the cast in the final chorus getting in place to watch the outtakes for the day. Peter Sellars's updating of the opera treated it as a cynical reflection on American imperialism in the Mideast.[18]

To turn this opera into a political satire because we no longer believe in the virtue of conquest has worked brilliantly with modern audiences, and I would not like to go on record as suggesting that such approaches are "wrong." The inherent ironies in the problem of Caesar make them feasible, and the opera does not entirely neglect those ironies. But at the same time I believe a wholly satirical approach to *Giulio Cesare* runs counter to both text and music if considered in their original context.[19] Many Britons in 1724 did not question imperialism as a means to their ends, especially Britons in the King's Theater in London, nor did they doubt that they were superior to Egyptians, any more than had the Romans depicted in the opera.[20] The opera celebrates Caesar's success in setting Cleopatra on the throne of Egypt in the place of her brother, the effete and treacherous oriental potentate Ptolemy, while simultaneously uniting with her in mutual love. Moreover, Cornelia and Sextus, the wife and son of Caesar's defeated enemy Pompey, are included in the *lieto fine*, after Sextus finally kills Ptolemy in vengeance for his father's death. Caesar gets no blame in any of it. The contrast with Addison's Caesar is most striking, and would have been immediately observable by London audiences in 1724. *Cato* was revived seven times in 1723–24, and ran at the same time as *Giulio Cesare* in February and April 1724.[21]

The difference between the two dramas is due, at least in part, to the fact that the King's Theater in the Haymarket was not Drury Lane. The virtues of *Cato* had been in some degree "more prosaic and middle class than romantic and aristocratic in their morality."[22] The King's Theater depended on the patronage of the nobility and upper middle class, "persons of the greatest politeness,"[23] who could afford the more expensive subscriptions, and who were interested not only in the prestige afforded by attending the event but also, and not least, in the music and acting. Handel was under constraint not to offend significant members of his audience, less because of the danger of government disapproval, than because the Royal Academy, for which he was orchestra director as well as composer, could not afford to lose investors to factionalism. Disturbances in the opera house were mostly about rivalries between singers rather than about politics.[24] As a result, Handel and Haym were called upon to produce an entertainment that took good advantage of the singers at hand and to find a middle ground that would reinforce the status quo rather than a moral and esthetic sermon to challenge it. This they did with notable success in the years 1724–26, with three of Handel's greatest operas, *Tamerlano, Rodelinda,* and *Giulio Cesare.*

Tamerlano and *Rodelinda,* adapted respectively from librettos by Agostino Piovene and Antonio Salvi, were in the modern style. *Tamerlano* comes very close to genuine tragedy. *Rodelinda* anticipates the themes of marital fidelity that became increasingly important after 1750.

Their model for *Giulio Cesare* was, in contrast, Bussani's old-fashioned seventeenth-century carnival libretto, which freely intermingled the comic and serious elements. Even more than Busenello's *Prosperità infelice*, it employed the positive elements of Caesar's character available from Plutarch.[25] The central plot of the opera is the developing romance between Caesar and Cleopatra. It is heroic and romantic in the aristocratic vein, and with its triumph of the central couple, it harks back more to the court festivals of the late Renaissance than the Arcadian celebration of the clement prince; with no censorious Cato on the scene to spoil things, this story about Caesar has an entirely different appeal than that in Addison's *Cato*.

The love affair between Caesar and Cleopatra was morally suspect, of course, and Plutarch reports that some people in Caesar's day thought the whole Alexandrian campaign was the unnecessary result of Caesar's extramarital infatuation (*Caesar* 48.3). Lucan paints Cleopatra in luridly negative terms as the "deadly Erinys of Latium" (10.59). In describing Caesar's affair he puts a negative spin on the Ovidian combination of love and war: "He let Venus have a place in his business, and mixed illicit sex and illegitimate offspring in with his campaign" (10.75–76). Cleopatra is an African Queen, whose dangerous sexual attraction for visiting Romans we observed in chapter 2. To make the affair into something more positive, therefore, Haym had to make judicious use of the ancient material.

The conflict between Caesar's military obligations and his passion for Cleopatra had been the central point at issue in act IV in Busenello's *Prosperità infelice* and might easily have been so in Handel's opera. In Haym's libretto, as in Bussani's original, Cleopatra's plans are initially connected to issues of power and sex rather than romantic love, since she intends to seduce Caesar and use him against her brother Tolomeo. "Fear not, with my looks I shall oblige Caesar more than he [Tolomeo] did with the head of Pompey," she observes (I.v).[26] Disguised as a maidservant named Lydia, she presents herself to Caesar as Cleopatra's agent. She succeeds at once, and celebrates her charms: "Beauty can whate'er it please obtain" ("Tutto può donna vezzosa"; I.vii). His attraction to her is reinforced when she sings him a ravishing love song at the beginning of act II, costumed as Virtue on Mount Parnassus and surrounded by a band of Muses playing on stringed instruments.[27] Much of act II, moreover, takes place in the morally ambiguous setting of gardens. The first is a pleasure garden disguised as a philosophical retreat. In "a garden of cedars, with prospect of Mount Parnassus" Caesar is serenaded by Virtue and the Muses (scenes i–ii), but the words that "Virtue" sings are all in the erotic language familiar from Poppea's garden of delights. In scenes iii–vi, Cornelia is confined by Tolomeo in a "garden belonging to the seraglio, to which corresponds that of the wild beasts." Finally, in II.vii–viii, Cleopatra feigns sleep in a garden, a "luogo di delizie," where Caesar finds her and expresses his longing. The whole opera might easily therefore become an erotic farce or satire on power in the manner of *Poppea, Agrippina,* or *Ottone in villa.*

But this was England eleven years after the premiere of *Cato,* not carnival in Venice. Handel and Haym put their hero in a less compromising moral position by depicting a growth in sincerity of passion between the lovers. Plutarch reports that other sources blamed the Alexandrian war not on Caesar's passions but on Ptolemy's eunuchs and ministers (48.3). That is the approach taken in *Giulio Cesare,* and it is made clear from the very first scenes. Caesar enters, hailed politely by the chorus as "our Hercules." He accepts their praise as his due in an opening aria, "Let Egypt's laurels wreath the conqueror's brows." He proclaims his victory over Pompey with his famous phrase from the campaign in Pontus: "Curio, Caesar no sooner came, but saw and conquered." He receives Pompey's wife Cornelia and his son Sesto, magnanimously accepting their freely offered surrender: "'Tis the prerogative of heroic virtue to pardon offences. . . . [T]he rage of war shall cease, and the conqueror o'ercome by the vanquish'd." Then Tolomeo's general Achilla unexpectedly presents Caesar with Pompey's head, to the consternation of all on stage. Caesar is as horrified as the rest. He announces that he will come to the palace, and in a rage aria ("Empio dirò tu sei") declares:[28]

> There I'll reproach the barbarous act,
> And bid him fly my sight:
> The prince whose soul is void
> Of pity and compassion,
> Deserves not to hold the reins of empire.

This episode has a historical basis. The sources agree that Caesar wept publicly at Pompey's murder and had those immediately responsible put to death. On the one hand, Lucan (*Pharsalia* 9.1062–1108) and Cassius Dio (*Roman History* 52.8) make it clear they think Caesar's grief was rank hypocrisy, given the enmity between the two men. Plutarch gives a different explanation (*Caesar* 48.2; and compare *Pompey* 80.5):

> Arriving at Alexandria just after Pompey's death he turned away in horror from Theodotus as he presented the head of Pompey, but he accepted Pompey's seal-ring, and shed tears over it. Moreover, all the companions and intimates of Pompey who had been captured by the king as

they wandered over the country, he treated with kindness and attached them to himself. And to his friends in Rome he wrote that this was the greatest and sweetest pleasure that he derived from his victory, namely, from time to time to save the lives of fellow citizens who had fought against him.[29]

Both Plutarch's passage and the scene in the opera are set in the context of the famous *clementia Caesaris* (chapter 1). In this light, Caesar's tears seem genuine; the picture of Caesar as capable soldier and magnanimous victor is maintained throughout the rest of the opera. Following the suggestion in Plutarch, Tolomeo and his agents are the villains of the piece, threatening our heroes with death and the attractive Cornelia with unwanted sexual attention, thereby playing roles equivalent to the Caesarians Sempronius and Syphax in Addison's *Cato*. In I.ix of *Giulio Cesare*, Caesar greets Tolomeo himself as court etiquette requires but makes his displeasure at Pompey's murder clear, and Tolomeo's treacherous replies do not fool him (I.ix):

> *Ptolemy.* Fortune, great Caesar, throws beneath your feet
>   The sceptre of the earth and bids you rule.
> *Caesar.* How shall I thank the mighty Ptolemy for such favour?
>   The rising sun
>   appears not with more lustre in heavens, than Ptolemy on earth.
>   But remember!
>   The least unworthy act, obscures the greatest glory.
> *Achillas.* [to Ptol.] (Mark! Even in your royal presence he upbraids
>   you.)
> *Ptol.* (Audacious Roman!)
> *Caes.* (I see he understands me.)
> *Ptol.* Those who attend, will straight conduct you to the royal
>   apartments
>   prepared for your reception. (He little dreams how near he
>   is to ruin.)
> *Caes.* (I read dissembled treachery in his face.)
>   [*aria*] As crafty huntsmen, in pursuit of prey
>   Unseen, and hushed in silence stalk along:
>   So those whom malice prompts to base designs,
>   Conceal from every eye, their dark intent.

His genuine respect for the memory of his rival is mirrored by his chivalrous passion for Cleopatra. He does not merely lust for the voluptuous "Lydia" in II.vii, while she appears to be asleep in the *luogo di delizie*, but wistfully desires that fate might have made her his wife and consort. In Bussani, Caesar, like Scipio in *Scipione affricano*, calls himself a captive of love.[30] In Handel's version, despite his infatuation, he is in better control of himself, for when Cleopatra-as-Lydia "awakes," he makes it clear that actual marriage with a maidservant is impossible. Caesar is, in effect, what Juba was in the *Cato*, the sympathetic heroic male—tough in war, full of principle, capable of the softer feelings of passion and love, but in control of those passions when duty calls.

That, coupled with Caesar's impressive arias, is certainly enough to carry audience sympathy, but Haym and Handel developed what they found in Bussani to take the characterization a step further. When the uproar of the first scenes has died down, after the initial triumph has been thoroughly spoiled by Pompey's head and Egyptian plotting against Caesar, Cornelia and Sesto, Caesar has a moment to contemplate an urn, set on a pile of military trophies, that contains the ashes of Pompey's head. The moment is solo and so the sentiments may be regarded as sincere:

> Great soul of Pompey, who with solemn pace
> Invisibly stalk'st round thy peaceful ashes,
> Thy glittering trophies, and all thy pomp and greatness
> Were but vain shadows, like what thou art at present.
> Here ends the vanity of human greatness;
> He who but yesterday
> Stretch'd o'er the world his victorious arms
> Now turn'd to dust,
> The narrow limits of an urn contains;
> We all, alas! derive our source from earth,
> To which we soon return. Unhappy life!
> How frail is thy condition!
> A breath gives being to thy feeble state;
> Which soon or late a blast destroys.[31]

The text of this passage, beginning "Alma del gran Pompeo," is Bussani's. In the first production of Bussani's text, Sartorio set only the first five lines through "ombra sei" ("like what thou art at present") as a brief and stately lament with a descending chromatic bass line (Monson no. 25). It is a solemn moment, but in its attenuated version does not generalize the experience beyond Caesar's immediate sorrow for Pompey. Handel by contrast set the entire passage as a simple and moving accompanied recitative. Caesar's entry into the scene is heralded by a pulsing chromatic line in the violins marked Largo that rises in lament and falls in a sigh that introduces "Alma." The passage looks like a simple commonplace on the mutability of human fortune, but it appears to take its inspiration from well-known lines of Lucan's *Pharsalia* (1.135–45):

> The shadow of a great name, [Pompey] stands like a towering oak-tree in a fruitful field, carrying the old trophies of a nation and the consecrated

gifts of generals; no longer clinging by strong roots, it is held only by its weight, and sticking bare branches into the air, it casts its shadow not with leaves but with its trunk. And though it totters, about to fall from the first strong wind from the east, while so many trees rise in strength round about, even so, it alone is worshipped. But in Caesar there was not just a name and reputation for generalship, but a virtue that could not hold still, and its single shame not to conquer in war.[32]

Lucan goes on to compare Caesar's inexhaustible energy to the lightning storm that destroys all before it, and which, by implication will take down the old oak tree that is Pompey. The once great man is now a pathetic trunk, a revered but strengthless shadow, and yet he is the only thing that stands between Rome and Caesar. Caesar, on the other hand, the irresistible, destructive force, is imbued with a kind of debased virtue and sense of shame.

Haym and Handel, following Bussani, adapted the passage and simplified its meaning to Caesar's advantage. A pun on the name Pompeius Magnus that begins Lucan's passage ("magni nominis umbra") is suggested in Bussani's first phrase ("Alma del gran Pompeo"), addressed to the soul of the great Pompey; Caesar goes on to play on Lucan's use of and the word "shade" (umbra) in lines 135 and 141 to suggest former life and glory that is only shadow: "Fur ombra i tuoi trofei / Ombra la tua grandezza, / e un' ombra sei."[33] Lucan's original picture of former glory about to fall becomes, in Haym's text, a reflection on the fall that is the lot of all human glory. Lucan's fundamentally anti-Caesarean sentiments are thus manipulated to create a recitative whereby Caesar can display his famous admiration for worthy opponents and his genuine grief at Pompey's death. Caesar feels deeply and reflects honorably on those feelings. Addison's Cato scornfully suggested that one learned only success and fortune from Caesar; but Handel's Caesar is capable of recognizing the mutability of that fortune and extending his reflections to self-knowledge. Pompey, too, had had success and fortune and now is reduced to ash. Caesar, one senses, feels that he is vulnerable as well.

This reflective moment passes immediately with the entry of Cleopatra as Lydia, but Caesar's reflections here prepare for the crisis in act III. Tolomeo defeats the forces of Caesar and Cleopatra, and Caesar's own fortune is indeed reversed. Forced to swim for his life, he is cast up onto a deserted shore, and reflects on his fate (III.iv). The lyrics again are commonplaces, but they are not in Bussani, and the scene and sentiments belong to Haym's and Handel's interpretation of the character.[34] With the music they express profound feeling and link the scene with the thoughtful reflection over the ashes of Pompey:

[*Accompanied recitative*] Propitious Fate, with tender pity mov'd,
Thro' boisterous waves, has brought me safe on shore;
Nor is it pleas'd as yet to cut my thread of life.
But whither shall I run to seek assistance?
Where are my shatter'd troops and legions fled,
That with resistless force were wont to conquer!
Alas, the monarch of the world is now constrained,
To wander in these desert plains alone.
[*Aria*] Sweet breezes with your gentle gales
 In pity cool my troubled breast;
And tell me quickly where to find
 The lovely idol of my heart.
[*Accomp. recit.*] But much I fear this melancholy sight,
Of bodies slain, portends a bad event.
[*Aria*] Sweet breezes with your gentle gales
 In pity cool my troubled breast.

The aria is not strictly da capo, and its structure is arresting. Accompanied recitative introduces the aria, which is not unusual, but it subsequently interrupts the lyric passages as well, after the B section ("And tell me quickly . . ."), before returning to the opening lines of the A section ("Sweet breezes . . .").

This episode, too, has a historical basis: "[W]hen a battle arose at Pharos [island, Caesar] sprang from the mole into a small boat and tried to go to the aid of his men in their struggle, but the Egyptians sailed up against him from every side so that he threw himself into the sea and with great difficulty escaped by swimming" (Plutarch, *Caesar* 49).[35] The surprise is that musically and thematically this scene forms a pair with Caesar's meditation over the urn of Pompey in act I. Haym and Handel create here a moment in which Caesar reflects on his fate, positive at this moment in ways that Pompey's had not been, but nevertheless still as fragile. Pompey's grandeur and triumphs had become mere shadow; alone, bereft of his troops, Caesar might easily suffer the same fate. Music evoking ocean waves in a gentle breeze with rising and falling phrases in the strings introduces the opening accompanied recitative "Dal ondoso periglio" (literally, "From the peril of the waves"), suggesting that the danger has indeed passed and that he has escaped drowning. Agitated sixteenth notes, that in Monteverdi would be *stile concitato*, support his anxious rhetorical questions about his troops and his isolation. The Italian reflects this better than the English translation ("But whither shall I run to seek assistance? . . .):

Ma! Dove andrò? e chi mi porge aita?
Ove son le mie schiere?

Ove son le legioni,
Che a tante mie vittorie il varco apriro?
Solo in quest' erme arene
Al Monarcho del mondo, errar conviene?

The waves return again for the aria, providing a gently mournful accompaniment for Caesar's lament and his fears for Cleopatra that swell to a climax with the phrase "oh Dio, al mio dolor" and then recede.

This sequence combines all the attractive qualities of Caesar's character. Uttered in extreme circumstances it confirms that his feelings for Cleopatra are genuine. His positive qualities as soldier and lover come out at this moment of ultimate crisis, expressed verbally and musically in a way that links back to his first accompanied recitative and reminds us of his thoughtful nature as well. He is, in this respect, his own adviser figure, the man of action taking the place of the Stoic philosopher. In his *Moralia*, Plutarch argues that Alexander the Great's achievements were not the result of Stoic destiny but rather of Alexander's own virtues and abilities.[36] So pronounced were these virtues, according to Plutarch, that they constituted a practical philosophy that was ultimately more influential and successful than the theoretical work of the professional philosophers: "For from his words, from his deeds, and from the instruction which he imparted, it will be seen that he was indeed a philosopher."[37] Caesar, I believe, may be seen as a similar case in this opera.

The resolution that develops from this is therefore the usual happy ending of *dramma per musica* rather than the qualified tragedy of Busenello's *Prosperità infelice di Giulio Cesare*. The Egyptian court finally collapses from internal betrayals. As a result, Caesar finds new troops immediately after the lament discussed above, and at the end of the scene he sings an aria in which the gentle waves of lament have become a C major raging torrent that carries all before it (III.iv): "As torrents tumbling from a rock, / With fury drive whate'er they meet." Caesar is Lucan's powerful force of nature, but here that force is spent on good rather than evil. Caesar saves Cornelia and Cleopatra from imminent danger of imprisonment and violation by Tolomeo. Sesto kills Tolomeo in hand-to-hand combat, thereby finally avenging his father. The last scene celebrates a genuine victory, recapitulating and improving upon the opening scene: Caesar and Cleopatra are united in love and victory, Caesar receives Cornelia and Sesto once again and honors them, and they conclude in the final chorus, "Joy and pleasure return to our hearts, every bitter woe has left my heart and all that remain are love, constancy and faith."

None of this would signify, of course, if Cleopatra was simply duping Caesar to win power. In such a case , Caesar would be in the risible position of Ottone or Claudio in *Agrippina* and *Ottone in villa*. But although Cleopatra begins her seduction as a play for influence over Caesar, her succession of arias, too, shows a growing sincerity of feeling for Caesar that balances her political aspirations. In the crucial scene II.viii, under the pressure of the attack from Tolomeo's men, she impulsively reveals herself to promise help to Caesar, whom she clearly loves and upon whom she depends. Her moving aria "Se pietà," which closes II.viii, asks for a blessing not so much on her own fate as that of Caesar: "In the meantime, just heaven, protect my hero, / For all my future joy depends on him." Her balancing aria in III.iii, "Piangerò la sorte mia," laments the apparent loss to Tolomeo of her own grand position but also "Cesare il mio bel nume."

Cleopatra can scarcely be included in the category of the faithful wife that we saw exemplified in Cavalli's Sofonisba, nor of the virginal lovers of Zeno's Sofonisba or Elvira. Her historical reputation prevents that. Her appearance as Virtue in the Parnassus scene has more than a touch of irony to it. The lyrics to her "V'adoro pupille" (II.ii) are the stuff of love poetry employing the images familiar to us from *Poppea* and *Scipione affricano,* and Handel's music for them is ravishing:

> Your charming eyes my ravish'd soul adores,
> The thrilling pain my heart with pleasure bears;
> When you with pity look, my sorrows cease;
> For you alone can heal the wounds you gave.[38]

Nevertheless, the theatricality of the scene evokes court masque or Renaissance intermedio and visually gives the seduction a formality that raises it to a royal or even divine level, and above mere carnality. Cleopatra is not an Agrippina or Cleonilla. What she shared initially with Poppea, as a seductress of a powerful man for her own advantage, is gradually transformed by her growing strength of character and the apparent legitimacy of her claim to the throne of Egypt. These elements of her character, which are set in opposition to the unwavering villainy of Tolomeo and his faction, leave no doubt about where our sympathies are meant to lie. Whereas Tolomeo threatens the life and virtue of Pompey's family, Cleopatra pities Cornelia and Sesto (I.viii) and allies herself with them.

Handel and Haym have thus solved the problem of Caesar for their aristocratic English audience. Caesar has taken a humane role like that played by Juba, the soldier-lover in Addison's play. He has also absorbed the role of philosophic adviser and thereby exhibits all the positive qualities that Addison had assigned to the historical enemies of Caesar. The libretto may occasionally verge on the melodramatic, but when joined with Handel's brilliantly humanizing music, the resulting opera contrives to do what Addison prescribed for his own drama, to give the mind a noble entertainment, which "cherished and cultivated that humanity which is the ornament of our nature." If a contemporary had been looking for politics in this opera, she might have equated Caesar with the king without causing offense. That equation was in fact made by a statue of George I commissioned for Rolls House by Delvaux, who showed the king in imperial Roman armor.[39] (Figure 5) I have argued elsewhere that in *Scipione,* produced two years later in the spring of 1726, Handel managed at once to make a political and moral statement consonant with the Hanoverian message while "neutralizing" the more heated political debates of the day.[40] Something similar is at work here: Caesarean—Hanoverian—*clementia* resolves the factionalism that Addison and his contemporaries had so decried. In the next chapter we will observe a similar operatic co-option of the story of the German Arminius and his opposition to Rome, used as a Whig hero in 1714 and subsequently by Handel in 1737 to represent the house of Hanover.

Il Catone in Utica

Pietro Metastasio dealt with the problem of Caesar in a wholly different way. *Il Catone in Utica* (1728) was first set to music by Leonardo Vinci at the Teatro d'Aliberti in Rome, and once again the story of Cato provoked strong public reaction. Metastasio was working under the influence of the Arcadian Academy but had taken the idea of returning tragic ideals to the stage a step further even than most French neoclassical dramas: Cato is shown dying on stage at the end of the opera. Metastasio was also probably inspired by Addison's *Cato,* which he would have known in Italian translation.[41] In the final moments Cato is on stage, mortally wounded by his own hand:

> *Catone.* Look . . . the day already fades . . . from my sight . . .
> *Cesare.* Rome, what a man you are losing!
> *Cat.* Carry me elsewhere . . . to die.
> *Marzia.* Come.
> *Emilia and Arbace.* What anguish.
> *Cat.* No, tyrant . . . you will not see . . . Latin liberty . . . die with me.
>   [*Catone, held up by Marzia and Arbace, exits dying.*]
> *Ces.* Ah! If it must cost me Cato's life, take back your gift, oh gods, the crown and the throne. [*Throws down his laurel crown.*]

But the public in Rome was used to the conventions of the *lieto fine,* and felt that at the very least deaths ought to take place tastefully out

Figure 5. Laurent Delvaux,
George I in Roman armor,
London, c. 1724. Conway
Library, Courtauld Institute
of Art. Used by permission.

of sight.[42] There was general dissatisfaction after the early performances of the original libretto that remind one of Aristophanic reactions to the alleged innovations of Euripides. A verse was found scribbled on the parapet of the orchestra, "Cruel Metastasio, you have gathered all Tiber's heroes in a sewer [*in un condotto*]." A note on the Pasquino advised the *Compagnia della Morte* to come to the Teatro d'Aliberti to take the body away for burial.[43]

The scandal around *Catone in Utica* suggests radical dramatic innovation, but Metastasio was working with precedents that made his move a bold but logical next step, not a sudden move into foreign territory. In the previous generation, librettists had been moving closer to what we conventionally regard as tragic action. In the 1690s Silvio Stampiglia in Rome and Matteo Noris in Venice adapted heroic-tragic stories of the early Roman Republic to the form of *dramma per musica*, which were set in the latest musical style by Alessandro Scarlatti and Bononcini. *La caduta de' decemviri* (*The Fall of the Ten*), *Muzio Scevola*, *Attilio Regolo*, and *Tito Manlio* all tell stories of adherence to patriotic principle that result in heroic self-sacrifice or the killing of kin. These librettos include wild romantic complications, conventional scenes of lowbrow comedy and the standard (and historically impossible) happy reunification of all the characters in the *lieto fine*. They also contain scenes of tragic violence or near-violence that would not become the norm for opera until very late in the next century. *La caduta de' decemviri* is especially striking in this respect. It tells the story of Virginia, whose father Verginius killed her rather than have her taken as a slave for the pleasure of the unscrupulous patrician Appius (Livy 3.44–50). Scene iii of act III follows Livy's narrative rather closely, as Verginius calls his daughter aside and, on stage, stabs her. There follows a popular uprising in which the forces of authority are overthrown by the outraged populace and justice restored. Although this is not how the opera ends, its combination of violence and overthrow would not sit comfortably on the opera stage until the 1780s.[44] (See chapter 9.) The violence and sacrifice of *Catone in Utica* is mild by comparison.

But there was an outcry, and Metastasio responded by reworking the third act; Cato left the stage to die two scenes before the end. In the *scena ultima* Marzia reports his death, and the center stage is given to a victorious but reviled and repentant Caesar:

> *Marzia*: I recall that I am bereft of all hope because of you: an orphan, desolate, and a fugitive. I recall that I swore to my father to despise you; and an even greater torment, I recall that I adored an ungrateful wretch.
> *Cesare*. How much I lose in a single day!
> *Fulvio*. When you triumph, all loss is easy.
> *Ces*. Ah! If it must cost me Cato's life, take back your gift, oh gods, the crown and the throne. [*Throws down his laurel crown*.]

In this form the libretto was a success, and subsequently it had a great run of popularity, being set, over the course of the century, in a wide variety of venues by many composers, including Hasse, Vivaldi, Graun, Jomelli, J. C. Bach, and Paisiello. Bach's version was especially successful, with at least eight productions between 1761 and 1772.[45]

Antonio Vivaldi took a final step in making the *scena ultima* palatable and eliminated Cato's death altogether for his 1737 production in

Verona; his reason was "to make the drama shorter and happier in the current spring season."[46] In Vivaldi's version of the final scene of the opera, Marzia tells Caesar she will continue to love him if he spares her father; Caesar assures her that he will do so, and a chorus, rather than Caesar, concludes the opera in a festive mode: "Let the torch of love shine, and let new peace make the Capitol joyful." This is an extreme version of what Italians at midcentury felt had to be done with Metastasio's rather daring and experimental libretto to make it agreeable, at least in the spring season. But Vivaldi's version with its conventional *lieto fine* makes a good test case for the argument here, because even Vivaldi maintains as central, and so as essential to the drama, a patriotic republicanism that is not generally supposed to emerge in opera until after the plays of Vittorio Alfieri. *Catone in Utica* is an early example of republican tragedy, and its consistent popularity is an important step toward the regular representation of republican themes and tragic death on the opera stage in the final decades of the century.

The action takes place in Utica in the last days of Caesar's African campaign. Historically, Cato and Caesar never met there: Metastasio's Utica is an imaginary place where his characters come together to represent the larger historical problems and conflicts. Cato has concentrated his forces in the city but is ordered by the new, pro-Caesarian senate in Rome to surrender. He refuses. Caesar has come into Utica to treat with Cato, and it emerges early in the first act that he and Cato's daughter Marzia are passionately in love with one another. But Marzia is also being courted by the Numidian Prince Arbace (who represents the younger Juba). Cato approves of the match with Arbace, and throughout the first two acts he keeps insisting that the marriage go forward, much to Marzia's distress. The end of the second act and the third act are taken up in part with Cato's anger against his daughter for her preference for Caesar. In this way Caesar the warrior and dictator, potentially the villain of a prorepublican drama, as he was in Addison's version of the story, has been turned structurally, at least, into a neocomic lover, complete with a soldier-rival in Arbace, and a cranky paterfamilias in Cato, who regards Caesar as a highly unsuitable candidate for son-in-law. To complicate matters further, Pompey's widow, here called Emilia, is also in Utica to seek vengeance against Caesar for Pompey's death. Her actions generally make peace and the legitimate consummation of Caesar's and Marzia's passion even more difficult. In act III, she lays an ambush for Caesar as he and Marzia attempt to escape Utica through an underground aqueduct—the motivation for the graffito in the Teatro d'Aliberti claiming Rome's heroes were in the sewer. Her plot is foiled at the last moment by Cato himself, who regards the treachery as dishonorable and un-Roman. Instead he proposes to fight Caesar hand to hand, but Caesar refuses out of his respect for Cato. At this point Caesar's troops storm and take Utica. Marzia concludes that as Cato's daughter she must recant her love for Caesar. Cato either does or does not commit suicide, and the opera ends.

Addison, to be sure, had invented romances for his secondary characters, but he had kept them within the Catonian camp, with the consequent warming of sympathy for Cato himself, and the improving conclusion was that whoever was virtuous and a defender of liberty was a Roman. Addison's play remained the tragedy of Cato and the Republic, and not of lovers caught between warring factions. Haym and Handel were dealing with Caesar's historical love affair with Cleopatra that had only to be manipulated with the help of a Plutarchan view of history to turn it into the stuff of heroic drama. But by any historical view, Metastasio's idea of a love affair between Caesar and the daughter of Cato is bizarre, and when combined, in Vivaldi's spring version, with a joyous ending, the drama appears to approach farce. The dignity of neoclassic tragedy, so prized by the Arcadians, seems as far away as ever, and the spirit of the seventeenth century still very close.

As an Italian, Metastasio was not dealing with a united country whose internal politics and leaders might be variously associated with those of the Romans, as were Addison or Handel in England. Italy, for centuries divided, ruled, and fought over by regional or foreign powers, had the Church of Rome as its only unifying institution, which controlled the intellectual life of the peninsula. Nathaniel Burt has pointed out that "the [Arcadian] Academy in a time of political despotism, confusion, and division provided Italy with a cultural unity and a measure of intellectual freedom. The Academy was a genuine republic of letters." Reinhard Strohm has suggested that opera in the late seventeenth and early eighteenth centuries was one of the few intellectual and non-ecclesiastical institutions to maintain and disseminate the traditions of Italian history, art, and literature. The librettists from the Arcadian Academy, beginning with Silvio Stampiglia, who based a series of successful librettos on stories from Livy about the legendary early years of Rome, succeeded as reminders of former national glory.[47] We observed in the last chapter the success of the Arcadian project in making Italian letters and Italian opera a European cultural phenomenon through the agency of the Italian *poeti cesarei* in Vienna.

Back in Italy, heroic tales from the early and middle Republic, such as the Scipio operas, might easily serve to feed nascent feelings of nationalism, and operas on imperial themes served as satire on foreign imperial courts, especially in staunchly republican Venice. But the stories from the fall of the Roman Republic, most of all those concerning Julius Caesar, when disunity and civil war tore Italy apart, present problems of the kind we have already observed above. Nevertheless, it is also a period full of drama, and the time when issues of liberty, tyranny, clemency, and duty became most acute for the Romans, and was therefore difficult to resist as a topic for librettists wanting to address those same issues while celebrating Italian history. The solution is once again in Plutarch, his balanced vision the one that Metastasio clearly adopted, for he remarked in his *Argomento* to *Catone in Utica* that one was unsure "whether we should more admire the generosity of Caesar, because he had such great respect for his enemies' virtue, or the constancy of Cato, because he did not wish to outlive the liberty of his country."

It is the romantic and nearly comic elements, obligatory in Italian opera since its beginning, that actually enabled Metastasio to present this balanced vision in a way that also addresses the serious issues embedded in the story of Caesar and Cato. They were two men who finally had no way of talking to one another, and by writing both Caesar and Cato into the plot, as neither Addison, Bussani, nor Haym had done, Metastasio represented the two forces that were tearing the Roman Republic apart. Metastasio's Caesar, as conqueror of Pompey and the senatorial party, is willing to do almost anything to win the virtuous Cato to his side—anything except give up his hard-won power. Cato for his part can never be won unless Caesar gives up himself and his power and returns to Rome as prisoner. There is seemingly no middle ground between the two, and that is made very clear in Metastasio's scene at II.x (Vivaldi II.viii), in which the two men meet and Caesar's determined diplomacy fails utterly.

The romantic subplot provides a middle ground for the audience, if not for Caesar and Cato, from which we can see Caesar as something other than tyrannical villain, and appreciate at the same time what it means for the rest of the world to be caught between two forces that refuse to agree. Marzia, as she mediates between father and lover, becomes the representative of that middle world as the peace negotiations fail and the two men part in anger. As the scene comes to a close, Caesar has with great patience endured Cato's belligerent refusals to accept peace with him on any terms at all. Caesar has offered to share his power with Cato and finally to cement a relationship by marrying Marzia (a political move that coincides with his own wishes). Cato reacts violently, crying, "Ah first may all the anger of the gods rain down on me, before the blood of one so disgraceful sullies my blood, before I allow a traitor to be joined to me, one who in his madness has nearly buried already our ancient liberty!"[48] Caesar, his patience at an end, starts to leave. Vivaldi's version (II.ix) edits Metastasio's longer scene but maintains its essence:

> *Marzia.* Oh, God! Wait! (to Catone) This is your peace? (to Cesare)
> And this your longed for friendship?
> *Cesare:* Accuse your father. He wants war.
> *Mar.* Oh, father . . .
> *Cat.* Be quiet; don't speak of that man!
> *Mar.* Caesar . . .
> *Ces.* I've already put up with too much.
> *Mar.* Ah, no! Quiet now your stubborn angers. Your rages cost too
> much weeping for the Latin wives, your hatreds too much blood
> for the unhappy people of Quirinus. Oh, let friend no more be
> seen to savage the impaled body of his friend. Oh, may brother
> not triumph over brother! Let the father no more fall next to the
> son whom he has killed! Enough at last of so much blood and
> weeping!
> *Cat.* It's not enough for him.
> *Ces.* Not enough for me! If you wish, there is yet time; I'll forget your
> insults, renew my promises, lay down my anger, and await your
> choice: ask me for war or peace—you will be satisfied.
> *Cat.* War. It's war I want.
> *Ces.* And war you shall have.*

Marzia as lover of Caesar and child of Cato is Metastasio's solution to the problem of how to view the personalities of the late Republic that he expressed in his *Argomento:* Through her, he is able to examine both. As Cato's daughter she is to be associated with her father's republican virtue and staunch refusal to give in to tyranny. Her frank admiration of Caesar, on the other hand, allows a view of his courage, forbearance, and political savvy. Both men can be claimed as worthy of Italy's grand traditions. This Metastasio could not have done if he had followed Addison's lead and made Caesar the villain in a true tragedy of Cato.

But Marzia is also caught in the middle, her words sounding like the pleas of the Sabine women who intervened to prevent their Roman husbands and Sabine fathers from slaughtering one another.[49] Because of her position, she becomes a tragic figure, representing not only her own anguish but also that of families and country ravaged for being similarly in the middle. The opera is, in part, the tragedy of Italy, for Marzia fails where the Sabine women succeeded, and this may well be what made Vivaldi respond to the story. The year before he set *Catone,* he had ruminated discontentedly in the dedication to his opera *Adelaide* about his "wretched Italy, which after the expulsion of her last Kings, had fallen to the point where she could no longer free herself from foreign subjugation."[50] Like

Elvira in *Scipione nelle Spagne,* Marzia is a fully drawn character who is nevertheless a symbol of the opera's message.

Metastasio's Caesar throws down his victory crown in shame and self-disgust at the death of Cato. Like the conclusion of *Giulio Cesare,* this ending appears to freeze history. Vivaldi, with his springtime conclusion to the opera, even rewrote history to eliminate the need for Caesar's penitence, but his librettist included in the final scene a new element that is perhaps more disturbing than that of the original. Pompey's widow, Emilia, her plot for revenge thwarted by Cato himself, is present in the *scena ultima* to witness Caesar's final gestures of peace. In the midst of the general reconciliation, she declares bitterly to Caesar, "The gods will take care to avenge us; perhaps the blow is not very far off. May Heaven hasten it for others' peace, and that hand that you least believe to be unfaithful, may that hand tear your breast." She then exits. Her parting words are a direct reference to Brutus's blow on the Ides of March and must cast its shadow over the brightly shining conclusion, not solving the problem of Caesar but only postponing it for a time. Vivaldi's is, after all, dynamic and not frozen history. Further unhappiness lies in the future for Marzia and Italy. This tragic juxtaposition of irreconcilable forces anticipates the moment in Cimarosa's *Gli Orazi e i Curiazi,* still two generations in the future, when the young woman in love will not merely be the unfortunate witness of war but a murdered victim, her body the object of forces still bitterly divided as the curtain goes down.

7 Arminius and the Problem of Rome

CORRADI, *GERMANICO SUL RENO*; ANONYMOUS,
ARMINIO (LONDON); SALVI/HANDEL, *ARMINIO*

The theme of resistance to tyranny, and a related nostalgia for the idealized liberty of the Roman Republic as expressed in *Il Catone in Utica*, had been present in opera since Monteverdi's *Poppea*. This was natural enough in dramas performed for the Republic of Venice, which regarded itself as the legitimate heir of ancient Rome as well as the sometime antagonist of papal Rome. Allegiance to republican ideals, however, conflicted with a number of ideological and practical considerations that demanded equal attention. One was an admiration for the military and artistic achievements of the Roman Empire, achievements that most early modern European nation-states strove to emulate. This admiration resulted in veneration of the better-respected emperors such as Augustus, Titus, or Hadrian, whose power as emperor nevertheless had superseded that of the Republican senate. The Romans themselves struggled with the contradiction inherent in the veneration of empire, and Caesar is the very embodiment of the problem, as we saw in the previous chapter.

A second consideration was the recognition that, however much liberty was an attractive ideal, the eighteenth-century reality was that everyone was the subject of a king, emperor, or pope, whose goodwill, and often whose money, made production of opera possible. The degree of autocratic control varied from venue to venue of course, but the reality of power had to be faced even by Venice, which, from the time she had begun to celebrate herself in opera, was nevertheless increasingly losing her grip on her own empire and was subordinate to other European powers. Hence Venetian librettos are largely dedicated to non-Venetian aristocrats; Agostino Piovene's dedication of his *Publio Cornelio Scipione* (1712) to *La Nobilità Veneta* is unusual if not unique.

A final consideration was that while the nations of Europe might admire Roman conquest as a model for their own imperial aspirations, their history also made them the victims of that conquest: England, France, Spain, and Germany had all been invaded and occupied. Caesar the conqueror was a problem for Rome; Rome the conqueror was a problem for the world. In consequence, those countries also had native heroes, freedom fighters who had opposed the very Roman military power that, in other contexts, those same countries admired and wished to emulate. Those heroes included Vercingetorix in France, Boadicea in England, and Arminius in Germany. In the view of Tacitus, these figures were foils against which Rome's own corruption and loss of virtue might be observed, barbarian enemies that better exemplified traditional Roman virtue than did the Romans themselves.

What I have called the myth of the clement prince has, in the operas thus far observed, mediated at least some of these contradictions. An operatic general or emperor who could recognize his duty and respect the individual liberty of his subjects while yet remaining in control offered a Senecan, neo-Stoic ideal in a world where there was no way around the fact of centralized, autocratic power. Individual liberty in opera is nearly always represented as love, and a beneficent conqueror like Scipio, by honoring the erotic and marital attachments of the conquered, deserved and justified his position. Operas about such princes end as celebrations of princely power. Their opposite numbers, such as Nero or Sulla, for whom personal desire is more important than public duty, do not deserve their positions, and operas about them were cautionary tales or carnival satire. The case of Caesar and Cato as it was presented in the early eighteenth century made clear the precarious nature of this myth. In the last chapter we observed how easily Caesar, the *fons et origo* of the myth of imperial *clementia,* might become a dramatic villain, and how in fact considerable care had to be taken if his positive qualities were to be maintained. The example of Cato, the native Roman freedom fighter, stood as a dangerous example of resistance to regal power and its threat to internal liberties.

This chapter examines a group of operas that looked at Rome as invader of northern Europe. They feature as dramatic hero the German leader Arminius—Arminio in Italian and Hermann der Cherusker to the Germans—who successfully defeated three Roman legions under Quinctilius Varus in the Teutoburger Forest during the reign of Augustus. Some years later, during a punitive campaign led by the young Germanicus Caesar, nephew of the emperor Tiberius, Arminius continued to cause trouble for Rome. But his wife Thusnelda was captured and taken to Rome, where she was displayed, along with her son by Arminius, in Germanicus's triumphal procession. The Arminius operas discussed here are Giulio Cesare Corradi's *Germanico sul Reno* (*Germanicus at the Rhine;* Venice, 1676), an anonymous *Arminio* (London, 1714), and Handel's *Arminio* (London, 1737), written for a libretto adapted from an original by Antonio Salvi. They represent a range of nationalist and libertarian feelings, for Arminius served as a hero for a more generalized aristocratic European audience before he was turned into the specifically German popular legend Hermann.

Arminius was, in Tacitus's eulogistic terms, "unquestionably the liberator of Germany."[1] He was a tribal leader of the Germanic tribe called the Cherusci, who occupied an area in northwest Germany around the middle Weser River between the Harz Mountains and what is now Hanover, a fact significant for British productions of operas about him. Early in his life he had enjoyed Roman citizenship and seems to have had command of Cheruscan troops in the Roman army. In 9 C.E. Arminius led the Cherusci in a revolt against Roman intrusions across the Rhine and lured three legions under the somewhat gullible Quinctilius Varus to their famous destruction in a narrow defile in the Teutoburger Forest.[2] The Germans slaughtered the Romans like cattle, said Velleius; it was the worst military disaster for Rome since Crassus's shameful loss to the Parthians two generations earlier. The half-burned body of the general Varus was mutilated and his head forwarded to the Romans through a German intermediary. Germanicus later found the bodies of the three legions left unburied, with evidence of the torture and execution of captives. Suetonius says that Augustus was "so greatly affected that for several months in succession he cut neither his beard nor his hair, and sometimes he would dash his head against a door, crying: 'Quinctilius Varus, give me back my legions!' He observed the day of the disaster each year as one of sorrow and mourning" (Suetonius, *Augustus* 23).[3]

Arminius's wife Thusnelda was the daughter of a pro-Roman Germanic chieftain named Segestes; relations between the in-laws were not happy. Tacitus's *Annals* provides the melodramatic details that were later to appeal to opera librettists: "Segestes . . . remained recalcitrant, and private enmity was exacerbated, because Arminius had carried off his daughter, who was promised to someone else, so the hostility of father-in-law and son-in-law was mutual" (*Annals* 1.55). During one of Arminius's uprisings, his German troops even cornered Segestes in his home fortress, where he would have fallen had he not been rescued by Roman troops under Aulus Caecina Severus, one of Germanicus's subordinate officers.

Thusnelda's sympathies were with her husband rather than her father, and Segestes ultimately recaptured her and turned her over to the Romans. Her brother, Segestes's son Sigimundus, seems to have switched sides at least two times, and he was finally marched in Germanicus's triumph in Rome along with his sister, while their father was treated as an honored guest at the celebratory banquet (Strabo, *Geography* 7.4.1). Arminius's own brother Flavus also served in the Roman army but remained loyal to the Roman side: The two brothers are reported nearly to have come to blows after shouting insults at one another in Latin from opposite sides of the Weser River.

Arminius remained at large and continued to head German resistance against Rome, fighting a series of battles against Germanicus and others. He lost those battles, but the cost of the victories to Rome ultimately convinced the Romans to restrict their efforts to conquer Germany. Arminius's tribe, the Cherusci, were for their part afflicted with internal dissentions like those of Arminius's family, and Arminius was killed by his own people in 19 C.E.

These are the historical facts that can be established. But already by Tacitus's day, three generations or so after the death of Arminius, history had begun to turn to legend among the German tribes. Tacitus himself wrote an admiring and tragical eulogy of Arminius that suggests legend rather than history, not least because he uses it to bring the second book of the *Annals* to a moving conclusion, after detailing the death of Germanicus and the general dissolution of the Roman court (*Annals* 2.88):

> The Roman evacuation of Germany . . . had induced Arminius to aim at kingship. But his freedom-loving compatriots forcibly resisted. The fortunes of the fight fluctuated, but finally Arminius succumbed to treachery from his relations. He was unmistakably the liberator of Germany. Challenger of Rome—not in its infancy, like kings and commanders before him, but at the height of its power—he had fought undecided battles, and never lost a war. He had ruled for twelve of his thirty-seven years. To this day the tribes sing of him.[4]

This passage was to provide the core for Arminius's subsequent reputation, beginning in the late Renaissance, when the texts of Tacitus were

rediscovered. Tacitus was following the Greco-Roman tradition of eth-
nographic writing that included an idealized picture of the relative freedom and simplicity of barbaric peoples, which, as Albrecht Dihle says,
"invites his contemporaries . . . to take a good look at themselves in
comparison."[5]

The dangerous and impressive thing about the Germans, in Tacitus's
view, was their tenacious hold on their natural liberties and the consequent threat to Rome. (See, for example, *Germania* 36.) In Tacitus's
Annals, Arminius's brother Flavus defends his loyalty to Rome with a
recitation of its advantages—that it brought him higher pay and military
decoration. Arminius sneers in reply that the reward for slavery is cheap
("vilia servitii pretia"; *Annals* 2.9). Hence, the admiring eulogy of Arminius is part of a larger pattern in Tacitus of exposing the gap between Roman ideals and Roman behavior by showing that the supposedly barbaric
Germans possessed the Roman virtues that the Romans themselves had
betrayed. A Roman author provided the means by which the apparent
contradictions in Europe's attitudes toward ancient Rome, delineated
above, might be mediated and the so-admired virtues and military power
of Rome transferred to its subjects.

German humanists of the sixteenth century, beginning with Ulrich
von Hutten, had interpreted the Arminius story as an allegory of German
unity and freedom from the tyranny of Catholic Italy, Spain, and France.
But the Thirty Years' War put an end to German unity for the time being.
Despite the use of Arminius's name by seventeenth-century academic
writers to call for a return to German freedom and unity, the single most
remarkable work in the baroque period was Daniel Caspar von Lohenstein's
lengthy two-volume novel *Grossmütiger Feldherr: Arminius* (*The Magnanimous General, Arminius*), published in 1689. Lohenstein's *Arminius*
has been described as formless and an "indigestible porridge" but also as
the most important polite novel of the seventeenth century.[6]

However, the specifically German transformation of Arminius into a
popular legend really only came of age in the mid- to late eighteenth century, and then into the nineteenth century, with authors such as Johann
Elias Schlegel, Friedrich Gottlieb Klopstock, Heinrich von Kleist, and
Christian Dietrich Grabbe.[7] External literary influence on Italian opera
librettos, particularly those of the early eighteenth century, came out of
France rather than Germany. George de Scudéry in 1643 wrote a tragicomedy titled *Arminius, ou les frères ennemis* that featured political and
amatory rivalry between Arminius and his brother Flavus; Jean-Galbert
Campistron wrote a popular *Arminius* in 1685, a transformation of the
Teutoburger narrative that was to be the direct and acknowledged source

of Salvi's *Arminio* opera for the Florentine court, the libretto adapted later by Handel. Hence, Arminius, his family, and their relations with Rome, were in this period acted out on French, Italian, and English stages, and their insistence on German liberty and unity were being used to address other matters.

In the case of Arminius dramas, much of the attention is given to invented crises in his relations with his wife Thusnelda, often due to difficulties created by Romans who wish to compete for her affections. Two of the librettos here, Corradi's *Germanico sul Reno* and the anonymous London *Arminius*, take as their basis the events surrounding Germanicus's relations with Arminius during his campaigns against the Cherusci. The action of Handel's *Arminio* is set just before the slaughter in the Teutoburger forest. They are interesting for the ways that they complement the republican attitudes toward liberty and tyranny in *Catone in Utica*; the English operas also appear to have relevance for the family lives of the nobility who sponsored their production. Beyond the immediate issues, and taken as a group, these operas have ramifications for the views of patriotism and national liberty expressed by late-century operas in the final two chapters.

Corradi's 1676 *Germanico sul Reno* for Venice is, as the title suggests, an overt celebration of the Roman Germanicus Caesar rather than of Arminius. The dedicatee is identified by his titles only: "Prince of Monaco, Duke of Valence, and peer of France." The dedication reads, "Heroes should be consecrated to heroes, and great souls seek for great princes as an object to show them off. I consecrate Germanicus to your most serene Highness, because in [your Highness] may be seen living the magnanimity (*generosità*) of Germanicus, it being right that the first splendor of Italy receive light for its rebirth from one who is not the least Sun of France." The frontispiece of the libretto (fig. 6) shows Germanicus on a canopied throne; the composition is that of the genre paintings of scenes of royal clemency familiar from the *Continence of Scipio* (fig. 1).

Arminius's role in this opera is therefore secondary. The historical center of the opera concerns Germanicus and his relations with his wife Agrippina, and with a subordinate officer named Floro, who represents the Roman troops. Tacitus (*Annals*, books 1 and 2) had related in detail how Germanicus had been sent to Germany partly to put down a serious mutiny among the Rhine armies. Accompanied by the famously chaste and noble Agrippina the elder and their son Gaius, nicknamed "Caligula" or "Little Boots" for the miniature army boots he wore, Germanicus managed to quell the mutiny and make popular reforms.[8] In the opera, Floro represents this mutiny, first suggesting to Germanico that

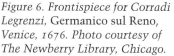

Figure 6. Frontispiece for Corradi Legrenzi, Germanico sul Reno, *Venice, 1676. Photo courtesy of The Newberry Library, Chicago.*

the troops will support him in a bid to overthrow the emperor Tiberius. When Germanico refuses in horror, Floro attempts a coup on his own, in the process making it appear as if Agrippina is being unfaithful to Germanicus on his (Floro's) behalf. The quelling of the revolt and defeat of Floro, and the happy reunification of Germanico and Agrippina, are the central events of the opera.

Connected to the main plot are the family relationships of Arminio, his beloved—here called Claudia rather than Thusnelda—and her father Segeste, who wishes Claudia to marry a Roman named Lucio. The famous intrepidity of Arminius and Thusnelda in the face of Roman threat is expressed here in terms of unflinching devotion to their mutual love. Initially, before Floro's true colors are revealed, the libretto plays with expectations that Arminio will be the villain, since he is the enemy of Germanico and Rome. In an early scene he captures Agrippina and

Caligula, who are wandering alone in the German forest. But Floro rescues them, and Arminio himself is captured. Imprisoned in a tower, he requests Claudia, who has disguised herself as a soldier in order to avoid discovery by her father and the Romans, to burn the tower down and rob the Romans of the satisfaction of executing him. She sets the tower alight but begs that Arminio fling himself down into her arms, which he does. Still disguised as a soldier, she then defends him from arriving Roman troops and he makes his escape.

Claudia and Arminio spend the rest of the opera thwarting in various ways Claudia's marriage to Lucio. In the end, Arminio rejoins the Germanicus plot by preventing Floro from shooting Germanicus with an arrow. Arminio and Claudia are rewarded by the magnanimous Germanicus, who declares Arminio his friend, unites him with Claudia, and promises them the emperor's pardon. The final triumph is Claudia's rather than Arminio's, since she and Agrippina sing the closing duet in praise of love. The overall shape of the ending, with forgiveness and even rewards for Rome's enemies because of their virtues, is familiar already from the *scena ultima* of *Scipione affricano*, written twelve years earlier. In that opera, however, the erring party was the somewhat pathetic Massanissa, and his sins were those of the overly passionate North Africans. Scipione the Roman, though tempted, remained constant in the face of that temptation. In *Germanico sul Reno*, the treatment of Arminio and Claudia/Thusnelda creates a Tacitean contrast between the brave and faithful German couple and the faithless and corrupt Roman Floro. In remaining faithful and protecting the authority figure Germanicus from harm, they set an example for the supposedly superior Romans.

Arminio's virtue is nevertheless a reflection of Roman virtue. The action and characters of the opera are surrounded by deities and abstractions of largely Roman and Italic nature. Time, Eternity, and Military Glory sing the prologue. Bellona, goddess of war and consort of Mars, appears over a triumphal arch raised in a celebration of Germanicus's victories (I.x). At the end of act II, Arminio conjures up the seer Aristaeus, a figure borrowed from the end of Vergil's *Georgics*, to foretell his future, and Aristaeus in turn brings Orpheus on stage to soothe and reassure Arminio for the apparent loss of his wife Claudia to Lucio. The opera concludes with the descent of Fama, who sings praises of Germanico. Arminio and Claudia bask in Germanicus's reflected glory, their own achievements absorbed into the ultimately Romanized world of the opera.

There is one more wrinkle, however. That Romanized world of opera does not belong exclusively to the Italians. In *Scipione affricano*, the dedicatee and analogue to the hero had at least been a noble Roman,

Lorenzo Colonna. Here, the dedicatee, like that of Zeno's later *Scipione nelle Spagne,* is a northerner: The prince of Monaco and the "Sun of France," the analogue to Germanicus in the opera, is the one who casts the light. As in Tacitus's analysis, Roman virtue and glory have moved out of the Roman sphere to the people of the North. The sources of Vivaldi's discontent two generations later for the plight of Italy (chapter 6) are already suggested in this and other libretto dedications that take as their subjects the aristocrats and royalty of northern Europe. Nevertheless, in this telling of the story, the dedicatee is at least identified with a Roman. In the two English tellings of the story that follow, Rome is the enemy, and the Germans are identified with those paying for the operas. The problem is to maintain a connection to Roman glory and virtue while admitting that Rome was the enemy. The solution lies in adopting a Tacitean admiration for barbarian virtue that equals but outshines the Roman.

Where *Germanico sul Reno* had celebrated Germanicus as a clement conqueror worthy of his superior position, the anonymous 1714 libretto *Arminius* for London is a celebration of Arminius as a champion of liberty against oppression.[9] The change of emphasis is instantly clear in the libretto's preface:

> Never human arm gave stronger shake to the power of ancient Rome, than that of stout Arminius. And if fortune had not too notoriously declared herself on the Roman side, they never had established themselves in Germany; where they found not the least security, as long as the unparalleled valor of this hero was acting against them: he sacrificed, for the liberty of his country, the Roman legions brought by Varus, and celebrated with the blood of the soldiers the funeral of their commander.

The action of the opera takes place while Germanicus is at the Rhine. Arminius's forces have been defeated, and the pro-Roman Segestes is in ascendancy. The plot features the rivalry between Segestes and the fugitive Arminius over daughter and wife, who is here called Ismena. There is much fear expressed of capture and being led in triumphal chains, a theme familiar from *Scipio affricano.* Here that theme is probably generated by the historical fact that Thusnelda really was paraded through Rome in Germanicus's triumph, but it is not developed into any kind of metaphorical language of love. Arminius tries to prevent Ismena's capture by having her kill both herself and her child. Her failure to do so results in her falling into the hands of Germanicus and her father Segestes, after which she remains adamant in her refusal to side with the Romans. A secondary plot involves the sister of Arminius who is called Cilene. Cilene induces the discontented Roman Cecina (that is, A. Caecina Severus, the commander mentioned in Tacitus who saved Segestes) to make an attempt on Germanicus's life. In the final scenes, Cecina is accidentally killed by Arminius's arrow—Arminius means to hit Germanicus; the event is perhaps adapted from Corradi. Arminius is captured, but the clement, noble, and generous Germanicus ultimately spares him and all ends happily.

This opera was produced more than a generation later than Corradi's libretto and shows the influence of the libretto reforms. A more serious tone comes from the near-tragedy of the loss of German liberty to Rome in which Arminius and Ismena/Thusnelda are swept up. Ismena's position is made clear in the first act (I.xi). She has been captured, and Germanicus wants her child by Arminius in custody as well, because "an infected branch from a rebellious stock, / May Rome o'ershade, and give its strongest forts a shock":[10]

> *Ismena.* Does haughty Rome then fear us still?
> Nay, fear us when we losers are? How great
> How illustrious is our fall!
> Freely, o Fortune, I'll forgive thee,
> If thou permittest to any of our race
> The honor to be feared by Rome.

Germanicus is impressed. He observes, "In spite of her captivity, / the undaunted dame with honor trims and feeds / the lamp of just expiring Liberty." Thus he frees her out of respect for her spirit. But her favor with Germanicus, and her inability to kill herself and her child, raise Arminius's suspicions of her loyalty. He reproves her with words reminiscent of his rebuke to his brother Flavus reported in Tacitus's account (2.6–7):

> *Ismena.* Ah dear Sir!
> *Arminius.* Humph! preserve that name
> For fortunate Germanicus (vile wretch)
> And offer to his servile yoke thy neck.
> *Ism.* Generous Germanicus broke my chains
> Himself, and me to liberty restored.
> *Arm.* A given liberty was ever vile.

In the final scenes, when Arminius has accidentally shot the rebellious Cecina and thus saved Germanicus's life, he remains a violently intransigent enemy to Rome, but Germanicus demonstrates a nobility of spirit that can recognize and even reward the bravery and free spirit of his enemy:

Germanicus. See now how differently a Roman heart
Beats with compassion in a noble breast.
Thou, both by fortune and by heaven,
By judge and justice are condemned:
Germanicus absolves thee, and at once restores
Thy wife, thy child, thy liberty and crown.

And so at the end, the result is the same as that in *Germanico sul Reno*: Arminius, won over by the magnanimity of Germanicus, swears eternal allegiance to Rome and Tiberius, and Germanicus thinks it is a second victory to have won over such a noble heart. Both magnanimous imperial power and German liberty are allowed to win.

This libretto appears to have caught the liberty-fever that had overtaken the London stage in the aftermath of the riotous reception of Addison's *Cato* in 1713, just a year before the production of this *Arminius*. Opera, as we have seen, was seldom so forthright as the spoken drama on immediate political issues, and so it is striking that this one so directly employs its legendary figures to utter the political catchwords of the day. But it is also interesting to note the limits of liberty. Liberty is legitimated as a gift of the imperial power that controls the stage. Personal and national liberty is respected, and patriots rewarded, but only in a context carefully circumscribed by the powers of the imperial monarch. On the Italian stage, that means the emperor Tiberius as represented by Germanicus; for the audience of the Queen's Theatre in 1714, it meant Queen Anne. In this regard, the dedication of the libretto to the Countess Godolphin, signed but probably not written by Johann Jakob Heidegger, is particularly interesting. She was Henrietta Godolphin, daughter of John Churchill, Duke of Marlborough and the daughter-in-law of Sidney, first Earl of Godolphin (d. 1712). During the reign of Queen Anne, Sidney Godolphin was a friend and supporter of Marlborough, the Whig champion, as we saw in connection with *Cato*; Godolphin strongly opposed Tory influence in the government, partly as a way to continue supporting Marlborough's prosecution of the War of the Spanish Succession. Furthermore, waiting in the wings as heir to the queen was the German George, elector of Hanover, the Whig candidate for the throne who became George I after Queen Anne's death on August 1, 1714. The theme of liberty in this opera is therefore of a piece with Whig ideology.[11] A celebration of Whig notions of liberty, coded as German liberty and featuring the German hero Arminius, who hailed from the area of Hanover, would seem to be no accident in such a political context.[12]

Twenty-three years later the subject of Arminius was visited again in a London opera: Handel's music for *Arminio* was first performed at the Theatre Royal in Covent Garden beginning in January of 1737. Its libretto was condensed from Antonio Salvi's much longer libretto for the grand duke of Florence in 1703. That libretto was in turn adapted from Campistron's French play *Arminius*. These texts set the tensions between Arminius and his father-in-law Segestes during the earlier confrontation with Quinctilius Varus rather than at the time of Germanicus's campaigns. The opera's conflicts are generated by the fact that Varus has fallen in love with Tusnelda (she is so called in these librettos) and attempts to win her away from Arminius, and by the tension created by Segestes, not only with Arminius and Tusnelda but also by his son Sigismundus. Sigismundus wants to be a dutiful son, but he is in love with Arminius's sister Ramise and, furthermore, has serious doubts about betraying the cause of German freedom. The *lieto fine* of the opera includes the report of the defeat of the Roman troops in the Teutoburger Forest and the reconciliation of Segestes with his children and Arminius. The *clementia* in this opera belongs to Arminius, who forgives Segestes for siding with the Romans rather than with a conquering Roman general.

These last two operas, therefore, move radically away from any glorification of Roman authority and instead celebrate the nobility of the German heroes. Salvi's libretto is fairly lengthy and contains much detailed discussion of Germanic patriotism and bravery in the face of oppression. Nothing is made of this in Salvi's preface, beyond describing Arminius as "this relentless defender of liberty" ("questo acerrimo difensore di Libertà"), but one may assume a general appropriateness of theme for a court that was in the Habsburg sphere of influence.

The version adapted for Handel retains many of Salvi's original aria texts but cuts the recitative to the bone and considerably weakens the plot, which becomes a sketch of the events without adequate motivation needed to explain them. Nevertheless, while there is no dedicatory letter, nor anything in the "Argument" that hints at the kind of politics one finds in the anonymous *Arminius* libretto of two decades earlier, the English translation facing the Italian inherits from Salvi's original much that is familiar from dramas that are the heirs to Addison's *Cato*. In I.iv, for example, Arminius has been captured by the Romans and appears in chains. Arminius defiantly asserts,[13]

> E're that Arminius will bend his brow
> In poor subjection to the Latian throne,
> Or will disclaim his country, and his gods
> Torments or slavery, shall end my days.

He concludes the scene with an exit aria on the same theme:

My Heart's so firm, so nobly great,
It seems [i.e., is equal to] the malice of my fate.
Fortune, her cruel power to try,
May take my life or liberty,
Wretched I may, but base will never be.[14]

Handel's music is a surprisingly quiet declaration in E major of Arminio's patriotism. The aria is in triple time, marked andante, with minimal counterpoint. In the A section, a steady rhythm of staccato quarter notes in the strings emphasizes Arminio's determination. They lengthen to half notes on the initial statement of *è forte questa cor* ("My heart's so firm"). Melismas and repetitions match *sorte* ("fate") against *forte* ("firm"), but *forte* finally wins the contest. It is a striking moment in a sometimes banal score. (Example 5).

Arminio is no less adamant in II.iv when Segestes suggests he yield peaceably to Rome:

Segestes. To give your country peace, will be your glory.
Arminius. How say'st thou? Glory! What to give it up,
    In slavish homage, to a tyrant's yoke.
Seg. Then death be thine—
Arm. Welcome and glorious in liberty.

In the third act (III.vi), Arminio is freed from Roman captivity by Sigismundus, who has deliberately defied his father Segestes in order to do so. Sigismundus returns Arminio's sword to him, with the words, "See, see, I render to your eager grasp / this faithful instrument of your renown, / And of Germania's liberty." Arminio, sword in hand, replies with an aria that combines patriotic valor with personal honor:

Now glory darts a guiding ray,
And injured honor points the way;
Or I will die with conquest crown'd,
Or die with sacred laurels bound.

Despite all the talk of liberty, the potential political ramifications of the action are not nearly as directly expressed as those of the 1714 *Arminius;* in fact, the lack of political themes in the *Argomento* may be a judicious choice, for the situation of the divided family in the opera is painfully close to what was going on in the royal family at the time. Relations between George II and Queen Caroline and their son Frederick, the Prince of Wales, were deeply strained over questions of money, public respect due to the prince, and perhaps even succession to the throne of England. Whig rhetoric in the House of Commons from George Lyttleton

Example 5 Haendel's Arminio

and James Pitt styled the prince a popular hero and a "patriot prince" as a balance to the power of Robert Walpole, who was allied with the king. In February 1737, as *Arminio* was on the boards, Frederick was trying to have his allowance from the king increased through action in the House of Commons. In the fall of 1737, six months after the production of *Arminio*, Frederick would actually be exiled from St. James Palace, deprived of his guard, and anyone holding an office from the king was forbidden to see him.[15]

Handel worked for royalty on both sides of the quarrel. He was the music teacher of Princess Anne, George II's and Caroline's eldest daughter. In the years before her marriage to Willem of Orange and removal to the Netherlands he had received her enthusiastic support as well as that of the queen. Part of the reason for their support was their opposition to the Opera of the Nobility, newly formed in 1733 and patronized by Frederick and his faction in competition with Handel's established Royal Academy. In 1733–34 the rivalry was intense and the royals took sides. The acerbic Lord Hervey reported, "The King and Queen were as much in earnest upon this subject as their son and daughter, though they had the prudence to disguise it or to endeavour to disguise it a little more. They were both Handelists, and sat freezing constantly at his empty Haymarket Opera, whilst the Prince and all the chief of the nobility went constantly to that of Lincoln's Inn Fields [which housed the Opera of the Nobility]. The affair grew as serious as that of the Greens and the Blues under Justinian at Constantinople."[16]

By the time *Arminio* was premiered (January 12, 1737), the pressure seems to have been a little reduced. Handel had written an anthem for the wedding of Frederick to Princess Augusta of Saxe-Gotha in 1736, and his opera *Atalanta* also celebrated that wedding. In 1736–37, both royal factions were supporting both opera companies, although they refused to appear on the same nights.[17] Reinhard Strohm has suggested that "the individual action of the piece—the fates of the devoted couple Armenio and Tusnelda—must be understood as referring directly to the Prince of Wales and his wife."[18] But exact identification of Arminio, the heroic and patriotic leader, with Frederick implies a corresponding political identification of the collusionist Segestes with George II, and would probably have given offense at a time when Handel had no reason to do so. Rather, reference to the royals in the opera is probably to be seen in the familial relations of Segestes and his son Sigismondo, and stress should be put on the message of reconciliation between estranged members of the governing family. Sigismondo is portrayed throughout as a prince whose loyalty to his father remains in balance with his patriotism and loyalty to German liberty. In II.vii, he saves Segestes's life from Arminio's angry sister Ramise. In reply to Ramise's reproaches, he says, "Witness ye Gods, I am all Truth and Love. But say, what can I act against a Father?" (This is a notable expansion of the Italian: "Son pien di fede. Ma contro il genitor?") His crisis and loyalty are further elaborated in a recitative and aria in III.iv that summarize all the conflicts of the opera:[19]

> *Sigismondo.* Hold, hold, oh Heavens! How is my soul perplexed!
> Oh Love! oh duty! oh my friend and father!
> Hapless Ramisa, and most hapless sister [Tusnelda]!
> The various thought's too great, then ease me, Death!
> > Duty pleads a mighty tie;
> > Love too pleads not in vain;
> > I know not whose will be the victory.
> > So save this heart—my duty wrongs;
> > To wound it—injures love.
> > Cruel to my soul's desire,
> > Or unfaithful to my sire,
> > Alas I ne'er can prove.

With the winning back of Segestes at the end of the opera, the German ruling family appears as the defender of national liberty, finally united against the power of Rome, which, if one were so inclined, might be identified with the Catholic Church and the yet-remaining threat of the Stuarts. Tacitus's vision of Germans with old Roman virtues are the heroic defenders against the tyranny of (new) Rome.

Handel's "surprising and not altogether successful" return to the heroic drama of *Arminio* after the fantasies of *Ariodante*, *Alcina*, and *Atalanta* is perhaps due precisely to a hope of family reconciliation and unity.[20] Ellen Harris has pointed out that there is a larger common theme of family trials and reconciliations in Handel's operas for 1737, which, in addition to *Arminio*, included *Giustino*, *Berenice*, and, in the next season back at the Haymarket Theatre, *Faramondo*. *Faramondo* in particular includes a father-son relationship in which the son saves his father from vengeance and the opera ends in family reconciliation.[21]

Yet the hope of family reconciliation—if that is indeed what is being promoted—is not naïvely expressed at the end of *Arminio*. In a rapid turnaround characteristic of many *lieti fini*, Segestes admits that Arminio's virtue overcomes his enmity, the two embrace, and Segestes pledges his faith. A similar reconciliation is to be assumed between Segestes and Sigismundo, as Arminio says, "Now let my sister and your son be joyn'd / In Hymen's sacred bands: much more I owe him / For the great gift of liberty and life." But father and son have nothing more to say to one another after this, nor is an embrace indicated in the stage directions. Musically, the greatest portion of the last scene is a happy duet between the reunited Arminio and Tusnelda, following which Arminio, completing his own act of *clementia*, declares, "And now let the heavens, at last, serenely smile, / Let joy and gladness every bosom fill." The final "Grand Chorus," by contrast, is not the cheerful celebration of success one finds in *Giulio Cesare*, and might expect here. It is rather—in the English translation at least—a wistful hope for peace:

> Sorrows but so late subsiding,
> Scarce our hearts receive the bliss;
> Yet virtue all our actions guiding,
> We shall find compleated peace.[22]

The English version is a paraphrase rather than an exact translation. The Italian begins with *dolcezze*, "sweetness," not *tristezze*, "sorrows"; "Sorrows but so late subsiding," is a meaning buried only very deeply in the Italian of the second couplet, "Cangia in gioia le tristezze." Handel's music in G minor is correspondingly subdued, the sense of *tristezza* dominating *gioia*, and turning the final "Generosa un bel valor," and its parallel phrase in English, "We shall find compleated Peace," into a meditative conclusion. Handel's opera, rather than taking sides, adopts a poetic role of adviser to princes, depicting the virtues of forgiveness and family harmony.

The noble and virtuous non-Roman had been a figure available to opera from the middle of the seventeenth century. We observed the type already in *Scipione affricano* with Siface and Sofonisba, and again in *Scipione nelle Spagne* with Luceio and Elvira. In those librettos the final point was that the conquered were subjects worthy of the conqueror and the conqueror himself was virtuously capable of recognizing and rewarding nobility in his subjects. Arminio and Claudia/Thusnelda play this subordinate role of noble subject in *Germanico sul Reno*. Produced in Venice, there was still some effort in the text to claim Rome for Italy, despite the dedication. In the English operas, by contrast, the ambiguity in Tacitus's ethnography and history toward both Germans and Romans was the medium by which the contradiction could be addressed between the Rome that was a model for successful imperial, autocratic power, and the Rome that was the enemy, the oppressor of their ancestors, and the seat of papist tyranny. Arminio and Thusnelda maintain their primitive virtues of patriotism and bravery and thus flatter the northern Europeans, who are their descendants, while basking in the glow of the Roman heritage that legitimates the power of their monarchs and aristocrats. The problem posed by Rome for her former subjects is solved through the mediation of history that has been transformed into legend and, finally, into myth through the conventions of the opera stage.

In the process of mediating the contradictions, these operas raise political and social issues that are not usually supposed to come to the fore until later in the century.[23] Politically the issue of liberty is most obvious in the *Arminio* operas. The English productions, working in the theatrical world created by Addison's *Cato*, might be regarded as outside the European mainstream, were it not that one can point to similar trends in Salvi's *Arminio*, from which Handel was working, and from Metastasio's *Catone in Utica*. What is striking is that mid- and late-century operas, those on Roman themes at least, retreat from the strident rhetoric possible in the early century; perhaps as a fashionable Enlightenment, republicanism was giving way to the increasing possibility of real revolution.

The other theme that appears here, supposedly a trend of mid- and late-century Enlightenment thought, is that of marital fidelity, as opposed to unmarried erotic and romantic attraction that is so often at the center of events in operas that inherit the sensibilities of the seventeenth and early eighteenth century, including those of Metastasio.[24] This theme is supposed to become visible in the midcentury—for example, in Calzabigi's and Gluck's influential *Orfeo ed Euridice* and *Alceste*—but like the theme of liberty, and the occurrrence of tragic violence, it is already present much earlier. Glimpsed already in *Scipione affricano* with Sofonisba and Siface, fidelity and the threat to marriage is a crucial issue for Arminius and Thusnelda; the assault on their marriage by both Segestes and the Romans defines a central issue of the opera, replacing the threat to unmarried romantic connections that one sees in so many earlier texts. The Arminius operas anticipate the conflict of married couples with authority that will be visited again in the popular *Giulio Sabino* (1781) and find their way into the next century in operas such as Beethoven's *Fidelio*.

8 Clemencies of Titus

METASTASIO, *LA CLEMENZA DI TITO*;

GIOVANNINI/SARTI, *GIULIO SABINO*

> Antiquity knew no better nor more beloved
> prince than Titus Vespasianus.
> —Metastasio, *La Clemenza di Tito*

Looking back on the history of Italian *dramma per musica* from a late-eighteenth-century perspective, the opera historian Stefano Arteaga asked, "Does ancient and modern theater have a character as interesting as Tito?" A contemporary's answer to this question might easily have been, "Yes: it has Cato."[1] The shadows cast in the early century by Addison's *Cato* and Metastasio's *Il Catone in Utica* had been long ones, since both dramas were produced continually throughout Europe and influenced the writing of spoken drama and librettos. The ramifications of this production history for later eighteenth-century opera will be deferred until the final chapter. The present chapter examines an ideologically very different text by Metastasio, his *La clemenza di Tito*, written for the emperor's court in Vienna in 1734. This libretto, one of the purest expressions of a prince's clemency, was performed for a century, set by more than forty composers between its premiere in Vienna and Giuseppe Arena's version for Turin in 1839. Mozart's 1791 version is merely the most famous. Voltaire particularly admired the scene between the aggrieved Tito and the guilty Sesto in III.vi, declaring it as good or better than anything in Greek tragedy and a worthy companion to the best work of Corneille and Racine.[2]

La clemenza di Tito, like the Cato dramas, exerted an influence on the production of new librettos over the course of the century, both those that celebrated autocracy as well as some that focused more on the myth of liberty than the celebration of the prince. That influence is visible nearly half a century later; for example, in Pindemonte's and Cimarosa's *Giunio Bruto*, premiered in Verona in 1781, and in Giovannini's *Giulio Sabino* for the same year in Venice, with music by Giuseppe Sarti. *Giunio Bruto* was not successful, even with additions by Haydn for a revival at Esterháza. But Sarti's setting of *Giulio Sabino* was one of the most popular operas of the later eighteenth century, precisely because it was able to combine successful Metastasian esthetic formulas with avant-garde, northern European trends in operatic and literary production that had begun to affect serious Italian opera in the second half of the eighteenth century.

This chapter examines the 1734 libretto of *La Clemenza di Tito* as a paradigm of Metastasio's style of *dramma per musica*, the style that came to be known as *opera seria*, which celebrated the ancien régime in its final, prerevolutionary phase. There is then a brief summary of esthetic trends in the midcentury that affected libretto production, prominently but not exclusively associated with the operas of Gluck. Finally, it observes the impact of these trends on Sarti's *Giulio Sabino*, an opera in some respects derivative of Metastasio's *Tito* but also exhibiting qualities that were to become standard in the early nineteenth century. This discussion, therefore, bridges the midcentury and looks toward the 1790s, when historical Rome began its final phase as an important operatic expression of political and social reality. Two further heirs to Metastasio's 1734 *Tito*, Cimarosa's *Giunio Bruto* and Mozart's setting of *La Clemenza di Tito*, are discussed in the final chapter as responses to the age of revolution.[3]

La Clemenza di Tito

Pietro Metastasio's *La clemenza di Tito* premiered in Vienna with music by Antonio Caldara as part of the celebration of the name day of Emperor Charles VI in 1734. By this time Metastasio had moved to Vienna after his successes in Rome in the 1720s to take Apostolo Zeno's place as the Emperor's *poeta cesareo*. Caldara, for his part, was the official court composer. The opera was therefore an unapologetic celebration of Charles's virtues, in much the same spirit as was Zeno's *Scipione nelle Spagne*. It is to Metastasio's considerable credit that such a text addressed issues broad enough to be attractive subsequently to so many different patrons and composers.

Part of the reason for the libretto's success was the appeal of Titus, an ideal prince who combined wise and effective governance with mercy and generosity, an emperor with virtues similar to those of the elder Scipio, and so in some respects an even better analogue than Scipio to the Habsburg emperor and representative of the imperial myth of the clement prince. In addition, he did not suffer the complications attending the history of Caesar or even of Augustus. Titus appears to have been a talented man and an engaging personality. For the Romans, he was the hero of the Jewish war, conquering Jerusalem and pacifying Judea for his father Vespasian in 70 C.E., for which he was celebrated posthumously with the arch of Titus in Rome. He succeeded his father Vespasian in 79 C.E., and out of respect for popular feeling he dismissed his Judean mistress Berenice, King Herod Agrippa's daughter, with whom he had been living openly in Rome before his accession to power. He dealt generously in relieving the victims of Vesuvius the same year. When members of the senatorial class conspired against him, he pardoned them, although the senate had condemned them to death for treason.[4] He reigned only two years, dying in the year 81. After his death he was regarded as the paradigm of the constant and merciful prince, the ideal Stoic monarch who put his duty before his personal desires. Suetonius declared him to be the world's "beloved and darling" (*Titus* 1.1).

In contrast to the legend, however, the historical record is not quite so perfect. Romans who idealized Titus chose to forget that before his accession to power he had had a reputation for private dissolution, susceptibility to bribery, and occasional ruthlessness (Suetonius, *Titus* 6.2–7.1). As a result, Titus did not escape carnivalesque treatment in seventeenth-century Venetian opera. Giulio Cesare Corradi, in his popular *Il Vespesiano* [*sic*] of 1678, made his Tito the subject of a not very dignified romantic subplot. In Corradi's libretto, Tito's brother Domiziano connives to take power from their father Vespesiano during the perilous year 69 C.E. Meanwhile, Tito pursues his infatuation with a foreign slave woman named Irene (a lower-class version of the historical Berenice) despite bring married to a noblewoman named Fulvia. Tito is finally forced to send Irene away and, thwarted by his father both in his attempts to put a violent end to his brother and to pursue the liaison, ends the opera with the pathetic line, "Ah, Titus alone is the imprint of every torment."[5]

But the characterization of Titus as hero and legend was the one that prevailed, just as it had for the Romans. Even before Corradi's opera, a *Tito* by Nicolò Beregan from 1666 had treated him with respect. Beregan's libretto is set in Jerusalem at the conclusion of the Jewish war; in the end, Tito matches Berenice, Queen of Judea, with her beloved Polemone, allies himself with the Roman matron Martia Fulvia, and all conclude with a chorus of "Viva, Tito, viva, viva!" In Paris in 1670, Titus's liaison with Berenice was the subject of competing dramas, Corneille's *Tite e Bérénice* and Racine's *Bérénice*, both of which stressed the emperor's self-sacrificing nobility. For the eighteenth century, as we noted above, he was a most fascinating dramatic character and an analogue to the Christian monarch, who might dream about conquering Jerusalem but would not think of allying himself formally with a Jewish consort. In this respect, Metastasio's opera differs significantly from others we have observed in which the Roman general is eager to marry the foreign princess. Even Scipio Africanus was included in that number, and in *Giulio Sabino*, a younger version of Titus becomes enamored of a Gallic noblewoman. In *Clemenza di Tito*, Vergilian values of empire and duty are firmly asserted over Ovidian *amor* from the outset, as far as Tito himself is concerned. If *Scipione nelle Spagne* had served to exemplify the Habsburg virtues of the young Charles in Spain, this text was emblematic of his mature virtues as emperor, and beyond that became a paradigmatic Enlightenment expression of the tribulations and ideals surrounding monarchical power.

As Metastasio's libretto forms the basis for comparison with operas in this chapter and the next, it is worth reviewing in some detail the plot as he originally conceived it. It revolves around a conspiracy promoted by Vitellia, a fictional daughter of the deposed emperor Vitellius. Vitellius had defeated Otho in 69 C.E., the year of the four emperors, and was in his turn overthrown and killed by the troops of Titus's father Vespasian. Metastasio's Vitellia is motivated by a complicated combination of unrequited love for Tito, a desire for revenge for her father, and lust for power. She believes she should be Tito's consort and empress of Rome. She is resentful that Tito prefers his Judaean mistress, the princess Berenice, and seizes on vengeance for her father's death as a way to justify her resentments. When Tito sends Berenice away, he offers his hand instead to Servilia, the sister of his friend Sesto. Even before the opera began, the furious Vitellia had been pressuring Sesto, who loves her passionately, to set the Capitoline on fire and murder Tito in the ensuing chaos. Further enraged by this second snub, Vitellia sends the conflicted Sesto to set the plot in motion, in collusion with an unseen co-conspirator named Lentulo. In the meantime, Servilia, in love with Sesto's friend Annio, refuses the emperor's hand, and so Tito in turn summons Vitellia to request marriage. Vitellia receives the news too late to stop Sesto; the first act ends with the burning of the Capitol and the apparent murder of Titus. Sesto at the last minute repents of his intentions but believes he sees someone else do the murder and is unable to prevent it.

In act II, it emerges that it was not Tito who was stabbed, but Lentulo, dressed in imperial robes in premature anticipation of the conspiracy's success. Tito summons Sesto, unaware of his participation in the plot. Sesto's cloak bears the identifying emblem of the conspiracy, so he exchanges it for Annio's and goes to Tito. Tito subsequently sees the mark of the conspiracy on the cloak Annio is wearing and believes he is guilty. This sets up the moral complications that drive the second act. Annio denies his guilt but does not wish to inform on Sesto, Sesto does not want Annio to be unjustly condemned but cannot admit his own guilt for fear of betraying Vitellia, and Servilia, believing that Annio is guilty, rejects him. Things unravel at the end of the act when it turns out that Lentulo did not die of his wound and has revealed Sesto's complicity in the plot. Sesto is arrested. Vitellia, now the emperor's betrothed, ends the act with an aria expressing her fear that Sesto will expose her.

Act III concentrates on the emotional turmoil of Tito and Sesto. The senate has convicted Sesto, and all that remains is for Tito to sign the decree for his death. Tito decides to speak with Sesto before condemning him. Their confrontation in III.vi is the emotional center of the drama and is the scene that so impressed Voltaire. Tito appeals to Sesto to explain himself, first as subject and then as friend. Sesto refuses to speak, not wanting to expose Vitellia, and asks only that Tito remember Sesto's former affection. Left alone, the angry and bemused Tito determines first that Sesto shall die, but then relents and resolves on clemency: "If the world wants to accuse me of some fault, let it accuse me of pity (*pietà*) and not of unmovable sternness (*rigore*)." In the meantime, Vitellia, urged by Servilia to plead for Sesto's life, has a crisis of conscience and in the final scenes she reveals her own guilt to Tito. Appalled, but resolute in his mercy, Tito forgives everyone, urges the union of Vitellia and Sesto, and is praised for his clemency.

It is well established that the outlines of Metastasio's plot owe more to Corneille's *Cinna* than to the historical events surrounding Titus. *Cinna* portrays a historical plot against the emperor Augustus that was thwarted. Augustus forgave Cinna and his fellow conspirators, and they subsequently became his friends and allies. This episode was developed as an extended philosophical exemplum in Seneca's *De Clementia* (1.9), an essay written to demonstrate to the young Nero the value of clemency over tyrannical cruelty (a lesson ironically deployed by Nerone for the benefit of Ottone and Drusilla at the end of *L'incoronazione di Poppea*). Metastasio, by his own account in his *Argomento* to *La Clemenza di Tito*, filled out details of character and events from other ancient authors—he lists Suetonius, Aurelius Victor, and Cassius Dio and his Byzantine epitomizer Zonaras. In addition, the fierce and volatile character of Vitellia comes from Racine's *Andromaque*, where a jealous Hermione urges Orestes, who loves her, to murder her betrothed, Neoptolemus, because he is pursuing Andromache. After Orestes complies, Hermione kills herself in remorse.[6]

In bringing the central plot of *Tito* over from Corneille, Metastasio had to cope with the differences between the history of Augustus and the legend of Titus. Cassius Dio (*Roman History* 66.18.4–5) somewhat cynically suggested that "Augustus would never have been loved if he had lived a shorter time, nor Titus if he had lived longer. For Augustus, though at the outset he showed himself rather harsh because of the wars and the factional strife, was later able, in the course of time, to achieve a brilliant reputation for his kindly deeds; Titus, on the other hand, ruled with mildness and died at the height of his glory, whereas, if he had lived a long time, it might have been shown that he owes his present fame more to good fortune than to merit."[7] This summarizes what Wilhelm Seidel has identified as the difference between *La clemenza di Tito* and its model *Cinna*.[8] Corneille follows closely the narrative in Seneca's *De Clementia*. Augustus the emperor struggles with the heritage of his brutality during the civil wars after Caesar's death and grows into his act of clemency through a self-conquest that is stimulated by the advice of his wife Livia. Seidel believes the play shows the process by which tyranny becomes mature and beneficent monarchy, a process we have seen in various ways expressed in opera through Scipio Africanus.

With Titus, therefore, Metastasio chose as a model for the virtues of his patron Charles a figure whose legend was less compromised than was Augustus's. Titus's virtues were a constant habit of mind that might be challenged by the conspiracies of friends but could be reasserted in even brighter tones at the end. Metastasio's Tito, in anguish over how to react to Sesto's betrayal, even cites Augustus as a counter example (III.vii): "Now what will posterity say about me? They would say that clemency was worn out in Titus just as cruelty was in Augustus or Sulla."[9] In consequence, he declares to the gathered cast of characters in the *scena ultima*, "Be it known to Rome that I remain unchanged: I know all, I forgive all, and I forget all."[10] The contrast with the corresponding lines in *Cinna* is instructive. Corneille wrote (V.iii.1696–1700), "I am master of myself as I am of the world. So I am and so I wish to be. O, Time and Memory, forever preserve my final victory. I triumph today over the most just wrath of any you can remember."[11] For Augustus there has been process. For Titus, as with Scipio, virtue is reasserted, not gained, and the central character by his own admission exhibits no change or growth.

Representations of stability are not the stuff of riveting drama, however, and Racine, in his preface to *Bérénice* (1670), had remarked that he had made something from nothing ("quelque chose de rien") to tell the story of Titus's virtue. Seidel has commented on Metastasio's subordination of the political message to the erotic complications of the plot, when compared with Corneille's play.[12] This is somewhat misleading: In Corneille's play, Cinna's love for Emilia drives him to conspire against Augustus, and Maximus's love for her results in the betrayal of the plot. Moreover, Livia claims it is her love for Augustus that makes her plead for clement treatment of the conspirators. Nor is *La clemenza di Tito* any less political than *Cinna*, given the circumstances of its original production. Rather, the difference is that the central interest is in the anguish of the conspirators, the primo uomo and prima donna, rather than in the spiritual growth of the emperor: The unrequited and conflicted Sesto and the emotional lability of the nearly sociopathic Vitellia provide the opportunities for a composer in Metastasio's text. One critic describes *La Clemenza di Tito* as one of Metastasio's least problematic librettos, but that is only true in respect of Tito himself;[13] Sesto and Vitellia present a welter of fascinating complications.

A sense of unease comes in part from the fact that, though Tito, from his height, can forgive and forget, his friends, who have violated his trust, cannot do so. Even if we ignore the fact that outside the drama Titus himself was shortly to die, by one account poisoned by his own brother Domitian (Dio 66.26.2), the text contains a good deal that is very unstable. Sesto in the end can satisfy neither his beloved Vitellia, for at the last moment, he was unable to carry out the planned murder, nor finally himself, whose last uncompleted line only refers to his bitter memories of what he has done: "How and when will I be able to hope that the bitter memories of my wrongdoings . . ." Vitellia has callously driven the man who genuinely loves her to the point of execution and has destroyed any possibility of marriage with Tito, which might have been hers but for her own misdeeds. The contrast with Zeno's Elvira (chapter 5) is most striking. Elvira was Justice herself returned to earth, the final arbiter and reconciler of the seemingly irreconcilable quarrel between Ovidian love and Vergilian duty that male honor provokes. Metastasio's Vitellia, like his Sesto, must be penitent and be shown the way to reconciliation by Tito in order for the ending to be happy. The king's subjects are not his moral equals, as they were in *Scipione nelle Spagne,* but errant children to be scolded and forgiven.

The union that Tito proposes between Sesto and Vitellia as his last act of reconciliation therefore seems just—the two surely deserve one another—but it is scarcely satisfactory. Despite Arteaga's assertion about Tito's positive qualities, we come perilously close to the satiric world of *Poppea,* with its makeshift marriage between Ottone and Drusilla and the knowledge that the happy ending will ultimately be cancelled by history. In consequence, the Vergilian tension between celebration of the prince's triumph and recognition of life's shadows is maintained even here. These sources of instability continued to fascinate composers and audiences with the characters as much as with the sublime clemency of Titus.

The Midcentury Reforms

We observed at the end of chapter 5 that Zeno's move to Vienna was part of the successful Italian cultural imperialism made possible by the Arcadian opera reforms that turned *dramma per musica* from Venetian carnival entertainment into a widely diffused European phenomenon. Tightening of dramatic structure and elimination of overtly comic elements produced an eminently exportable product that served the social interests of the ancien régime and provided a suitable vehicle for the singers and musicians. While it is unfair to say that the structure of Metastasio's dramas was inflexible, a pattern emerged in which scenes began with recitative dialogue and concluded with da capo exit arias that encapsulated the emotion or thought of the character at the moment just before he or she leaves the stage. Metastasio wrote some choruses and duets, but his *opera seria* was principally a vehicle for soloists. His librettos turned this pattern into an effective combination of neoclassical drama and singable, even speakable poetry that appealed profoundly to the midcentury mood. *La clemenza di Tito* is a prime example. Other Roman subjects treated by Metastasio, in addition to *Catone in Utica,* were *Ezio* (1728), *Adriano in Siria* (1732), *Attilio Regolo* (1750), and the overtly mythical *Romolo ed Ersilia* (1765).

However fictionalized the action of operas such as *La Clemenza di Tito* might ultimately be, they nevertheless present historical figures in situations described by the ancient historiographers. Librettists called such action *verisimile*: reasonable invention based on what was probable. But not quite a century after the introduction of the historical Nero

onto the opera stage, critics were beginning to wonder about the suitability of history for musical drama. In 1755 Francesco Algarotti, in his
neo-Aristotelian *Saggio sopra l'opera in musica* (Essay on the Opera),
asked if "the trillings of an [aria] flow so justifiably from the mouth of a
Julius Caesar or a Cato as from the lips of Venus or Apollo."[14] Algarotti
thought myth and remote legend were subjects more suitable as sources
for plots and vehicles for song, and recommended particularly Metastasio's *Didone abbandonata* and *Achille in Sciro*. It should be noted that
neither Algarotti nor his followers were rejecting the Metastasian style in
its essentials. They merely wanted subjects that they perceived as more
appropriate for the genre of sung drama, and in this respect, Metastasio's
own late *Romolo ed Ersilia* makes the recommended shift away from
historical to legendary. They also aspired to improve opera's dramatic
impact by limiting the singers' control of the arias and to refine the lyric
portions as an emotional tool.[15]

Algarotti's most notable adherents were Christoph Willibald Gluck
and his librettist Raniero Calzabigi, working in Vienna and Paris. These
two experimented with librettos that made use of mythic subjects and
began to incorporate French elements of ensemble, chorus, and ballet,
and to employ a dramaturgy that, once again, supposedly brought opera
closer to the putative ideals of Greek drama. Gluck's reform operas favored
subjects from Euripides and Ovid: Alcestis, Paris and Helen, Orpheus and
Eurydice, and Iphigenia, both in Aulis and among the Taurians. Elsewhere,
French-influenced courts at Vienna, Stuttgart, Mannheim, and Parma in
the 1750s and 1760s were generating new styles of presentation associated
especially with the composers Tommaso Traetta and Nicolò Jommelli.
These composers were attracted to librettos that reflected Enlightenment
demands for genuine emotion and purity of expression in drama. Mythological stories recommended by Algarotti seemed more appropriate for
the expressions of universals than the historical plots favored by Metastasio and his imitators in their dramas of political and erotic intrigue. In
Gluck's operas one may also note an emphasis on domestic, married love
in contrast to the romantic free-for-all normal in seventeenth-century
opera and, as we have seen, still an important part of the machinery of
Metastasian *dramma per musica*. By adapting mythic stories such as
Orpheus, Alcestis, and Iphigenia, the operas of Gluck and Calzabigi focused on family issues that were fundamental to Greek tragedy, but that
included the emphasis on domestic fidelity that was part of neoclassical
art and the Enlightenment.[16]

Literary influences arriving from England were also having a transforming effect on Italian librettos; the last quarter of the century saw

the development of the Gothic novel and the morose reflections of the English "graveyard" poets, such as Edward Young and Thomas Gray, whose respective "Night Thoughts" and "Elegy Written in a Country Churchyard" gained a wide readership on the continent. The result for Italian operas written on Roman subjects was an increased fascination with emotional scenes set in graveyards, ruins, and dungeons, which gave the stories an atmosphere of Gothic romance rather than social reality.[17] Sarti's *Giulio Sabino,* produced in Venice in 1781, combines these trends nicely by putting a husband, wife, and children together in an underground chamber and then a dungeon before reverting to the still popular *lieto fine.*

Giulio Sabino

The libretto of *Giulio Sabino* is usually ascribed to Pietro Giovannini, who is otherwise unknown. The composer was Giuseppe Sarti, whose score received publication in 1783 and became a standard in the repertoire in a way more familiar from the nineteenth century than was the usual practice with *opera seria.* It was one of the most popular operas of the late eighteenth century, achieving a combination of older and newer literary and musical fashions that made it both accessible and brilliantly contemporary. In just the next five years alone it appeared in Florence, Pisa, Bologna, Esterháza, Barcelona, Vienna, Warsaw, and Naples.[18]

Julius Sabinus, a Gallic nobleman of the Lingones tribe (in the area of modern Langres), claiming descent from Julius Caesar, took advantage of the chaos of the year 69 C.E. to declare Gallic independence from Rome and raise a rebellion.[19] He was defeated by other Gauls who opposed the revolt, and so, to avoid capture and punishment, he burned his country estate to the ground and encouraged the belief that he had committed suicide in the ruins. In reality he hid himself in caves nearby, and lived there for nine years. His devoted wife Epponina maintained the pretence of grieving widowhood to protect her husband for nearly a decade, in the meantime working tirelessly to pave the way for his pardon, apparently even taking him to Rome in disguise. When that failed, she lived with him underground, bearing him two sons. In the year 79, about the same time Titus sent Berenice away from Rome, they were discovered, and Epponina made a final plea before the emperor Vespasian. Both Plutarch and Dio report that the family received no mercy and were executed.

Epponina emerges as the central figure in the ancient sources: Plutarch, calling her Empona, says the name means "Heroine" in her Gallic language. Tacitus in his sardonic way remarked that Sabinus had been as ready to flee from the battle as he was to begin it with reckless haste, but he speaks admiringly of the noble example set by Epponina. Dio reported, "She threw her children at Vespasian's feet and delivered a most pitiful plea in their behalf: 'These little ones, Caesar, I bore and reared in the monument, that we might be a greater number to supplicate you.' Yet, though she caused both him and the rest to weep, no mercy was shown to the family."[20] Plutarch tells the story of Sabinus and Epponina in his "Erotikos," an essay in the *Moralia,* and depicts a defiant Epponina in her final plea before the emperor, noting that "the audacity and pride of her words abolished pity in the spectators and roused Vespasian to a high pitch of fury: she renounced all hope of survival and challenged him to exchange his life with hers, declaring that she had lived more happily in the underground darkness than he had on his throne."[21] Plutarch uses the story as a dramatic defense of heterosexual married love and the fidelity of women, arguing pointedly against the homoerotic love of Plato's "Symposium" as the one right vector for love of beauty and ultimately truth (see chapter 2).

This story probably first appeared in European spoken drama as *Sabinus, treurspiel* in Amsterdam in 1702, followed by others with greater frequency after 1735. It gained particular notice on the opera stage in the decade just before Sarti wrote his version. *L'Epponina,* by Fattiboni, performed in 1770 to music by Bevilacqua, was followed by Chabanon's *Sabinus* (1773; based on *Eponine,* a tragedy by the same author with music by Gossec), an anonymous *L'Epponina* (1779; music by Giordano), and an anonymous *Tito nelle Gallie* (1780; music by Anfossi).[22] Sarti's setting was the most successful operatic version of this particular tale over the next thirty years, although there were others.

As the title suggests, Sarti's opera shifts the heroic lead from Epponina to Sabinus. It is set in and around Lingona in Gaul. The principals are Giulio Sabino, his wife Epponina, and the young Tito, son of the emperor Vespasian, who commands the Roman troops at Lingona. Tito, believing Sabino long dead, loves Epponina. The secondary roles are Sabino's sister Voadice; Arminio, governor of Lingona and Sabino's confidant; and Annio, Tito's prefect and confidant. Arminio and Voadice are romantically involved. Annio, secretly passionate for Epponina, is the real villain of the piece, and he continually attempts to get her to Rome and away from Tito and Sabino.

In act I Sabino emerges after many years from his hiding place under the ruins of his castle to meet with Arminio, who is planning a revolt against the Romans under Tito. Sabino learns that Epponina has been a suppliant to Tito, and thinks that she has been unfaithful to him. Tito, for his part, deceived by a letter forged by Annio, believes that his father Vespasian has ordered Epponina to be sent to Rome. He is torn between his perceived duty to his father and his desire to have Epponina close to him. Sabino confronts Epponina with her supposed infidelity, and Tito overhears him. To prevent his discovery by the Romans, Epponina pretends Sabino is a Gallic warrior named Orgonte. In this disguise Sabino joins the Roman troops, swearing darkly that his actions will be surprisingly prompt and fierce. Tito in the meantime cannot bear to send Epponina to Rome and urges her to escape into the forest. She and Sabino meet once again and resolve their misunderstandings. But Epponina must escape, and they conclude the act with a grief-stricken farewell duet.

Act II is crowded with incident. Annio attempts to bring Epponina back. Sabino as Orgonte intervenes and is arrested. Annio insists Sabino-Orgonte was molesting Epponina, and Tito orders him imprisoned. Arminio's rebellious troops rescue Sabino on the way to prison and return him to his wife and children in his subterranean hiding place. There Tito and the Romans discover them, and Sabino's real identity is revealed. He is sent again to prison, but while Epponina pleads with Tito for Sabino's release, he tries unsuccessfully to escape once again. Tito angrily condemns Sabino and Epponina to death in an act-finale trio.

In act III the Gallic revolt has been quelled and Arminio has been captured. Tito, feeling betrayed on all sides, nevertheless offers Epponina her life and her children's if she will marry him. She rejects him defiantly, and Tito declares she must die, but only after watching Sabino's death. She declares that if she and Sabino die together, she will be content. Left alone, Tito resolves that a woman's virtue must not surpass his own. His reputation and the honor of the empire demand that he find a solution without appearing either tyrant or coward. Consequently, after Sabino and Epponina, introduced by a sad march, bid an extended farewell in a gloomy torture chamber, the scene changes suddenly and miraculously into a bright royal hall. Tito forgives everyone, and in return Sabino swears his allegiance to Tito and Rome. The final chorus, consisting of passages that alternate *tutti* and duet, celebrates Tito's mercy and declares, "The Gaul, the German, once enemies of Rome, will pledge faith to Caesar their friend."[23]

There is much that is familiar in this opera. Structurally, its libretto might be by Zeno or Metastasio. It has three acts, six characters, and no chorus. Except for the act finales, there are no ensemble pieces. The *lieto fine*, a celebration of imperial clemency, remains firmly intact. The rivalry between the authority figure and the primo uomo for the attentions of the prima donna, as well as the authority figure's struggle to overcome his passions, are all part of the familiar myth. Specifically, the betrayed Titus Vespasianus, who is angry but finally merciful, seems to be a direct heir to Metastasio's Tito.

Nevertheless, there is a distinctly late-century mood to this opera that is different from the earlier treatments of similar subjects, and the continued popularity of *Giulio Sabino* was the result of the ways in which Giovannini and Sarti responded to, and even anticipated, the shifting trends and tastes described above. Flexibility in arrangement of arias and recitative allows for smoother dramatic transitions than is often allowed by exit arias.[24] The libretto reflects the intellectually fashionable revolutionary spirit of the times in its presentation of the opposition to Rome by Sabinus and Arminio.[25] It also finds in the source material an ideal vehicle with which to explore the growing public interest in gloomy ruins and morose sentiment that are in accord with the late-century interest in Gothic literature. Whereas Metastasio had had to pull his actors out of the sewer in *Catone in Utica* in order to make it palatable to his audiences, now the subterranean dungeon becomes the site of the central scenes in the opera. Most important, Sarti's music is appealing and effective. The best moments are reliably linked to emotional crises and dramatic high points in the libretto, thereby achieving the emotional focus that Calzabigi and Gluck had advocated.

The very nature of Sabinus's story makes the theme of patriotic resistance to oppressive imperial power impossible to miss in this opera. Arminio's rebellion against Tito is suggestive of (or perhaps suggested by) the historical rebellion of Sabinus against Vespasian in 69. The names of the non-Romans in the cast look dangerous (the events associated with the name Arminio were described in the previous chapter). His sister Voadice (Boadicea), for example, bears the name of a warrior queen of Britain.[26] Together with Sabinus, leader of the Gallic rebellion, they give the impression of a northern Europe united against the power of Rome and participate in the myth of liberty we saw operative in the *Arminio* operas and which will become even more important for the operas in the final chapter.

Sabino utters explicit defiance against the oppressor while he is disguised as Orgonte (I.ix): "From my earliest days my country's fierce nature taught me to bear arms. I have despised Rome, I followed Sabinus to the final battle after I spilled half my blood in his defense." Tito, like Scipio in Spain, immediately offers his admirable opponent a place in the army. Sabino replies at length, first in accompanied recitative, delivered in vigorous bursts, and punctuated by staccato statements from the winds and emphatic sixteenth-note runs in the strings. He appears to boast about his soldierly prowess, but it is really a veiled threat against Tito: "You will see what use I will make of this sword. Who knows if you have ever seen light shine more deadly than from this blade." He ends the scene with a defiant aria: "[On the field of battle] you will see who I am; no, I'm not telling you empty words. This hand is deadly. Maybe the one who fears it less ought to tremble at it more." The aria places Sabino in a position of hero like Luceio in *Scipione nelle Spagne* and puts him on a par with Epponina as an active agent in the action—he is thus rescued from the secondary position he holds in the ancient sources.

Yet *Giulio Sabino* is not a stridently libertarian opera, particularly if compared with the earlier *Arminio* operas or the first version of *Catone in Utica*. "Orgonte's" autobiographical outburst is really meant as a personal threat against Tito, because of the Roman's interest in Epponina, rather than as a statement of national pride. Sabino's and Epponina's defiance is couched in terms of keeping the family unit together in the face of the threat from Tito and, secondarily, from Annio. The opera concentrates on the pathos in the face of separation, torture, and death. Sabino's and Epponina's laments dominate the opera. The contemporary favorite number from the opera appears to have been Sabino's emotional aria to his two little sons in II.ix, "Cari figli, un altro amplesso."[27]

Moreover, Tito is no tyrannical monster. Like the Scipios of Minato and Zeno, he is a young man in love who finds himself caught between the demands of power and passion. He honors Sabino's bravery and is willing to allow Epponina's escape at the end of act I rather than have her be sent captive to Rome. He only insists on her death and Sabino's when he finds himself rejected and betrayed by everyone. Tito's three arias—one per act—show a range of personal emotions that follows the dramatic build of the action, from real distress at the need to send Epponina to Rome (I.vi; "Già vi sento"), to an angry warning that he will not allow his goodwill to be taken advantage of (II.vi; "Tigre ircana in selva ombrosa"), to a final determination not to be bested by Epponina in a contest of virtue and mercy. In Sarti's setting, this last (III.iii; "Bella fiamma") is a simple and moving decision to put aside his passion for Epponina in favor of his reputation, birth, and imperial honor:

> Lovely flame, that sets my breast alight, that implants a new kind of desire, I understand well what you ask of me.
>   You, my friend, that send me to glory, that crown courage and faith, scatter forgetfulness on my passion.

Within the limits of his role, he is dramatically more interesting than Metastasio's Tito, whose emblematic status as Good Emperor gave him

an almost naïve and unwavering virtue that, except in his private confrontation with Sesto, removes him from emotional interest. This Tito
is still young and is given scope by the librettist and composer to express
his natural emotions. But in giving Tito this role, the libretto also has
removed his connection to historical events and specific historical role:
Titus never actually confronted Sabinus in Gaul. No longer identified
as Titus the clement emperor, Tito becomes merely a Roman general in
love, lacking even as much anchor in historical events as had Scipio in
Spain, Germanicus on the Rhine, or Caesar in Egypt in their respective
operas.

The historical specificity attaches instead to Sabino and Epponina,
whose story of marital fidelity and endurance to protect the family unit
at the center of this opera is part of the historical record. But even here
there is a retreat from the more immediate concerns of legitimization of
power we observed in La clemenza di Tito or the other eighteenth-century operas we have observed on Scipio, Caesar, or Cato. This removal is
partly due to the nature of the story itself, that a woman hid her husband
in an underground chamber for nine years and had two children by him
in secret. The nine-year span of Sabinus's life underground, even if historically accurate, is also a traditional number, a multiple of three. The
obscurity of the source story when compared with the histories of the
late Republic or early empire, the opera's setting in the ruins of Sabino's
burned estate surrounded by the forests of Gaul,[28] the devoted married
couple threatened with separation or death, their two young children in
danger of being orphaned or worse, and their sudden release at the elev-
enth hour all give the opera a "once upon a time," folktale quality.

This is in part a result of the archetypical nature of its source in
Plutarch. His Moralia treats Sabinus's story as a culminating exemplum
of the faithfulness of women.[29] The Plutarchan passage differs radically
from the Senecan exemplum that stands behind La clemenza di Tito,
which, through the example of Augustus, addresses the effective deploy-
ment of power through mercy. Plutarch's language is suggestive of tragedy, myth, and moral fable rather than history. His Epponina plays her
role as grieving widow as if competing in a tragedy (suntragoideito tei
doxei tou pathous) and in her passion for Sabinus she "practically lived
in Hades with her husband" (oligon apedei suzein en Aidou t'andri). The
execution of Epponina's family is the act of an evil prince who finally
pays for his wickedness with the reciprocal extinction of his own family:
"So Caesar had her killed; but after killing her he paid the penalty as his
whole family was utterly destroyed in a brief time." This is only margin-
ally true: Vespasian did die that year, but peacefully in his bed, cracking

a joke with his last words (Suetonius, *Vespasian* 23.4). Titus died in 81 C.E. after a two-year reign, but he was much heroized; Vespasian's second son, Domitian, who succeeded Titus, was one of the more monstrous emperors, but he ruled in Rome in until 96 C.E. Plutarch sacrifices strict historical accuracy to give his story a moral.

Giovannini and Sarti adopt Plutarch's moral interpretation of the story and finally move it in the direction of a fairytale in which Tito mixes the roles of evil prince and fairy godfather. The former role comes to its climax when he declares that if Epponina will not give into his desires, she must die after watching Sabino die first. The latter role finally overrides the former in the recitative and aria "Bella fiamma." It is also suggested throughout the opera by the scenery: Tito's quarters in the opera provide brief but important contrasts to the gloom of Sabino's scenes in his ruined underground hideout, and in his place of execution. The chambers of Titus are above ground and full of space and light. In I.iii, and probably again in III.i–iii, Tito appears with Annio in a "magnificent pavilion that occupies the whole stage" from which is visible the Roman encampment. The *scena ultima* provides even greater contrast, as to the astonished wonder of Sabino and Epponina, the gloom of the torture chamber is magically converted, accompanied by the sound of a cheerful *sinfonia*, to "a royal chamber, illumined and full of people," where Tito, who had become the villain, liberally dispenses forgiveness and reconciliation. The final scene of the opera resolves into the miraculous and ahistorical, as the family is united rather than destroyed, tragedy is avoided, and, in the process, France and Germany (suggested in the opera by the names Sabino and Arminio) become sworn friends and allies of the emperor. The Vergilian shadows in the *scena ultima* of Metastasio's *La clemenza di Tito* find no place in the brilliance of the last scene of *Giulio Sabino*, where sentiment triumphs. The miraculous spectacle reminds one more of the theophanies that had been so common in the operas of the seventeenth century, and was last seen by us in *Agrippina*, than of the soberer *scene ultime* of Metastasian-style *opera seria*.

In these respects, therefore, the opera takes on the qualities of remoter myth recommended by Algarotti, even while seeming to present a story in the tradition of Metastasian historical drama of erotic intrigue and final clemency. *Giulio Sabino* appears to have been a success in its combination of all the late-century trends, and it points in the direction of operas of the early nineteenth century, such as *Norma* or *La Vestale*, which use Rome while separating it from historiographical specificity. But it does not commit to the more radical of these trends. While it is not a wholehearted celebration of imperial authority, as the Viennese dramas of Zeno and Metastasio had been, given the temporal proximity of its production to the revolutions in America and France, it is a surprising step back from the patriotic liberty dramas of the earlier century, such as *Catone in Utica* or the anonymous London *Arminio*. The fairytale quality of the opera provides an assurance of familial stability under established authority in such a way that it celebrates the family rather than the authority. We will have to look beyond to the operas of the 1790s to find more explicit working out of the connections among tragedy, liberty, patriotism, and monarchy.

9 The Revolution and the End of a Myth

Although the two stories that I have called the myth of the clement prince and the myth of liberty might seem fundamentally incompatible, in practice they were almost always combined, since their natural opposition was an effective source of dramatic conflict. Usually the result was that republican or nationalist resistance was overcome by imperial clemency and generosity after the authority figure has struggled and succeeded in conquering his own desires. A variation on this theme—observed in the operas on Julio-Claudian subjects and discussed in more detail below—occurs when the monarch is corrupt or self-indulgent. Operas about Nero or Lucius Cornelius Sulla the dictator are negative examples in the manner described by Livy, showing "base things, rotten through and through, to avoid," but are ameliorated by a last-minute change of heart and clemency by the tyrant.[1] The cases in which the two myths were not so reconciled—*La caduta de' decemviri* or *Catone in Utica*, for example—constitute experiments with tragic endings that appeared with some frequency from the 1690s through the 1720s. But these ran counter to the prevailing taste, and new librettos in the mideighteenth century maintained the *lieto fine*. Tragic endings began once again to appear, along with the esthetic and political changes that came at the end of the century.

As the last chapter showed, midcentury shifts in esthetic and musical taste were already beginning to challenge the form and content of *opera seria*. The political upheavals that followed the French Revolution further challenged *seria*'s most basic ideological assumptions as well, and therefore also its representation of ancient Romans. As we noted, ensemble pieces and choruses were employed to elaborate and intensify the more usual recitative and exit aria format of Metastasian-style librettos. These choruses, which brought more people on stage to share in the action, were an indicator of the renewed interest in the values of Greek tragedy, for which choral song had been a vital element. In some cases at least, as the century came to its close, the chorus also became a sign of the age of revolution, where *il Popolo* played an important role. Late-century librettists such as Francesco Salfi and composers such as Domenico Cimarosa were republicans in their politics and used the new operatic forms to promote political ideas and rhetoric inherited from the American and French revolutions.

Revolutions do not suddenly spring full grown and armed from their societies' heads, and it is not surprising that the interest in the republican myth of liberty that intensified in the last decade or so of the century is already observable in operas written before the revolutions occurred. The trend is apparent in two opera texts with plots taken from Roman republican history: Giovanni de Gamerra's *Lucio Silla* (music by Mozart for Milan, 1771) and Pindemonte's *Giunio Bruto* (music by Cimarosa; Verona, 1781), already indicate new directions a serious opera might take. Neither one is a revolutionary text, any more than is *Giulio Sabino*; de Gamerra even submitted his *Lucio Silla* to Metastasio for approval.[2] But they both depict resistance to tyranny, internal (*Lucio Silla*) and external (*Giunio Bruto*), in combination with an increased tragic sensibility that appears to derive from Greek tragedy. These two operas serve to introduce discussion of the three operas written in the 1790s that exemplify possible approaches to Rome in the decade following the French Revolution.

In *Lucio Silla*, de Gamerra, known to his contemporaries as the *poeta lagrimoso* for his emotionally dark sensibilities, set a recognition scene (I.vii–viii) in a gloomy burial place for heroes of the Roman past ("Luogo sepocrale molto oscuro co' monumenti degli eroi di Roma"). The original designs by Fabrizio Galliari show a large enclosed chamber with looming grave monuments.[3] Giunia, daughter of the dead populist leader Marius, is being pursued by her father's enemy, the dictator Silla (Lucius Cornelius Sulla). She brings offerings to her father's grave, accompanied by a chorus of aristocrats; together they pray to the spirits of the Roman heroes to avenge Roman liberty:

> *Chorus.* Come forth from these urns, oh honored souls, and in anger avenge Roman liberty.

Giunia. Oh, beloved shade of my father, if you hover here around me, let my prayers and sighs move you to pity.

Chor. The arrogant man, who tightens the bonds on the Capitol, may he be cast down from his throne today as an example for all time.

Giu. Oh Father, if the wicked Sulla was always the object of your hatred while you were alive, since Giunia is your daughter, because she has Roman blood in her veins, she comes with a suppliant's heart to your urn.

Instead of the ghosts of dead heroes, however, Giunia discovers her living lover Cecilio, an exiled enemy of Silla she had thought was dead. The scene ends in reunion and a conventional lovers' duet, but the scene as a whole includes several of the coming trends in opera: choral exchange with a character, Gothic gloom, and a taste for republican liberty.

In addition, it is especially striking that these scenes appear to reproduce deliberately the outlines of the prologue and choral entry of Aeschylus's *Libation Bearers* (lines 1–263), the second play of the *Oresteia*. In that play, Orestes, son of the murdered Agamemnon, returns from exile to visit his father's grave. He hides himself when his sister Electra enters, accompanied by a chorus of mourning women, to bring offerings to the grave of her dead father. In dialogue with the chorus, she deplores the tyranny of her murderous mother Clytemnestra and her lover Aegisthus. Orestes reveals himself, there is a joyful reunion, and the two then plot the deaths of Clytemnestra and Aegisthus. The similarities between this scene and the act II ending of *Lucio Silla* are so near that de Gamerra must surely have written it in reference to Aeschylus's tragedy, though it is a momentary evocation of mood rather than an indication of fundamental change, for the opera does not end in vengeance and tragedy.[4] Silla repents of his tyranny and retires, restoring liberty to Rome. He forgives attempts against his life and unites the lovers amid general rejoicing, and so the opera is structurally similar to *La Clemenza di Tito*.

By contrast, Pindemonte's *Giunio Bruto* does end tragically, in some of its versions at least. The story comes from the earliest years of the Roman Republic.[5] The agents of the deposed king Tarquin suborn members of the Roman aristocracy in an effort to return Tarquin to power. Among these are the sons of Lucius Junius Brutus, who, after the rape of Lucretia, led the drive to expel the king. The plot is discovered, and the sons of Brutus were executed before their father's eyes along with the other conspirators. It is a hard-hearted story of rough, republican virtue. In the later eighteenth century, it was the subject of Vittorio Alfieri's play *Bruto Primo* and Jacque-Louis David's painting *Brutus* (1788–89), which shows a stoically removed Junius Brutus at the dramatic moment when the bodies of his sons are being returned home.

It had not, however, been popular as a subject for opera. Pindemonte and Cimarosa were adapting the most recent version available, a libretto of a generation earlier by Mariangelo Passari (music by Nicolà Logroscino; Rome, 1749).[6] In Passari's version, there is only one son of Brutus, who betrays Rome at the behest of Tarquin's daughter Tarquinia, whom he loves. Passari contrives a last-minute forgiveness for Brutus's son at the rueful pleas of Tarquinia. The structure and personnel of Passari's plot thus mirror those of La clemenza di Tito. It might also be thought to prove Algarotti's point about the unsuitability of history for opera, as the stern founder of the Roman Republic is the subject of a plot that becomes progressively sillier and more sentimental as it goes on until the whole point of the original story is finally abandoned.[7] Pindemonte's 1781 version, and an adaptation for a London pasticcio in the same year, make some effort to return to the spirit of the ancient tale and end tragically with the (offstage) execution of the son. But already in 1783 in Pisa, the lieto fine was restored.[8]

Nevertheless, and despite the happy endings, all the versions of Giunio Bruto, beginning with Passari's, contain hints of things to come. First, they celebrate Roman liberty and the triumph against tyranny. Passari's opera ends in choral rejoicing on a political note: "May heaven make Roman liberty everywhere prosperous. And on this day may justice and Mercy be seen to surround us." The London pasticcio ends on a cold note, with a chorus addressed to Brutus: "Let the son die, may Rome's liberty live eternal. Great hero, may Tarpeian prosperity thrive through you." The opening scenes of the 1783 version from Pisa include an exit aria for Brutus that celebrates Rome's defiance:

> Yes, let that arrogant king shake, and let him threaten war and death; Roman liberty will always arise more powerfully.
> And one day every king, every people will tremble for their own destiny at the name of the great Latin people alone.[9]

Second, whether or not Brutus's son is finally executed, we are now in the realm of tragic actions among great families that begins to look more like the internecine quarrels of Greek drama than had much of earlier opera. Moreover, the period in which the events took place constitutes the Roman version of the legendary Greek tragic world that Algarotti had thought was the most suitable subject for opera. Stories of this kind come from a remote period of Rome, the historicity of which even Livy, who conscientiously reports them, remained unconvinced.

As a result, the medium of quasi-legendary subjects from the Roman Republic could serve to combine the esthetic trend in opera away from historical subjects with the apparently contradictory impulse toward political realism that came from the revolutionary thinkers and writers of the late century. Enlightenment notions about liberty and patriotism resulted in texts that espoused resistance to tyranny and a patriotic wish for Italian autonomy, applied locally if not yet nationally. This trend was then given focus, beginning in 1775, by the works of the playwright Vittorio Alfieri. Inspired by Addison's *Cato*, among other things, Alfieri wrote overtly political dramas meant to urge his fellow Italians toward ideas of liberty and self-determination. He took mythological and historical subjects from biblical and Greco-Roman antiquity, as well as stories from later European history; his Roman plays were *Virginia, Ottavia, Sofonisba, Bruto primo* (dedicated to George Washington), and *Bruto secondo*. Unlike the usual heroic dramas of the day, Alfieri's plays could end in death and tragedy; they are all focused on the defiance of tyranny, whether internal or external.[10]

Scena Ultima

The final scenes of three librettos will serve to illustrate how these late-century themes are manifested in the representation of ancient Rome in the last decade of the century. The operas in question are Mazzolà's and Mozart's setting of Metastasio's *La clemenza di Tito* for Prague (1791), Francesco Salfi's libretto *La congiura pisoniana* (*The Pisonian Conspiracy*) for Milan (1797), and Antonio Sografi's and Domenico Cimarosa's *Gli Orazi e i Curiazi* (*The Horatii and the Curiatii*) for Venice (1797). The first two constitute polar opposites: *Tito* is stolidly traditional in its message, whereas *La congiura pisoniana* is openly revolutionary. *Gli Orazi* stands somewhere in between the two, looking forward to the spectacular tragedies of the Italian nineteenth century in which the female lament ends in female death.

The libretto for Mozart's *La clemenza di Tito* was adapted from Metastasio's original by Caterino Mazzolà for the coronation of the Habsburg emperor Leopold II as King of Bohemia in September 1791. Mazzolà created a two-act version in which the action is essentially the same as the original. But the verbal motivation and characterization were much reduced by the elimination of recitative and condensation of action, leaving the subtleties to be worked out in the music.[11]

The *scena ultima* follows Vitellia's tormented rondò "Non più i fiori," in which she contemplates the consequences of confessing to her culpability in the plot to murder Tito. It begins with a grand choral entry celebrating Tito:

> That you are the thought and the love of heaven and the gods, great hero, has been shown in the brief turn of this day.
> But, happy Augustus, there is no reason for wonder, now that the gods thus watch over one who is like them.

Metastasio opened and closed his last scene with this chorus. Mazzolà put it only at the beginning of the scene, then mostly maintained Metastasio's recitative, up to the moment when Tito announces, "Be it known to Rome that I remain unchanged: I know all, I forgive all, and I forget all." At that point Mazzolà wrote his own words and Mozart set it in an ensemble finale that includes Tito's solo, combinations of the other characters, and chorus:

> *Vitellia, Servilia, Annio.* Oh generous! Oh noble! Who ever approached such grandeur? This surpassing goodness brings tears to my eyes.
> *Tutti. (except Tito).* Eternal gods, protect his sacred life. Preserve Rome's good faith in him.
> *Tito.* Eternal gods, cut short my life on that day when I no longer care for the good of Rome.

After the first statements of the final *tutti* and Tito's solo, the two are interwoven into a final grand statement of Tito's constancy and the public prayer for his continued life as protector of his city. The sentiments expressed—and the sentimentality, which is not in Metastasio's version—are in all respects perfectly conservative. It is an imperial *lieto fine* of the kind that we have seen in Habsburg operas since *Scipione nelle Spagne.* Mazzolà's Sesto remains unforgiving of himself, and the Vergilian shadows in Metastasio's original are still faintly visible in him and in Vitellia, but the praise of Tito's *clementia* is not compromised, and the chorus, far from tragic, reinforces the joyful imperial message. Whatever might be happening in Paris at the time, revolution is presented as a nonstarter in Prague due to the presence of an emperor who is at once subservient to the greater good and the source of that good. Any novelties in the opera are artistic, not political.

In fact, Mozart's *Tito* was so proper that it was not even a success with the people it was supposed to celebrate at the premiere. A high court official declared that it was "the most boring spectacle." The empress Maria Luisa reportedly called it *porcheria tedesca* ("German rubbish"). That is perhaps apocryphal, but she did write in a letter the day after the premiere that the "grand opera was not so grand, and the music very bad, so that most of us went to sleep." The court's was not to be the final word on either the quality of the music or the continued vitality of Metastasio's text, since the opera apparently was received with increasing enthusiasm during its run in Prague through September 1791.[12] The reaction at the premiere was nevertheless symptomatic of a larger truth: The usefulness of the Roman myth of the clement prince in its eighteenth-century form was waning. Neither the creators nor the intended receivers of the opera were attached to the imperial message, as they had been in the age when *Tito* was first written. Mozart himself, although he had a standard classical education and was eager all his life to write *opera seria*, had no great interest in antiquity.[13] He felt that Mazzolà's reduction of the Metastasian original had been necessary to make it a "real opera." The libretto itself had not even been the court's first choice for the coronation opera; the impresario's contract for it had suggested *Tito* in case a new libretto on other subjects could not be written in time. Leopold II had a taste for serious opera, which he had acquired while ruling as grand duke of Tuscany in Florence, but his first choices for his new *seria* troupe in Vienna were mythological or exotic in the modern style: Nasolini's *Teseo a Stige* (*Theseus at the Styx*) and Prati's *La vendetta di Nino* (after Voltaire's tragic *Sémiramis*).[14] *La clemenza di Tito* was perfectly safe and appropriate but no longer interesting, at least to its first patrons.

To others, however, a different kind of Roman story remained very interesting. By the later 1790s the rising tide of revolutionary fervor inspired a series of Italian operatic texts, of which Salfi's *La congiura pisoniana* was an early example and a model for others.[15] Adapted in part from a French play by Gabriel-Marie Jean-Baptiste Legouvé titled *Épicharis et Néron, ou Conspiration pour la Liberté* (Paris, 1794), it was written for La Scala in 1797, the winter after the French army of Italy under Napoleon seized Milan from Austria.[16] The libretto conflates several episodes from Tacitus and Suetonius to tell the fall of Nero as an allegory for both the fall of Louis XVI and the expulsion of the Austrians from Milan. Its librettist, Francesco Saverio Salfi, was in Milan as a fugitive from Naples, where he had been convicted of association with Jacobin and Masonic groups. The composer, Angelo Tarchi, whose music for *La congiura* does not survive, had already written music for innovative librettos such as *Virginia* and *Il Conte di Saldagno*, which made use of choruses, ensemble, and spectacle and brought tragic death on stage.[17]

The frontispiece of *La congiura pisoniana* (fig. 7) makes its revolutionary agenda perfectly clear, declaring that the opera is being produced "under the auspices of the French Republic" and including a figure of La Libertà. "Citizen" Salfi's preface is addressed to "The People of Milan." The evening included a ballet titled *Giunio Bruto* on the subject of Brutus's expulsion of the Tarquins from Rome. Like the title page, the ballet and a crucial scene of the opera featured a statue of La Libertà.

The action of the opera is based on a failed conspiracy against Nero, associated principally with a senator named Piso, that occurred in 65 C.E. Salfi combined the planning and subsequent discovery of the conspiracy with the burning of Rome (63 C.E.) and the fall of Nero (68 C.E.). In the last scene Nero has committed suicide and his body lies on stage. Piso (Pisone) and the Greek slave woman named Epicharis (Ecaride), who had played a major role in inspiring and planning the conspiracy, arrive on

Figure 7. Frontispiece for Angelo Tarchi, La congiura pisoniana, *Milan, 1797. Photo courtesy of The Newberry Library, Chicago.*

stage, newly freed from prison, with the People and the rebellious praetorian guard:

> *Final scene. Ecaride [enters] accompanied by maidens, and Pisone by*
> *conspirators. The People carry symbols of liberty in triumph.*
> *The praetorian guard follows.*

> *Chorus.* New Amazon of high courage [*Novella amazon d'alto valor*],
>   you receive the exultation of our hearts. You women who were
>   victims of slavery, let her victory be an example for you. If you
>   will ever be fierce and free, you will also always be the more dear
>   and beloved.
> *Flavio (seeing Nerone stabbed and on the ground).* Look, there he is!
> *Pisone.* Oh, heavens! He lies in his own blood!
> *Ecaride.* That blood announces our peace at last. Where the wicked
>   tyrant has fallen, may liberty now arise.
> *Pisone.* Ah may every other trouble of oppressed humanity be ended.
> *Both.* Let everyone promise over the tyrant to live free or die [*viver*
>   *libero o morir*].
> *Tutti.* May every cruel one always suffer the same revenge.*

The overthrow of Nero and the appearance of his corpse onstage is
celebrated with an ensemble and choral finale in the style that had been
used in Paris earlier in the decade to glorify the revolution.[18] This vision of
the overthrow of authority by the combined forces of the People and the
aristocracy, represented respectively by Ecaride and Pisone, would have
been unthinkable in any other performance context than one controlled
by France at the end of the century. The operas of republican Venice
such as *L'incoronazione di Poppea* and *Agrippina*, had, over the years,
suggested by implication that such an ending to Nero's story would be
just, but even Venice did not present it so openly. In 1789, however, on
the eve of the French Revolution, Gaetano Sertor wrote a *Morte di Cesare* for Venice in which Caesar was assassinated offstage and his body
exhibited; even so, the opera ended with Antony letting slip the dogs of
war and inciting a chorus of Hispanic guards to vengeance against the
conspirators. Sertor's epilogue assures his audience: "Do not concern
yourself, Venice; today the Roman Republic only makes a spectacle of
her misfortunes as you watch, but does not dare to compare herself with
you."[19] All the same, the door was now open for *La congiura pisoniana*
to exhibit openly the conclusion of a violent Roman political story. Its
final tableau is still a *lieto fine*, but one made possible by the death of
an emperor, a political hijacking of the *opera seria* for a use that is in
diametric opposition to that of *La clemenza di Tito*.

Nor was *La congiura* an isolated case. In 1797, the same year it appeared in Milan, an anonymous adapter rewrote Sertor's *La Morte di Cesare* for Venice so as to co-opt it for the new political order. The *scena ultima* was completely rewritten to show the onstage murder of Caesar, following which there is a celebration around the statue of Pompey the Great between Brutus and a split chorus that sounds as if it is a riposte to the glorification of Caesar found in Handel's *Giulio Cesare*. It begins, "Shade of Great Pompey [*Ombra del gran Pompeo*], you are avenged, you have conquered. See the oppressor of Rome dead at your feet." It closes with a chorus like that of *La congiura*:

> *Tutti.* Fearlessly we ask of heaven either death or liberty.
> *One part.* For her we will fight.
> *Second part.* For her we will triumph.
> *Tutti.* We swear, and swear again, either death or liberty [*o morte, o libertà.*]

In point of fact, and contrary to conventional wisdom, onstage death in opera had always been popular. In the seventeenth century, ballets of gladiatorial combats appeared with some regularity, and in *Scipione affricano* it provided a body that gave Siface his disguise and allowed him to take on his false identity as a slave. Villains could be killed off with impunity, as was Tolomeo in *Giulio Cesare*. But killing primi uomini and prime donne was another matter. The ground was laid with Metastasio's revised *Catone in Utica* and with his *Didone abbandonata*, in which a maddened Dido rushes into the flames of her burning palace. Both operas were produced continuously throughout the eighteenth century all over Europe; *Didone* reached a peak between 1750 and 1752, with seven productions in Turin, Venice, Brunswick, Genoa, Bologna, Vienna, and Barcelona. In Venice alone there were eight revivals between 1725 and 1787, all by different composers.[20] In Mattia Verazi's *Sofonisba* (music by Tommaso Traetta; Mannheim, 1762), the title character took the poison and in the *scena ultima* left the stage before dying. As we have seen, in some versions of *Giunio Bruto*, Brutus's son goes off stage to be executed. Hence, the step to showing onstage death in the climactic scene was not a great one. It needed only the requisite shift in taste to make it happen.

The final step was taken in the 1780s and 1790s with a series of "Morte" operas, like *Morte di Cesare* and Antonio Sografi's *La Morte di Cleopatra*.[21] In the latter, Antony falls on his sword offstage, but we see Cleopatra take the asp from a basket of fruit, apply it to her breast, and toss it away. The opera concludes with the onstage expiration of Antony and Cleopatra in each other's arms before a horrified ensemble that includes Augustus and Octavia:

Tutti. O fatal, terrible day!
Augustus. How unhappy and unfortunate I am!
Tutti. Ah, let's flee from this room of fear, death and horror
  [*di spavento, di morte, d'orror*].

In the Vergilian teleology that constituted the Roman ideal, the African Queen—Dido, Sophonisba, Cleopatra—finally had to die in order for Rome to survive. Now it was possible to show those deaths, rather than sequester them offstage.

The death of a Roman woman, on the other hand, was a different thing. There had been suicidal Lucretias and dying Agrippinas in cantatas (the young Handel wrote "Agrippina condotta a morire" and "Lucrezia" while in Italy). Frigimelica-Roberti's Lucretia had died in *Il trionfo della libertà* (Venice 1707), and Agostino Piovene's Agrippina was murdered by assassins as the curtain fell on his *Nerone* (Venice 1721). Such experiments with tragic denouements had failed to please in the longer run, however. That may be in part because quasi-historical Roman women such as Lucretia or Virginia who died tragically tended to do so just in advance of the overthrow of authority, and the world of opera had not yet been the venue for such events to be dramatized. Even that taboo began to change with operas such as Tarchi's *Virginia* for Florence in 1785.[22]

In 1797 Antonio Sografi, author of *La morte di Cleopatra*, wrote *Gli Orazi e i Curiazi* for Venice. The music was by Domenico Cimarosa, who had provided the score for Pindemonte's *Giunio Bruto*, and it was produced at La Fenice some months before the French Republican army under Napoleon captured the city. It tells a story from legendary Roman history of the battle between Rome and her mother city Alba Longa. Under King Tullus Hostilius, two sets of triplets, the Roman Horatii and the Alban Curiatii, decided the outcome of hostilities by doing battle with one another. A single Roman Horatius emerged victorious. On his triumphal return to Rome he found his sister weeping angrily because one of the Curiatii her brother had killed had been her fiancé. In fury Horatius killed her on the spot; subsequently brought up for trial, he was defended by his father, who declared that his daughter was a traitor to Rome. As a result, Horatius was given a relatively light and largely symbolic penalty. The main sources of the story are Livy (1.24–26) and Dionysius of Halicarnassus (*Antiquities* 3.13–22), but Sografi was also deriving many of his ideas from Corneille's play on the same subject titled *Horace*.

The *scena ultima* of *Gli Orazi* ends the action at the moment of Marco Orazio's murder of his sister Orazia and leaves the stage in chaos. The murder is witnessed by a large crowd that includes their father,

Publio Orazio, Sabina, Marco Orazio's wife, and choruses consisting of Roman matrons, the senate, and the people of Rome:

> *Orazia [leaping onto high place].* Oh, gods, if you are just, avenge me. *[furiously]* Make Rome pay for her wicked citizens a penalty worthy of their crimes. Rain your anger down upon her. Blast with lightning the household gods and temples, and all the boastful display that gathers in his breast, and may he never receive in his destruction that pity which he did not grant to another.
> *M. Orazio.* But first you will pay, wicked girl, with a pierced breast, the well-deserved penalty for your crime. *[He stabs her and throws her down the steps.]*
> *P. Orazio & Sabina [to M. Orazio].* Just gods! What have you done?
> *Matrons [crying out against M. Orazio].* Pitiless man!
> *M. Orazio [with a fierce gesture].* I have performed the duty of a Roman.
> *People, Senators, Chorus.* Live, oh brave man. You have served your country.
> *P. Orazio, Sabina, Matrons.* Dreadful day! of death and horror!
> *People and Senators.* Exalted day! of glory and honor!
> *[Last choruses sung in alternation.]*
>> *M. Orazio remains steadfast in the middle of the scene with a fierce gesture, P. Orazio and Sabina in an attitude of grief attended to by Licinio. The matrons cry out against P. Orazio, the people and senate praise him, part of the people goes up the stairs, horrified by the murder of Orazia, etc. In such fashion, with the confusion, joy, and consternation of the various characters of the immediate scene, the action ends.* *

This opera and its last scene are a grand synthesis of all the late-century trends we have observed in this and the previous chapter. Like *Giulio Sabino*, this is a story removed from the historical figures Algarotti had thought should be avoided, in this case because the story was taken from remoter Roman legend. Formally it ends in an action ensemble that includes soloists, some moments of duet, and finally opposing trios that are reinforced at the last by a split chorus. The choruses represent the People in all their manifestations, from nameless crowd to the patriotic hero and his family. A lack of resolution was observable at the conclusions of *La morte di Cesare* and *La morte di Cleopatra*, and even in *Il Catone in Utica*, caused by the tragic deaths of the title roles. Here the uncertainty is heightened to its utmost by the "confusion, joy, and consternation of the various characters," and by the quarreling, divided chorus that proclaims simultaneously the victory of Roman duty and patriotism, and horror at the pitiless murder of kin.

That kin is, moreover, female and a citizen woman. In *Didone abbandonata* and *La morte di Cleopatra,* the dying woman was a foreign threat to Rome that was eliminated. In *Gli Orazi e i Curiazi,* the threat to Rome is an internal one, and the victim of a brother who had declared in an earlier scene, "Neither father nor wife nor family nor friends live as far as I am concerned; the fatherland has all my affections, and in that I find everything." Marco Orazio's words sound as if Cato might have uttered them, and, even more, they are in the spirit of revolutionary patriotism of Alfieri's spoken tragedies; passages such as this caused Friedrich Lippmann to declare that the republican spirit of ancient Rome found an unprecedented and more powerful expression in these late-century operas.[23] Leaving aside the question of whether this is strictly true for *Gli Orazi*—the story takes place in Rome's regal period, not in the Republic, and King Tullus's position is never challenged by the Romans[24]—the degree to which Marco Orazio is willing to sacrifice family for country is remarkable. Metastasio's Cato was willing to disown his daughter because of her love for Caesar. Brutus in *Giunio Bruto* was willing to let the state punish his son for treason. But Orazio's murder of his sister takes matters a step further than these. Certainly liberated Italians of the day could read this excess as republican patriotism; in the preface to the 1798 Genoese production addressed "To the Free Citizens," Francesco Benedetto Ricci wrote, "My mind exults in presenting to you a drama and a ballet, both worthy of the sacred fire of liberty, which burns in you. 'The Horatii and the Curiatii' will serve you as a measure for preserving intact your faith and love for your country."

As noted, opera had begun to show symptoms of a renewed and informed interest in Greek tragedy. Here the combination of politics and violence turned inward against a citizen woman whose passions have carried her away appears at last to be in accord with the more excessively violent Greek tragedies, in which tensions in family and state come to a bloody climax: wives kill husbands, sons kill mothers and vice versa, fathers sacrifice daughters. But even in Greek tragedy violence is not done before our eyes, and there is usually a price to pay for it afterward: The triumphant escape of Euripides' Medea in a dragon chariot with the bodies of her children is unusually disturbing. To end this opera with an unrepentant Marco Orazio standing above the crowd, steadfast and with a fierce gesture, was pretty strong stuff, even for postrevolutionary Europe, and adjustments were sometimes made. On the one hand, it was revived in Venice at La Fenice in 1798 and 1800 with the ending unchanged. In autumn of 1800 in Trieste, the curtain closed right after Orazio's speech and the murder of Orazia; no ensemble discusses ramifications of any kind. But Milan saw a revised finale in 1798 in which Orazio, having stabbed his sister, immediately cries, "Sacred gods, what have I done?" He throws down his sword and covers his head with his cloak, while the Roman matrons exclaim in fury and horror. He then runs from the scene in confusion, and the closing chorus raises its hands and eyes to heaven and concludes, "Sacred law, you preserve the State. / Ah, often private emotion / changes justice to madness." It was in this form that the opera came in 1802 to Paris, where it received formal publication.[25]

At this point in musical history, opera is no longer "early" and we have reached the further limit of our subject. The nineteenth century, never-theless, did not immediately cease producing either *opera seria* or an-cient Roman subjects in opera.[26] *La clemenza di Tito* found an audience on the continent and was the first of Mozart's operas to be produced in London.[27] As we have noted, the last new setting of Metastasio's *Tito* was still to come in 1839. Rossini set an *Adriano in Palmira*. Spontini wrote *La Vestale*, and Bellini *Norma*. Beethoven's first attempt at opera was for a libretto titled *Vestas Feuer*. Cherubini composed for *Il Quinto Fabio, Adriano in Siria*, and *Giulio Sabino*. Giovanni Pacini's *L'ultimo giorno di Pompeii* (Naples, 1825) was a success, partly for the cataclys-mic eruption of Vesuvius that killed everyone at the end. It was said of Saverio Mercadante, a popular composer beginning in the 1820s, that "in subjects taken from Roman history, [he] felt at ease and his imagination had space to roam. He seemed to envisage with surprising clarity those severe customs, those virile sentiments, those robust practices which made the Roman people conquerors and governors of the world."[28] As late as the 1840s, his *Virginia* could sufficiently ruffle the censors' feathers to be suppressed, although it was finally performed in 1866.[29] The librettos for *Virginia* and for Mercadante's *Orazi e Curiazi* (1846) were written by Salvatore Cammarano, who also wrote the librettos for Donizetti's *Lucia di Lamermoor* (1835) and Verdi's *Il Trovatore* (1852), indicating how the old was still sitting side by side with the new.

Some of these were reactionary pieces written by people who rejected the contemporary romanticism (Rossini and Mercadante, for example); others were in the new tragic-romantic vein that had less to do with the imperial ethos of Rome than with the family tragedies of the Greeks (Spontini, Bellini). But it is also true that the subject matter was itself reaching its limits, and a general modern impression that no operas were written on Roman historical subjects between Mozart's *La Clemenza di Tito* and Arigo Boito's *Nerone* (posthumous, 1924) is forgivable. The "Roman" titles of the nineteenth century were not the ones that survived as public taste chose its favorite operas and composers, and as the canon of classics was being formed. The seeds of change in focus and treatment in the Roman operas of the 1770s and 1780s came to fruition in the aftermath of the French Revolution and the fall of Napoleon, and the pervading cultural sense that historical Rome was an interesting source of operatic stories had all but vanished by the mid-nineteenth century. This was partly due to simple exhaustion; in 1828 Vincenzo Bellini sneered that "Caesar in Egypt" was a subject that was "old as Noah."[30] The stories of Rome migrated to other venues and left Roman antiquity on the opera stage as another exotic land to be visited from time to time but not to be embraced as one's own.

Licenza *(Epilogue)*

In June 2006 a production of *Lucio Silla* premiered at Teatro La Fenice in Venice as part of the year's celebrations of Mozart's 250th birthday; the production moved to the Salzburg Festival in July.[31] The set and costumes suggested the late eighteenth century. The main piece of scenery was a large, Vitruvian-Palladian structure in tan and white, with a central arch, trabeated entrances on either side, an attic storey, and empty pedimented niches that provided texture but no human features. It stretched the width of the stage and could be rolled backward and forward to indicate a change of scene, or turned around, its obvious features as a stage property thus exposed. The bare walls of the stage were also exposed, and the lighting was stark. The set was covered with what initially appeared to be sawdust left from set construction but turned out to be a dusting of stage snow that sometimes swirled appealingly around the long cloaks of the singers as they walked. The whole effect was bleak and shabby, presumably meant to emphasize the destructiveness of Silla's dictatorship. At the conclusion of act I, when the chorus entered with Giunia at what was supposed to be the *luogo sepolcrale molto oscuro*, they appeared in rags and proceeded to pull Etruscan-style urns from under the floorboards as they called upon the dead. In the *scena ultima*, Silla's recantation and *clemenza* was forced from him at knife's point, subsequent to which he was killed and his body carried around in a chair while the chorus sang its (now ironic) celebration of his virtue and glory. On the whole, the production gave the impression that the stage director and set designers had been told they were doing *Les Miserables* on a low budget.

The present writer was not alone in his distaste and disappointment at what he had seen.[32] At the curtain call the night of the premiere, there were boos of protest audible amid the applause when the production staff took its bow. At the price one pays for tickets, it is reasonable to expect an internationally acclaimed opera house to provide a mise-en-scène that, if not lushly extravagant, at least complements the music and in some stimulating way provides an equivalent to the style of the period it is supposed to be presenting.[33] But putting consumer economics aside, there are more substantial reasons to feel aggrieved. In discussing Handel's *Giulio Cesare*, I was unwilling to declare the innovative Peter Sellars or Bayerische Staatsoper productions "wrong," however removed they seemed to me to be from the political emphases of Haym's and Handel's original. They each provided a picture that went with the words, and they did not change the ending to suit their own purposes. This *Lucio Silla* was a different matter. Mozart's opera is not a Brechtian fable about the overthrow of oppression. It is an *opera seria*, a variation on what I have called the myth of the clement prince, the text of which was read and approved by Metastasio himself. It is a story of love endangered and an eleventh-hour return by a bad ruler to repentance and good behavior. To change it to a story of forced confession and assassination makes nonsense of the whole, both dramatically and musically. George Bernard Shaw complained of watching operas whose producer either "does not know the story of the opera he has in hand, or has become cynically convinced that an opera is in itself such a piece of nonsense that an extra absurdity or two cannot matter much."[34] Shaw was objecting to careless production values in London stagings of operatic warhorses, but change his "opera" to "*opera seria*" and the point is applicable in cases like that of the 2006 *Lucio Silla*. An assumption on the part of directors and designers that the plot they are presenting is absurd, or that audiences are not intelligent enough to detect for themselves the problems of power that lie beneath the stability and poise of eighteenth-century musical drama, and that in consequence they have to have it hammered home with a deliberate brutalization of the production concepts, is insulting at best, to both the audience and the dramatic work.[35]

I would not complain about the Fenice *Lucio Silla* if I thought it was the only modern stage production to have had the problems I have identified; frequent attendees at performances of Shakespeare or Wagner will recognize the phenomenon. These sorts of ruminations, however, expose themselves to accusations of subjectivity or pedantry or both. The more important point here is to observe the degree to which *opera seria* about the ancient Romans was based on assumptions—on a myth, in the language of this book—that are no longer current and are difficult to make palatable to a postmodern audience. It is not a new problem. In Paris in 1791, a public outcry stopped a production of Metastasio's *Adriano in Siria* set by Méhul. Jacques-Louis David is supposed to have declared at the time that the Parisians would rather tear down the Opéra than see kings in triumph there.[36] But it may be that more recent enormities perpetrated by the Sullas of the twentieth century have made it impossible to celebrate autocracy seriously, even as an evening's vehicle for musical entertainment, and that the assassination of the tyrant is the only way to create a dramatic *lieto fine* in the world as we know it now.

For the myth of republican liberty, the story of individual and national struggle for freedom remains a vital one. As a result, operas in the carnivalesque, Venetian mode are less difficult to package, and approaches to autocratic power such as one finds in Monteverdi's *Poppea* or in the mockeries in *Agrippina* or *Ottone in villa* need little doctoring to be understood these days. (Though doctoring they receive nonetheless: There are always those who cannot resist making the obvious more so.) But the Arcadian imperialist project with its clement princes ran its course a long time ago. Sometimes the sheer quality of the music and the depth of human feeling such operas express can carry the day anyway: Handel and Mozart were especially adept at this, and the musicality and humanity of *Giulio Cesare* or *La clemenza di Tito* survive on their own. In many a case, however, modern productions deconstruct their subjects in a way so as to remind us again that Plautus and Terence, not Sophocles and Aristotle, were the real fathers of *dramma per musica*.

APPENDIX: PASSAGES FROM
UNPUBLISHED ITALIAN SOURCES

The following passages are the originals of the translations marked with an asterisk (*) in the text.

Chapter 1

Page 20. *Lettere di Apostolo Zeno*, 2nd ed., no. 434, vol. 2, p. 443.

Questa sera va in iscena la mia Ifigenia. Non vi potete immaginare la congiura fatta per gittarla a terra. Le scene non sono finite; gli abiti o sono vecchi, o non forniti; i musici poco la sanno; le decorazioni non sono state eseguite giusta la mia intenzione: ma con tutto questo, e con quanto ne può succedere, due cose assai mi consolano; l'una che l'Augustissimo Padrone la gradisce sommamente, e l'altra che il mio libretto letto da tutta la corte è grandemente piaciuto: onde se sopra il teatro non farà l'effetto che dovrebbe, la colpa non sarà mia.

Chapter 3

Page 57. Francesco Sbarra, *Alessandro, il vincitore di se stesso*, II.vi.

Alessandro. Mio caro,
    Hò à togliermi la vita?
Aristotele. Anzi la morte.
Al. Et hò a dar contro me
    Sentenza sì crudel?
Ar. Così coviene.
Al. Ch'io sia con mè severo?
Ar. Anzi pietoso.
Al. Ch'io cerchi il proprio danno?
Ar. Il proprio bene.
Al. Ed io, ch' à gli altri impero,
    Di me stesso sarò crudo tiranno?
Ar. Son tiranni i tuoi sensi.

Chapter 4

Page 75. Corradi, *Il Nerone*, preface.

Asceso Nerone sul trono di Roma, si fè credere à suoi Popoli per il Solone di que' tempi; mà cadutagli di mano la bilancia d'Astrea, in breve convertì il nome di Giusto in quello del maggior Tiranno del Mondo. Lo spogliare di sostanze la plebe per vestire la superbia dei suoi caprici fù il minore d'ogni delitto. Stupri, morti, e ruine continui trionfi di quell'anima indegna.

Chapter 5

Page 91. *Scipione nelle Spagne* I.xvi.

    Scipione. Quel, che ti pende al fianco,
        Peso guerrier, pria tu mi cedi.
    Luceio. Intendo.
        A ceppi di Cardenio
        Lieto succedo. Eccoti il ferro, e sappi
        Che tormelo dal fianco
        Mia virtù sol potea.
    Sofonisba. (Virtù funesta!)
    Sci. Giurati amico mio. La legge è questa.
    Sof. (Respiro.)
    Luc. (Acerba legge,
        Che mi toglie fin l'odio
        Di un mio rival, per liberarne un' altro.)
    Sci. Tanta pena ti costa
        L'amistà di Scipion?
    Luc. Più, che non pensi.
        Ma lo vuole il destin. Giuro . . .
    Sci. Sù questo
        Brando lo giura: indi il gradisci in dono.
    Luc. Giura Tersandro; ed or tuo amico io sono.
        E sia pegno di fè questo, che or prendo
        Illustre acciar, tuo dono,
        E in serviggio al guerrier fianco appendo.

Page 92. *Scipione nelle Spagne*, III.ii.

    Scipione. Roma punir non usa
        Un atto di virtù.
    Luceio. Virtù, che nuoce
        al pubblico interesse, è fellonia.
    Sci. Diemmi il Senato autorità sovrana.
    Luc. Quì del campo è il poter, non del Senato.
    Sci. Di campo io sono il Duce.
    Luc. Un furor cieco
        Libero è da le leggi, e tutto ardisce.

Sci. Deh! fuggi, amico, io te ne priego.

Luc. Ovunque
Non ripugni il dover, mi è sacro il nome.

Page 92–93. *Scipione nelle Spagne* III.ii (continued).

Luceio. [To Sofonisba] Qual testimon de la mia fede esigi
Per mio rossor? Pur ti ubbidisco Andiamo.
Si abandoni Cartago.
Perdasi un bel morir. Scipio lo chiede:
Sofonisba lo brama.
Lo impene la mia fede. Andiamo. Hai vinto . . .
Nel voler partire s'incamina da la parte dovè Scipione,
e vedutolo si ferma in atto pensoso.
(Ahi! che fo? dove vò? giudice è Scipio
Di mia viltà.)

Sofonisba. Che più ti arresti?

Luc. Muori. *frà se tenendo sempre Sof. per mane.*
(E muori anche con l'odio
De la tua Sofonisba:
Mà non mancar, Luceio, al tuo dovere.)

Luc. (*va a Scipione*)

Scipione. (Irresoluto è ancor.)

Sof. (Torno à temere.)

Luc. Signor, deh! mi perdona
Questa mia debollezza. Un troppo amore
Quasi mi fè tradir la mia amistade.
eccoti Sofonisba. A te Consorte
Io la feci: io la lascio; e vado a morte.

Page 99. *Scipione nelle Spagne, scena ultima.*

Scipione. Mà, Luceio, qual posso
Rendere à merti tuoi premio bastante?
Non l'hò che in Sofonisba. Io te la rendo.

Luceio. Perdona. Sofonisba è già tua sposa.

Sci. Esser dovea.

Luc. Tù ne hai la fè.

Sci. Tu il core.

Luc. Il dover tua la fece.

Sci. E tua l'amore.

Sof. (Gare che son mio affanno.)

Page 99. *Scipione nelle Spagne, scena ultima* (continued).

Scipione. In sì illustre litigio
Nostro giudice omai sia Sofonisba.

Luceio. Ella saria giudice insieme, e parte.
In Trebellio mi accheto.

Sci. Egli è Romano.
Cardenio eleggo.

Luc. Ei meco
   Hà commune la patria.
Sci. Eleggo Elvira.
Luc. Son pago. . . .
   Elvira. Al grande assalto or ti apparecchia, o core.
Sci. & Luc. Bella.
Sci. Da tè dipende—
Luc. A te te s'aspetta—
Sci. Di due cori il riposo.
Luc. Il giudicio sovrano.
Sof. (Per Luceio ella avvampa. Io spero invano.)
Elv. Trà Luceio, e Scipion virtù fin' ora
   Contese con virtù; gloria con gloria.
   Pari n'è il vanto. Or solo
   Sì eroiche gare amor trà voi decida.
   Egli che unì con immortal catena
   Di Sofonisba, e di Luceio i cori,
   Ne annodi anche le destre
   L'Iberia applauda, e l'Imeneo si onori . . .

Page 100. *Scipione nelle Spagne, scena ultima* (continued).
Sof. & Luc. E già trovo in amore,
Scip, Elv., Card. Ed io trovo in virtude,
   à 5. Il mio riposo.
   E' sempre in sè beato,
   Quando è virtù l'amor.
   Di sua fortezza armato,
   Ei troverà il diletto
   O' nel suo stesso affetto,
   O' nel suo stesso onor.

Page 104. *Scipione nelle Spagne, Licenza* (1744).
Fia, per cui salga all'etra il tuo gran NOME.
Scipio in Ennio il trovò. Questo sol vanto,
Manca al tuo onor: degno di Carlo il canto.
   Qual ribomba
      Eroica tromba
   Al tuo NOME, Augusto CARLO?
   Taccian gli altri. Egli a se stesso
   Degna tromba è si gran NOME.
Può sua gloria appien lodarlo:
E virtù rammenta in esso
I trofei, che più del serto
Crescon freggio alle tue chiome.
   CORO
CARLO il tuo NOME Augusto
   il pregio tuo maggior . . .

Chapter 6

Page 130. *Il Catone in Utica* (Verona, 1737), 2.9.
>*Marzia.* Oh Dio! t'arresta.
>>Questa è la pace? *a Cat.* e questa
>>L'amistà sospirata? *a Ces.*
>*Cesare.* Il padre accusa;
>>Egli vuol guerra.
>*Mar.* Ah, Genitor.
>*Cat.* T'accheta:
>>Di costui non parlar.
>*Mar.* Cesare—
>*Ces*: Ho troppo
>>Tolerato fin'ora.
>*Mar.* Ah, nò, placate
>>Ormai l'ire ostinate; assai di pianto
>>Costano vostri sdegni
>>Alle spose latine, assai di sangue
>>Costano gl'odi vostri all'infelice
>>Popolo di Quirino, ah, non si veda
>>Sù l'amico trafitto
>>Più incrudelir l'amico, ah, non trionfi,
>>Del germano il germano; ah, più non cada
>>Al figlio che l'uccise il padre accanto.
>>Basti alfin tanto sangue e tanto pianto.
>*Cat.* Non basta a lui.
>*Ces. a Cat.* Non basta a me! Se vuoi,
>>V'è tempo ancor, pongo in oblio le offese,
>>Le promesse rinovo,
>>L'ire depongo e la tua scelta attendo,
>>Chiedimi guerra, o pace,
>>Soddisfatto sarai.
>*Cat.* Guerra, guerra mi piace.
>*Ces.* E guerra avrai.

Chapter 9

Page 175. *La congiura pisoniana, scena ultima.*
>*Ecaride accompagnata da donzelle, e Pisone da*
>*congiurati. Il popolo porta in trionfo le insegne di*
>*libertà. Seguono le guardie pretoriane.*
>Coro
>>Novella amazone
>>D'alto valor

Accogli il giubbilo
Del nostro cor.
Donzelle, vittime
Di servitù,
Vi sia di esempio
La sua virtù.
Se fiere e libere
Sarete ognor,
Più care e amabili
Sarete ancor.

Flavio vedendo Nerone trafitto nel suolo.
Eccolo!

Pisone. Oh ciel! Nel proprio sangue ei giace!

Ecaride. Quel sangue annunzia alfin la nostra pace.
Dove cadde il reo tiranno,
Sorga ormai la libertà.

Pis. Ah finisca ogni altro affanno
Dell' oppressa umanità!

à 2. Sul tiranno ognun prometta
Viver libero o morir.

Tutti. Possa ognora egual vendetta
Ogni barbaro soffrir.

Page 178. *Gli Orazi e i Curiazi, scena ultima.*

Orazia. Salendo in una eminenza.
Numi se giusti siete
Vendicatemi voi. *furibonda.* Fate che Roma
Paghi degl' empi Cittadini suoi
Pena condegna ai lor dilitti. Piombi
Sopra lei l'ira vostra. Fulminate
E lare e i templi, e quanto il fasto aduna
Entro 'l suo sen, e non ritrovi mai
Ne' precipizi sui
Quella pietà che non concesse altrui.

M. Orazio.
Ma pria tu pagherai
Empia col sen trafitto
La pena ben dovuta al tuo delitto.

la ferisce e la precipita dalla gradinata.

P. Orazio, Sabina.
Giusti Dei! Che facesti!

le MATRONE *inveindo contro M. Orazio.*
Spietato!

M. Orazio in atto feroce.
Il dover d'un Romano ho compito:

Popolo e Senatori. Coro.
Vivi, o forte; alla patria hai servito:

P. Orazio, Sabina, Matrone.
  Giorno orrendo! di morte d'orror.
Popolo e senatori.
  Giorno eccelso! di gloria d'onor.
     alternativamente.
M. ORAZIO *rimane immobile nel mezzo della scena in atto feroce,* PUB-
LIO *e* SABINA *in attitudine di tristezza assistiti da* LICINIO. *Le matrone
inveiscono contro* ORAZIO, *il popolo e i senatori lo esaltano, parte del
popolo và sulle gradinate innorridita per l'uccisione di* ORAZIA *ec. In tal
modo con la confusione, allegrezza, e consternazione de' varj personaggi
della scena stessa termina l'azione.*

NOTES

Chapter 1. Ancient Rome in Early Opera

1. Sartori's catalogue of Italian librettos written before the year 1800 lists in excess of twenty-five thousand items. These are mostly operatic, but they include other musical events, such as serenades, cantatas, intermezzos, and so forth (Sartori, *Libretti italiani* 1:ix). The operatic documents include original librettos, reprints, revivals, and adaptations.

2. On the Venetian operas, see Rosand, *Opera*, 184–88. On the London *Muzio Scevola*: Dean and Knapp, *Handel's Operas*, 368–84, and Burrows, *Handel*, 109–10. Bononcini composed act II and Handel act III. Act I was set by Filippo Amadei, a lesser but respectable composer also working in London at the time.

3. Wiseman, *Myths of Rome*, 10–11. For a more theoretical approach to defining myth in reference to opera, see Feldman, *Opera and Sovereignty*, especially 227–83. In Feldman's view, "myths are not particular tales, in and of themselves. At most they are uses of tales that are taken to be traditional, disseminated as such, and deployed for political or other kinds of legitimating purposes. . . . In this sense myths are privileged narratives" (228). Feldman believes, as I do, that eighteenth-century opera was engaged in the business of "turning histories into myths," but my narrative begins the process already in the seventeenth century. Unfortunately, Feldman's complex treatment of later eighteenth-century opera came out while the present book was in its final stages of production, and so I only engage with it very superficially to indicate where readers may find an alternative and more expansive view of that period.

4. Ketterer, "Why Early Opera Is Roman."

5. On Hellenistic kingdoms and their relation to Greek and Roman literature, see Green, *Alexander to Actium*, especially 171–86; Hutchinson, *Hellenistic Poetry*, especially 277–354; and Clausen, "Callimachus and Latin Poetry."

6. Tacitus, *Annals* 4.34.

7. Livy, "Praefatio" to books 1–5, *The Early History of Rome*, trans. Aubrey de Sélincourt (Harmondsworth: Penguin, 1971), 34. This approach to antiquity was still viable in 1798, when Francesco Benedetto Ricci posited a moral purpose for opera based on ancient practice. In his preface to the libretto of *Gli Orazi e i Curiazi*, addressed "To the Free Citizens" of Genoa, he wrote, "The most remote times have had their spectacles made to raise the spirit and to decry their depraved habits."

8. On Ovid's relegation to the Black Sea and his ironic relationship with the Augustan literary program, see Conte, *Latin Literature*, 340, 355–57. For a summary of approaches to the political Ovid with basic bibliography, as well as a chal-

lenge to a political reading, see Thomas Habinek, "Ovid and Empire," in Hardie, *Cambridge Companion to Ovid*, 61. On Propertius, see Conte, *Latin Literature*, 334–36.

9. Dihle, *Greek and Latin Literature*, 348; the assessment of Dio is on pages 348–50.

10. See Jones, *Plutarch and Rome*, 124–26, on Plutarch's social class in Greece, which had an attitude that was "both Greek and Roman," and "interests and sympathies [that were] bound up with empire." Dihle, *Greek and Latin Literature*, 193, describes Plutarch as among those Greek intellectuals who "cast off those reservations concerning Roman Imperialism which they had cherished for centuries" and "became [the empire's] most loyal supporters."

11. On the invention of opera in Florence about 1600, see Carter, "Seventeenth Century," 1–8; Kimbell, *Italian Opera*, 53–62; Sternfeld, *Birth of Opera*; Donington, *Rise of Opera*, 103–40.

12. Barbara Hanning, "Dafne," Grove Music Online (accessed Dec. 4, 2006).

13. Curtis, *L'incoronazione di Poppea*, vii, calls this the "Clorinda cadence," which was taken up by later composers as a mark of special moments.

14. For the variety of names applied to the new genre in its early years, see Rosand, *Opera*, 35–36.

15. The seminal study is Bianconi and Walker, "Production, Consumption and Political Function," especially 259–74, on political and civil functions of opera.

16. The operas are, in order of reference, Monteverdi's *Arianna* and *Il ritorno d'Ulisse in patria*, Cavalli's *Il Giasone*, Zeno's libretto *Scipione nelle Spagne*, Legrenzi's *Germanico sul Reno*, and Polarollo's *Il ripudio d'Ottavia*.

17. Calcagno, "Censoring *Eliogabalo*," 375. Calcagno's article documents an interesting case where the *lieto fine* was probably inspired by the politics of a particular opera house rather than by esthetic considerations.

18. Skippon, *Journey*, 520. For further discussion of the comic elements in early Venetian opera, see Rosand, *Opera*, 60–65, 189–90. For the comic pattern in Zeno's operas, see Sala di Felice, "Zeno," 111–12, and generally my arguments in "Why Early Opera Is Roman." For a different perspective, see Hoxby, "Doleful Airs of Euripides," and note 23 below.

19. Vincenzo Nolfi, preface to *Bellerofonte* (Venice, 1642), cited from Fabbri, *Il secolo cantante*, 131.

20. On the change of taste, see Kimbell, *Italian Opera*, 181–89. For a sample of Arcadian complaints about late-century opera, see the passage by Giovanni Maria Crescembeni quoted in Rosand, *Opera*, 275.

21. See also Smith, *Tenth Muse*, 63–73. "Thus, what took place in the last two decades of the seventeenth century and the first two of the eighteenth was not a thoroughgoing housecleaning, but a pruning and repotting, accompanied by a great amount of philosophical flim-flam about Greece and the pastoral perfection" (64).

22. The Arcadians made a veritable religion of not mixing genres, but elimination of comic elements was a trend already noticeable in, for example, productions of Minato's libretto *Scipione affricano*. The first version in 1664 included a comic servant named Lesbo. By the 1678 Venice production this role had been eliminated.

23. Although modern criticism has sometimes called certain Euripidean plays

with happy endings comic, to call them comedies would have made no sense to a fifth-century Athenian, for whom comedy meant the social and political Old Comedy of playwrights such as Aristophanes. Nevertheless, in this connection see Hoxby, "Doleful Airs of Euripides," which argues for a formative role of Euripidean tragedy in early modern ideas of the tragic and its role in opera. One might ask if Euripidean "melodramas" such as *Iphigenia among the Taurians* or *Alcestis* were appealing to the theorists and librettists because they fit an already established tragicomic pattern or whether they helped establish that pattern. But they are undeniably an influential part of the opera reforms of the eighteenth century, first through the French neoclassical dramatists and then through theorists such as Algarotti. (See chapters 8 and 9.)

24. Smith, *Tenth Muse*, 40.

25. Reinhard Strohm, *"Tolomeo*: Handel's Opera and the Rules of Tragedy," in Strohm, *Dramma per musica*, 209.

26. Konstan, *Roman Comedy*, 15–32, gives a concise summary of the conventions of the ancient genre and its issues.

27. See Rosand, *Opera*, 2n1, for the first five years of Venetian opera.

28. Cicero, *Letters to Atticus* 8.16.2.

29. The appearance of the word *clementia* in late republican discourse is conveniently described by Konstan, "Clemency as a Virtue," 340–41; on the new shrine, see 341–42. Plutarch, *Caesar* 57.4; Appian, *Civil Wars* 2.106; Cassius Dio, *Roman History*, 44.6.4; and "Clementia Caesaris, aedes" in Steinby, *Lexicon topographicum urbis Romae* 1:279–80. The establishment of this cult was notable, as it was the first addition of a cult to a virtue to Roman religious life since the early second century B.C.E. See Fears, "Cult of the Virtues," 846–49.

30. Konstan, "Clemency as a Virtue," 342; *Res Gestae Divi Augusti*, Section 34. For a general treatment of imperial use of virtues, see Fears, "Cult of the Virtues."

31. "Tu regere imperio populos, Romane, memento / (hae tibi erunt artes), pacique imponere morem, / parcere subjectis et debellare superbos." This passage, and especially the last line, is important for the discussions in chapters 3 and 4.

32. The episode of Alexander's clemency is in Plutarch, *Alexander*, 21, as well as Arrian, *Anabasis of Alexander* 2.11.9; Diodorus, *Bibliotheke* 17.36.2; Curtius, *History of Alexander* 3.11.4–5; and Justin, *Epitome* 11.9.12. Scipio's continence is reported in greatest detail in Livy, *History of Rome* 26.50, Polybius, *Histories* 10.16, and briefly in Valerius Maximus, *Memorable Deeds and Sayings* 4.3.1. For a list of the many early modern representations of these scenes, see "Die Enthaltsamkeit des Scipio," in Pigler, *Barockthemen* 2:424–29; "Alexander d. Gr. und die Familie des Darius," in Pigler, *Barockthemen* 2:357–59. Burt, "Opera in Arcadia," 146–47, remarks on "the visual record in Tiepolo of the operatic ideal."

33. See Panofsky, *Hercules am Scheidewege*, 37–166. There is an excellent summary of the characteristics of seventeenth-century Neostoicism in Heller, *Emblems of Eloquence*, 146.

34. On Hercules as a Stoic hero: "As the best of models they accepted Hercules, the man rightly deemed a god, who traveled over all the world, purging it of every lawlessness, and bringing with him justice, holiness and peace." Arnold, *Roman Stoicism*, 295–96 and n. 161. Seneca, *De Constantia* 2.1, is directly to the point: "Our Stoics declared [Ulysses and Hercules] sages [*sapientes*], unbeaten in their

labors and disdainers of pleasure, and victors over all terrors." Other relevant ancient citations include Cicero, *De Officiis* 3.25; Seneca, *De Beneficiis* 1.13.3; and Epictetus, *Discourses* 3.26.32.

35. Compare Dean, *Handel and the Opera Seria*, 56: "[Metastasio's] librettos aimed at dignity and a lofty humanism in the spirit of his age, and were designed to present a standard of conduct suitable to princes, based on the classical Roman virtues."

36. I am counting the versions listed in Brunelli's *Tutte le opere di Pietro Metastasio*, 1:1498–99.

37. The fortunes of the libretto that we know as Handel's *Giulio Cesare*, for example, are described with fascinating detail by Monson, "'Giulio Cesare in Egitto.'" The mutations that could be imposed by a composer on his own operas are exemplified by what happened to Handel's *Giulio Cesare* over the course of the years 1724–35 in London, described succinctly by Dean and Fuller, *Giulio Cesare in Egitto*, x–xi. See also the review by McLauchlan, "Giulio Cesare in Egitto," for further information on authorial changes.

38. Newberry Library catalogue number Case ML50.2.A74 S35 1703. The title page of the original reads: "Arminio / Drama per Musica/ rappresentato / nella Villa / di / Pratolino. / In Firenze, MDCCIII / Nella Stamperia Di Sua Altezza Reale. / Appreso Pietro Antonio Brigonci" (Sartori, *Libretti italiani*, no. 2787). The adapter's hand has crossed out "nella Villa / di / Pratolino" and replaced it with "da rappresentarsi / nel Teatro di Via del Cocomero / nel Carnovale dell'anno 1716 / sotto la protezione del A[ltezza] R[eale] del Ser[enissi]mo Gran Principe di Toscana." (Cf. Sartori, *Libretti italiani*, no. 2792.)

39. This is the standard conception of these *arie di baule*, but recent work suggests the business of choosing and performing the "baggage aria" may have been as much an appeal to audience taste and expectations as it was an expression of a singer's ego. See Brown, "On the Road"; Freeman, "Farinello and His Repertory"; and Poriss, "Making Their Way Through the World," especially 198–201 on seventeenth- and eighteenth-century practice.

40. John Rosselli, "Opera as a Social Occasion," 305, in Parker, *Oxford History of Opera*. Rosselli's entire essay, 304–21, is an excellent introduction to the colorful and varied experience of opera going before Wagner. See also Feldman, "Magic Mirrors and the *Seria* Stage," for an anthropological interpretation of audience attendance at the opera as a social ritual.

41. Kimbell, *Italian Opera*, 250–78, for example, does this with settings of Metastasio's libretto *L'olimpiade*. See also Powers, "Il Serse trasformato"; and Heller, "Queen as King." For a chronological analysis of the Achilles and Deidamia story from Statius in early opera librettos, see Heslin, *Transvestite Achilles*, 1–55.

42. On the character of the libretto as both a performance document and a poetic text to be read, see, for example, Freeman, *Opera Without Drama*, 24–25.

Chapter 2. The Coronation of Poppea

1. For the purposes of this book, *L'incoronazione di Poppea* means the opera as it is printed in Alan Curtis's edition, *L'incoronazione di Poppea*, including the coronation scene, the theophany of Venus and Amor, and the famous final duet

of Poppea and Nero, "Pur ti miro." There exists no securely established copy of the libretto or score from the first productions in 1643, and so discussion of the opera's text and music depends on widely dispersed librettos and scores of later dates. Fabbri, "New Sources for 'Poppea'," has made a compelling textual argument that the final duet, "Pur ti miro," usually thought not to be Monteverdi's, was nevertheless part of the 1643 production. There are convenient summaries of the sources and problems in Curtis's edition (v–ix), with more detail in his "*La Poppea impasticciata*" and Carter, *Monteverdi's Musical Theatre*, 263–69. For more extensive analysis, see Rosand, *Monteverdi's Last Operas*, 61–68 (on the librettos) and 88–128 (on the scores).

2. For the relation between *L'incoronazione di Poppea* and the pseudo-Senecan tragedy *Octavia*, see Rosand, "Seneca," and Heller, "Tacitus incognito," 69–70.

3. Ottavio Rinuccini (1562–1621) was the first opera librettist, having produced the texts for Peri's *La Dafne* and *Euridice*, as well as Monteverdi's *Arianna*. All these show strong influence from Ovid's *Metamorphoses* and *Heroides*. See Sternfeld, *Birth of Opera*, especially chapter 1, "Orpheus, Ovid and Opera," 1–30.

4. For the operas produced in these years in Venice, see Rosand, *Opera*, 2n1.

5. Carter, *Monteverdi's Musical Theatre*, 270.

6. Fabbri, *Il secolo cantante*, 112; Rosand, *Opera*, 110–33.

7. They were Malipiero's *L'imperatrice ambiziosa* and Pallavicino's *Le due Agrippine*. See Fabbri, *Il secolo cantante*, 110, and Heller, *Emblems of Eloquence*, 147–50.

8. Rosand, "Seneca," 34, describes the significance of the new historical material: "As a historical libretto . . . Poppea assumes a special gravity and responsibility beyond any fiction of plot. For this libretto sets up particular expectations of verisimilitude. Its characters, unlike their mythological or pastoral counterparts, demand to be measured against reality."

9. Donington, *Opera and Its Symbols*, 37–38.

10. Rosand, "Seneca," 40, and Rosand, *Monteverdi's Last Operas*, 330–37; Fenlon and Miller, *Song of the Soul*, 74, 87–89. Giuntini, "L'amore trionfante," 351, regards it as the victory of virtue inspired by love rather than by Senecan Stoicism, as exemplified by Drusilla and Ottone's devotion and loyalty, for these are virtues that survive rather than die.

11. Carter, *Monteverdi's Musical Theatre*, 271–72, was speaking of the writings of Loredano, Busenello's contemporary recently adduced as background for the Incogniti readings of the opera. Some less moralistic approaches to the opera include that of Donington, *Birth of Opera*, 232–35, who regards *Poppea* as a kind of skewed fairy tale, or even mythic *hieros gamos* (sacred marriage) in which we celebrate with the triumph of the lovers; and Carter, who places it in the spirit of the so-called paradoxical encomium; that is, praise of what cannot otherwise be praised (*Monteverdi's Musical Theatre*, 275–77). Heller concludes that "in this construction of the political Seneca, there is little persuasive endorsement of the Neostoic moral program, as argued by Fenlon and Miller, or support of the republican cause that one finds in the *Octavia*" ("Tacitus Incognito," 72–73).

12. I have treated the two elements individually and in somewhat greater detail in Ketterer, "*Militat Omnis Amans*," and "Neoplatonic Light."

13. Lindberg, *Theories of Vision*, 95, observes, "Much of the light imagery of Western thought can be traced ultimately to Plato's *Republic*, where Plato points

out that knowledge of the eternal forms is acquired by a process analogous to vision of the imperfect material world." See also Ketterer, "Neoplatonic Light," 3–8.

14. Kristeller, *Eight Philosophers*, 47–8; Lindberg, *Theories of Vision*, 95–96. The Aristotelian system was chiefly set out in the *De Caelo*; see Ross, *Aristotle*, 95–99.

15. Leclerc, "Du Mythe platonicien," 114–16.

16. Hanning, "Glorious Apollo."

17. The definitive work on the 1589 intermezzi or intermedi is Saslow, *Medici Wedding of 1589*; on the cosmic interpretation, see especially 20, 31, and 34–35. For the Platonic elements, see also Donington, *Rise of Opera*, 62–67.

18. *Asolani*, p. m, quoted and translated by Robb, *Neoplatonism*, 186 and 206–7.

19. Plato, *Timaeus*, 45c–d; Plato, *Timaeus; Critias; Cleitophon; Menexenus; Epistles*, vol. 9, trans. R. G. Bury (Cambridge, Mass.: Harvard University Press, 1989), 101, 103.

20. Lindberg, *Theories of Vision*, chap. 1, especially 3–6; also 88–89, and 95, quoted above in note 14. Examples of the Platonic theories are those of Grosseteste and Bacon (Lindberg, *Theories of Vision*, 94–103 and 113).

21. Translation by John Ciardi, *The Purgatorio* (New York: New American Library, 1957). See also *Paradiso* C. 1.46–54.

22. May, *D'Ovide à Racine*, 119–24.

23. Plato, *Lysis, Symposium, Gorgias*, vol. 3, trans. W. R. M. Lamb (Cambridge, Mass.: Harvard University Press, 1967): 109.

24. Bellori, *Lives of Annibale and Agostino Carracci*, 48. The original is in Bellori, *Le vite de' pittori*, 48. For an assessment of Bellori's analysis, see Allen, "Ovid and Art," 358.

25. Comic sources of a poetic diction for love-as-war are described in Murgatroyd, "Militia Amoris," 66–67; and Fantham, *Comparative Studies*, 26–33.

26. See further McKeown, *Ovid: Amores*, vol. 2, on poem 1.9, especially 257–60 for the development of the idea of love as war.

27. Lines 1–2, 7–8, 17–22, and 25–30. Translation adapted from Ovid, *Heroides and Amores*, 2nd ed., trans. G. Showerman and G. P. Goold (Cambridge, Mass.: Harvard University Press, 1986), 355, 357.

28. The definitive study of the form is Copley, *Exclusus Amator*.

29. Monteverdi, foreword to the book 8 madrigals, translated in Strunk, *Source Readings* 4:157–59. Commentary on the style and its relation to "Il combattimento" may be found in Rosand, "Monteverdi's Mimetic Art," 132–37; Chafe, *Monteverdi's Tonal Language*, 234–246; and Ossi, *Divining the Oracle*, 211–42. The score of "Il combattimento" is available in Malipiero, *Tutte le opere di Claudio Monteverdi*, vol. 8.

30. "Pizzicato" is not a term Monteverdi had. The instructions in the score read, "Here put aside the bow and pluck the strings with two fingers."

31. Sandbach, *Stoics*, 28. See also chapter 1.

32. Fenlon and Miller, though, concerned with the Stoic and Tacitean elements in the opera, do not discuss the prologue. But on the importance of the prologue, see Giuntini ("L'amore trionfante," especially 348–49), with whom I am in greater agreement.

33. On the character Drusilla, see Heller ("Tacitus Incognito," 63n74), who suggests the name elicits memories of Caligula's sister. There may also be reminiscences of a Drusilla in Ariosto; see Fenlon and Miller, *Song of the Soul*, 42–43.

34. "Dopo il girar delle giornate oscure, / è di giorno infinito alba la morte." The image here is not strictly Stoic; orthodox Stoics were indifferent to death, which was obliteration, or else reserved judgment on its nature. Seneca reverts to Platonic ideas of the afterlife. See Rutherford, *Meditations of Marcus Aurelius*, 248–55, for a summary and bibliography of Stoic and Senecan views of the afterlife; also see Ketterer, "Neoplatonic Light," 9n31.

35. Busenello's scene is suggested by Tacitus's account (*Annals* 15.62), where he reports that Seneca recalled his followers "from tears . . . to strength, asking what had happened to the precepts of his wisdom, what had happened to reason, that had meditated so many years over impending evil."

36. This is a main point for Rosand, "Seneca." She provides a more developed appreciation in *Monteverdi's Last Operas*, especially 174–83 and 330–37. See also Fenlon and Miller, *Song of the Soul*, 74–79; Chafe, *Monteverdi's Tonal Language*, 314–15.

37. Giuntini, "L'amore trionfante," 350; Heller, "Tacitus Incognito," 72–73.

38. On the comic pattern, see chapter 1; Ketterer, "Neoplatonic Light," 8–10 with nn. 30 and 38.

39. Compare Rosand, *Opera*, 329–30 and n. 13: "In Poppea's aria 'Speranza tu mi vai' (I.5) a vivid trumpet figure is heard several times in association with the refrain 'Per me guerregia Amor' and thus becomes thematic of the aria." I would add further that the phrase is thematic of the opera.

40. Chafe, *Monteverdi's Tonal Language*, 325, points out the tonal similarities of Nero's passages with those of Poppea in I.v ("Per me guerreggia Amor"), a linkage that suggests that Nero's *concitato* passages are also meant to be part of the "campaign of Love."

41. Ovid, *Metamorphoses* 4.256–70.

42. Ottone's character has provoked widely different reactions from critics, ranging from "Monteverdi's favorite" (Kretzschmar, "Monteverdi's *Incoronazione di Poppea*," 519) to Carter's view that he is a musically weak character in whom Monteverdi had lost interest by the third act (*Monteverdi's Musical Theatre*, 281). He is the subject of more extended discussion here in chapter 4.

43. Even if one eliminates the final duet "Pur ti miro," this duet for Poppea and Nerone in III.v constitutes a triumph of eroticism. "Pur ti miro" merely restates its conclusions. I maintain this in spite of the fact that Heller, "Tacitus Incognito," 73–91, has shown that the only real musical-sexual climax comes in II.v in Nerone's and Lucano's celebration of the death of Seneca. Heller suggests a centrality of this scene in its formation of a "homosocial—if not blatantly homoerotic—world" (84) in which Lucano's historical attachment to Roman republicanism (90) "stands for Venice's own" and gives "his voice an oratorical advantage granted no other character in the opera. . . . Nerone and Lucano construct, albeit only momentarily, an alternative society, not unlike the Incogniti themselves; a male republic, devoted to artistry and sensual pleasure, dedicated to freedom of expression and patriotic service, and committed to the exclusion of women—however desirable or dangerous." Heller grants this scene and Lucano's participation the thematic centrality that Rosand gives to Seneca. Without

challenging Heller's very thorough analysis of the important place of Lucan and his *Pharsalia* in Venetian republican ideology, I would make three observations. First, Lucan was supposed to have informed on his own mother in exchange for immunity from charges when he was caught participating in the misbegotten Pisonian conspiracy against Nero in 63 C.E. (Tacitus, *Annals* 15.56; see chapter 9 for the conspiracy), and so historically he is as tainted as any of the other characters in the opera. Second, none of the more serious aspects of the historical Lucan, including his republicanism, are overtly invoked in this scene. Third, Lucano stimulates Nerone to climax with fantasies of Poppea's mouth, not of himself or other men. His role as virtual pander in this admittedly shocking scene is, in my view, a brief, satirical debunking of yet another cultural icon rather than a serious reminder of the superiority of Venetian republicanism. In any case I do not believe that it trumps the rapturous passion of Nerone and Poppea in III.v, which dramatically is their private triumph before the public and cosmic climax of the coronation.

44. There may be a hint of what is to come, but it is muted: The nurse Arnalta, reflecting on her own life after Poppea's triumph (III.vi), concludes, "Were I to live again, I'd choose to be born a noble and die a slave. Those who must quit the high life weep when it's time to die but those who have to serve are luckier, because they welcome death as a release from toil." This must be a reflection on the fall of Ottavia, which occurs in the scene just before, but it may also be intended as a subtle reminder of Poppea's own violent end to come as empress.

45. Ketterer, "*Militat omnis amans*," 392–93.

46. This topos in the Roman elegists is called *recusatio,* or "refusal to write epic." For further background, and the development of this idea in opera, see chapter 3.

47. Compare Chafe, *Monteverdi's Tonal Language,* 308: "Love has two sides, one public and one intimate, the former allied particularly to the Nero/Poppaea relationship and imperial power. . . . [The closing duet] 'Pur ti miro' . . . is the necessary 'public' expression of their love that ends the opera."

48. On this ambivalent self-representation by Venice, see Heller, *Emblems of Eloquence,* 2–5; Rosand, *Myths of Venice,* 44–46 and 117–19; and Kallendorf, *Virgil and the Myth of Venice,* 81–84. Another example of reference to the two Venuses in Venetian opera (Cavalli's 1667 *Eliogabalo*) is described by Calcagno, "Censoring *Eliogabalo*," 369–73.

49. Fenlon and Miller, *Song of the Soul,* 93.

50. For example, Tacitus, *Annals* 13.42; Cassius Dio, *Roman History* 61.10, 61.12, 62.2; and see Syme, *Tacitus* 2:550–52.

51. For example, Bauman, "Eighteenth Century," 34; Kimbell, *Italian Opera,* 185.

Chapter 3. Scipio in Africa

1. The opera opened in February, so the libretto is dated 1664 by the Venetian calendar. For the libretto, see Brown, *Italian Opera Librettos,* vol. 8. For the score, see Brown's facsimile edition: Cavalli, *Scipione Africano.*

2. On Grossi, see Heriot, *Castrati in Opera,* 129; Barbier, *World of the Castrati,*

85; and Michael Tilmouth, "Grossi, Giovanni Francesco ['Siface']," *Grove Music Online* (accessed Dec. 4, 2006).

3. Ellen Rosand and Herbert Seifert, "Minato, Count Nicolò," *Grove Music Online* (accessed Dec. 4, 2006); Cavalli, *Scipione Africano,* "Preface," n. 3. Powers, "Serse trasformato" (Pt.1, 485–86), describes differences between the 1664 and 1678 versions.

4. This included Minato's *Pompeo Magno,* dedicated to Maria Mancini Colonna, "Prencipessa Romana Duchessa di Tagliacozza, &c"; Beregan's *Il Tito,* dedicated to Lorenzo and Maria Colonna, and to Filippo Giuliano Mancini Mazarini; and Noris's *Zenobia,* also dedicated to Filippo Giuliano Mancini Mazarini. Cavalli's *Giasone,* produced in Rome in 1671, was dedicated to Maria Colonna, but in honor of Lorenzo's election to the order of the Toson d'Oro. For Minato's connections with Colonna, see Tamburini, *Due teatri per il principe,* 60–61, 72, 92–96, 151–58, 166–67.

5. *Dizionario biografico degli Italiani* 27:352–61. For the Colonnas' historical connection with papal Rome and Spain, see Dandelet, *Spanish Rome,* 202–10. Dandelet describes a resurgence of Spanish influence in Rome in the fifteen years prior to the production of *Scipione affricano,* with an accompanying use of Roman history and legend as "both a story and stage to reflect on [Spanish Habsburg] destiny as modern heir to the Roman empire" (202). Since the Renaissance, the Colonna family had been making use of Roman history to assert their own legitimacy (Grafton, *Rome Reborn,* 91).

6. For Habsburg claims on Scipio, see Trevor-Roper, *Princes and Artists,* 28; and Tanner, *Last Descendant of Aeneas,* 116.

7. On Scipio Africanus, see Scullard, *Scipio Africanus,* and Walbank, "Scipionic Legend." For the sake of clarity we should note that Scipio Africanus the Elder is not the protagonist of Mozart's serenata "Il Sogno di Scipione." That episode, adapted from the final passages of Cicero's *De Republica,* features Scipio Africanus the Younger, the adopted grandson of Cavalli's Scipio.

8. Livy, 30.12.17–18. Livy's Numidians were a people living in North Africa west of Carthaginian territory, not the land south of Egypt, which was also known as Numidia. On Livy's adoption of this stereotype, see Haley, "Livy, Passion, and Cultural Stereotypes."

9. This presentation of ancient heroines is discussed by Garrard, *Artemisia Gentileschi,* in her "Chapter Four: Lucretia and Cleopatra," especially 210–16, and 244–77 (on Cleopatra). In reference to opera generally, the fundamental treatment is Clément, *Opera, or the Undoing of Women.* For early opera, see Heller, *Emblems of Eloquence.*

10. For discussions of the theme in drama, see Ricci, *Sophonisbe dans la tragédie,* and Axelrad, *Le thème de Sophonisbe.* Niderst in Corneille, *Théâtre Complet* 3:1, 231, lists seven dramas that follow Trissino's and lead up to Corneille's. For a more complete list of works on Sophonisba, see Stroup and Cooke, *Works of Nathaniel Lee,* 1:458n3.

11. "Der Tod der Sophonisbe," in Pigler, *Barockthemen* 2:433–35.

12. On comparison of Sophonisba to Cleopatra, see Butler and Scullard, *Livy, Book XXX,* 96, note to section xii.16: "The Egyptian princess Arsinoe was forced to walk in chains in Julius Caesar's triumph in 46 B.C. Doubtless the fall of Cleopatra, which had occurred during Livy's lifetime, was vivid in his memory as he

composed this account of Sophonisba." See also Pelling, *Life of Antony,* 17n66 and 314. Moscovich, "Cassius Dio on the Death of Sophonisba," shows verbal parallels in the presentation of the two women observable in Dio's accounts.

13. Translation by David West in Horace, *The Complete Odes and Epodes* (Oxford: Oxford University Press, 1997), 54–55.

14. Compare also V.ii.207–19: *Cleopatra*: Now, Iras, what think'st thou? / Thou, an Egyptian puppet, shall be shown / In Rome as well as I: . . . Saucy lictors / Will catch at us like strumpets, and scald rhymers / Ballad us out o' tune. The quick comedians / Extemporally will stage us, and present / Our Alexandrian revels: Antony / Shall be brought drunken forth, and I shall see / Some squeaking Cleopatra boy my greatness / I' th' posture of a whore.

15. On Dido as a literary response to Cleopatra, see Pelling, *Plutarch's Life of Antony,* 17, who cites Jasper Griffin, *Latin Poets and Roman Life* (London: Duckworth, 1985), 183–97.

16. Trissino's Sophonisba regards Dido as her first ancestress, whereas the Romans are the descendants of that Aeneas who deceived "unhappy Dido" (*la infelice Dido*) and in deceiving and abandoning her was the cause of her death (prologue, 35–39). Mairet reworks Dido's curse against Aeneas and the Romans from *Aeneid* 4.607–29 into a curse by Masinissa against Scipio and the Romans just before he commits a very ahistorical suicide at the end of the play (V.viii).

17. Disce, puer, virtutem ex me verumque laborem, / fortunam ex aliis.

18. Walsh, *Livy,* 94; and Scullard, *Scipio Africanus,* 27.

19. For Ovid's explicit reference to *Aeneid* 1.1, see McKeown, *Ovid: Amores* 2:11–12.

20. We have already observed this refusal to write epic poetry, or *recusatio,* in *L'incoronazione di Poppea* (chapter 2). Generally couched in a declaration of disability as the result of a god's command, the *recusatio* was a trope inherited by the Romans from Hellenistic poetry. It was common in Latin lyric and elegiac poetry, practiced by Horace (*Satires* 2.1, *Odes* 4.15), Propertius (*Elegies* 2.1 and 3.3), and even Vergil himself in his earlier poems, the *Eclogues* (6.3–12). See Lucas, "Recusatio"; and Wimmel, *Kallimachos in Rom,* 162–67. Roman *recusatio* is sometimes read as resistance to the Augustan program, but McKeown, rightly I believe, insists that in the *Amores* it is simply a humorous assertion of Ovid's own program and intentions (McKeown, *Ovid: Amores* 2:7–11).

21. Viva, Viva, Scipione . . . Vinse 'l Fato latino; & esser vol / De' Romani trionfi / Partiale 'l Destino.

22. Le Vittorie del Tebro / Il Fato le commanda, / La Fortuna le deve: / Altro non fà chi à guerreggiar s'accinge / Per l'impero Romano, / Che à i doni del Destin stender la mano.

23. Scene designations differ between libretto and score, especially in the first half of act 1. Notation indicates the scene numbers from libretto/score, as, for example, here: 1.4/5.

24. *Siface.* Dite ò Cieli, s'è l'istesso / Quel destin, che Rè mi fè, / e ch' infausto e crudo adesso / Mi legò tra ferri 'l piè. . . . / [*recit.*] Sfortunato Siface! In pochi istanti / E regno e moglie e libertà perdei; / E m'è rimasto , oh Dio! / Tanto di mondo à pena / Quanto misurar breve catena. (This is the score's text, pp. 13–14. In the third line of the stanza, the libretto reads, "E che misero, e depresso.")

25. Con acutissima / Saetta d'or / Quell' alma asprissima / Deh pungi Amor; / Onde sen' fuggano, / E si distruggano / I suoi rigor (p. 81 of the score).

26. Vibran dardi più pungenti, / Che di Scitia le saette / Due vezzose pupillette. // Più che Marte con sue schiere / Fà prigion 'l Dio bendato / Con un crine inanellato. (p. 37 of the score.)

27. Se non seppe 'l Dio de l'armi / Trionfarmi / Men sarò d'un nudo arciero / Prigioniero. // Se l'ardor d'un Dio feroce / Non mi nuoce, / Men potrà lascivo Infante / Farmi amante. (p. 49 of the score.)

28. Glover, *Cavalli*, 92–94, notes that this technique is typical of Cavalli.

29. Ma quai ritrovo, ò Cieli, / Apparati funesti? / Vase, catene, e fogli? / Ah forse questi / Son di Scipion gl'inchiostri? (*Legge:*) "O con queste catene in aspra sorte / Stringiti prigioniera; / O con questo velen bevi la morte." / Misera, oh Dio, che sento? / Così dunque i tuoi doni, empio Latino, / Crudelmente ritogli? / E de la cieca inesorabile Diva / Imitando i vestiggi / Alletti gl' infelici e poi gl' affligi? / Quest' e la Libertà, questo e lo sposo / à cui mi riserbasti? (108–9 of the score.)

30. O voi, che portate / De l'amoroso ardor / Acceso il cor / Sperate pur sperate, / Eh, non sono d'Amor / Lunghe le noie, / Hà principio di duol, e fin di gioie.

31. The opera was first produced in 1651. Quotes here and below are from the revised and expanded 1654 edition: *Alessandro, Il vincitor di se stesso*, tragico-media musicale di Francesco Sbarra (Lucca: F. Marescandoli, 1654).

32. An anachronism: Cato the Elder was a contemporary of Scipio Africanus the Younger, not Scipio Africanus the Elder. The character of Cato may be an inheritance from Trissino's *Sofonisba*, where he appears as Scipio's adviser and the sober voice of reason.

33. Compare the stichomythic argument between Nerone and Seneca in *Poppea* (I.ix).

Chapter 4. Otho in Arcadia

1. It is not entirely certain that Vincenzo Grimani was the libretto's author; see Sawyer, "Irony and Borrowings," 531n1. I have accepted Grimani's authorship, but any interpretation based on that assumption must remain tentative.

2. The libretto for *Agrippina* is in Harris, *Librettos of Handel's Operas*, vol. 1; the score is printed in the German Handel Society edition (Leipzig 1874). The libretto and facsimile score of *Ottone in villa* are in John Hill's edition. Hill describes the debt of *Ottone in villa* to *Messalina* at xvii–xxi.

3. *Galba* 19.2. Other sources on Otho besides *Galba* include Plutarch, *Otho*; Tacitus, *Histories*, especially 1.46–2.49, and *Annals* 13.12, 13.45–46; Suetonius, *Otho*; and Cassius Dio, *Roman History*, 63.10–15.

4. Montaigne, *Complete Essays*, 198.

5. Harris, *Handel and the Pastoral Tradition*, 11.

6. Poggioli, *Oaten Flute*, describes the inclusion of Christian (105–34) and Stoic (187, 192) transformations of the pastoral in the early modern period. Both these influences are essentially antithetical to the eroticism of the pastoral, focused as they both are on spiritual purity and the transcendent triumph of the soul, which have nothing to do with the worldly wish fulfillment of the pastoral impulse. Nevertheless, the boundaries of Christian, Stoic, and pastoral systems are

extremely permeable, and the pastoral elements in opera can shift easily from one mode of reference to another without serious violation of feeling.

7. Foley, Homeric *"Hymn to Demeter,"* 33–34, on the Greek tradition connected with the abduction of Persephone. In Roman literature, see Ovid's *Metamorphoses* for multiple examples, including 1.588–600 (Io), 1.689–708 (Syrinx), 2.833–875 (Europa), 5.385–408 (Proserpina).

8. The English and Italian traditions are parallel rather than dependent on each other. Henke, *Pastoral Transformations,* 19–32, especially 31. Henke proposes the rubric "tragicomedy in the pastoral mode" to describe such dramas that are not strictly pastoral but that participate in pastoral themes or sensibilities (45).

9. Harbison, *Reflections on Baroque,* 151–52. Harbison makes his observation by way of demonstrating a rococo substitution of storm music for the underworld journey as the place where emotional conflict and intensity in Rameau's operas collide.

10. By one account, this is an inversion of the historical situation. The reason Otho was sent off to govern Lusitania was his practice of locking the doors against Nero's access to Poppaea rather than being closed out himself (Suetonius, *Otho,* 3.2).

11. On the intersection and mutual suitability of the chivalric and pastoral traditions, see Harris, *Handel and the Pastoral Tradition,* 5–8; Cody, *Landscape of the Mind,* 10, quoting J. Huizinga, *Men and Ideas,* trans. J. S. Holmes and H. van Marle (New York: Meridian, 1959), 85.

12. Fenlon and Miller, *Song of the Soul,* 24–25 with 74–75.

13. The others are Giulio Cesare Corradi's *Il Nerone* (1679), Matteo Noris's *Il ripudio d'Ottavia* (1699), and Francesco Silvani's *La fortezza al cimento* (1699). Noris's *Nerone fatto Cesare* was revived in Florence in 1708, where Handel could have heard it (Dean and Knapp, *Handel's Operas,* 80).

14. See Rouvière, "L'équation vénitienne." On the transitional nature of the libretto, see also Strohm, "Händel in Italia," 167; Saunders, "Handel's 'Agrippina'"; Dean and Knapp, *Handel's Operas,* 118.

15. He composed this cantata, known also by its opening words "Dunque sarà pur vero," about 1708, but details are lacking. Burrows, *Handel,* 418.

16. Dean and Knapp, *Handel's Operas,* 119. Wolff called the scenes in Poppea's bedroom "pure comic opera" ("già pura opera buffa") in "L'opera comica," 43.

17. One might expect a change of scene here, but none is indicated in the libretto or in the autograph score (Dean and Knapp, *Handel's Operas,* 116n4).

18. Strohm, "Händel in Italia," 169–70. For Grimani's career, see *Dizionario biografico degli Italiani* 59:658–662.

19. Habsburg connections with imperial Rome are discussed in fuller detail in chapter 5.

20. Saunders, "Handel's 'Agrippina'," 253, challenges Strohm's interpretation. In any case, since Grimani's authorship is not certain, political interpretations of the opera based on the events of his career are speculative.

21. Mellers describes Claudius as "the authentic man-god of the heroic world, played by a bass of gargantuan range" (*Masks of Orpheus,* 74). Mellers's comparison of *Poppea* and *Agrippina* (74–75) is flawed in several of its details—Nero was not Claudius's son, and the bass range labels Claudius as something other

than a man-god—but his analysis is helpful in its perceptions about the role of Ottone.

22. For the libretto and score of *Messalina,* see Selfridge-Field, *Messalina.* The errant atoms in this passage are Lucretian, but Lucretius denies that nature consists of four elements (*De Rerum Natura* 1.705–829). More relevant is *Metamorphoses* 1.5–31.

23. Stormy weather seemed to please Vivaldi. Stormy seas form the titles of concertos RV 98, 253, 309 (lost), 433, and 570. There are also two motets on the subject: RV 627, "In turbato mare irato," and RV 632, "Sum in medio tempestatum." Sawyer, "Irony and Borrowings," 546, mentions the imagery of weather and sailing in *Agrippina.*

24. Di tempestoso mar, nel gran periglio / Rimase assorta l'Aquila latina. / E Claudio il tuo consorte / Nell' occidio commun provò la morte.

25. L'infido mar, geloso / Che restasse alla terra un tal tesoro / Lo rapì a noi.

26. Qual portentoso / fulmine è questi? / Ah, ingrato / Cesare, infidi amici, e Cieli ingiusti!

27. *Coro*: Lieto il Tebro increspi l'onda / Sotto i rai del novo allor. / E festeggi sù la sponda / Pien di gioia il Dio d'amor. / *Giunone*: D'Oton, e di Popea sul lieto innesto / Scende Giuno dal Cielo à sparger gigli; / E nel Talamo eccelso io lieta appresto / Vassalli à Claudio, e alta Roma i figli. // V'accendono le Tede / I raggi delle stelle; / Esse per tante fede / Risplendono più belle.

28. See Ketterer, "Neoplatonic Light," 21.

29. Most notably, Sawyer, "Irony and Borrowings," especially 544–57, argues that Handel's self-borrowings for the reconciliation scenes between Poppea and Ottone in act III suggest the composer's doubt about its permanence. Sawyer also believes (534) that the "bitter-sweet languor" heard under Nerone's renunciation of passion in III.xi undermines his expressed intentions and suggests his amorous behavior will return. For the ironies of Handel's music in this opera, see also Mellers, *Masks of Orpheus,* 75.

30. Zimmerman's words in the chapter epigraph and here are from her "Eros and Psyche" episode in *Metamorphoses,* 76.

31. Pastoral elements in Vivaldi's music include the lengthy echo scene in II.iii, which is typical of pastoral pieces (below, note 39); and three arias in one sceneset that are in *siciliana* style. See Hill, *Ottone in villa,* xvi and xxxiii.

32. I owe this observation to Wendy Heller. Muraro, *Venetian Villas,* reviews the history of these villas and their grounds with lavish illustrations. Muraro says (92) that the gardens assumed an increasing importance in the plan of these villas, "so much so that the villa could be reduced to a scenic backdrop destined to be seen as a background to the garden."

33. See especially Plutarch's *Otho,* 3, for his identification with Nero, as well as his even-handed and mild treatment of both aristocracy and military.

34. The scenes used were I.i–ix and III.xi–xvi. See Hill, *Ottone in villa,* xvii–xxi.

35. Hill, *Ottone in villa,* xx–xxi.

36. Treated in detail in Heller, *Emblems of Eloquence,* 263–94. Cleonilla's opening recitative marks her at once as what Heller calls (266) "a particular type of heroine [from the late 1670s and early '80s]: the lascivious, promiscuous, and intelligent woman—usually juxtaposed with a foolish, tyrannical ruler—who

embodied those qualities associated with both the courtesan and the more negative aspects of Venus as Venice."

37. Hill, *Ottone in villa*, xiii, argues that the music mocks the thought and hides what Caio really feels. But it is true also that the echo foreshadows the real echo scene where he will confront those feelings for us more openly.

38. Poggioli, *Oaten Flute*, 4; Harris, *Handel and the Pastoral Tradition*, 2–11.

39. On the echo technique, see Sternfeld, *Birth of Opera*, 197–226; and "Echo," in *MGG Sachteil* 2:1623–38. Mary Térey-Smith, "Echo, 2. Compositional Use and Performing Practice," Grove Music Online (accessed Dec. 4, 2006).

40. Barkan's analysis of the Ovidian passage in *Gods Made Flesh*, 47–52, has been helpful here.

41. For a Narcissus reference in which the desired object is actually one's lover rather than oneself, see Ronsard, *Amours* 20, quoted in Barkan, *Gods Made Flesh*, 220. The lover wishes he could be a Narcissus, and she a fountain in which he might plunge himself all night long (& elle une fontaine / pour m'y plonger une nuict à sejour.)

42. The mirror appears later, in II.vi. Cleonilla is discovered sitting in a rustic lodge, admiring her own image in a mirror: "Happy is my countenance, not because it adorns its proud brow with pretty gems and flowers, but because it only dresses its hair with the hearts of unfortunate lovers." The broken hearts of her conquests rather grotesquely replace the decorative flowers she had gathered for her bosom in the first act.

43. Hill, *Ottone in villa*, xiii.

44. Ibid., xvi.

Chapter 5. Scipio in Spain

1. Negri, *Vita di Apostolo Zeno*, 118. Zeno dealt with Clerici again when he was negotiating the terms of his moving to Vienna to become *poeta cesareo* in 1718 (*Lettere*, no. 412, vol. 2, pp. 401–4). In 1710 Zeno was writing by commission in Venice. For the text of *Scipione nelle Spagne* I have used his 1710 libretto printed in Barcelona.

2. If so, it was not the same setting as Caldara's score for the 1722 production in Vienna. See Freeman, *Opera Without Drama*, 287n2; and Sala di Felice, "Zeno," 82–83, on the context and setting of the 1710 production.

3. A 1740 setting by Leo (Sartori no. 21297) and a 1768 production in Milan with music by Bartoni (Sartori no. 21300) are, judging by their cast lists, versions of Piovene's 1712 libretto *Publio Cornelio Scipione* rather than of Zeno's, despite being titled *Scipione nelle Spagne*.

4. Trevor-Roper, *Princes and Artists*, 28 and figure on page 29. See also Strong, *Splendour at Court*, 94–95 and figures 74–75, for arches in Naples and Rome celebrating his connections with Scipio, the latter hailing Charles V as the *Tertio Africano*.

5. See Tanner, *Last Descendant of Aeneas*, 98–118; Matsche, *Die Kunst im Dienst der Staatsidee* 1:273–371.

6. Matsche, *Die Kunst im Dienst der Staatsidee* 1:68–78.

7. Ibid. 1:74, on clemency and justice as Habsburg ideals.

8. On Zeno's life and career, see Sala di Felice, "Zeno"; and Fehr, *Apostolo Zeno*.

9. In Boccabadati's *Scipione* (I.i) she is reported to have flung herself into the sea from a mere terrace, so Zeno's tower is a deliberate change.

10. This is Zeno's choice, based on Arcadian principles, as Boccabadati's play has comic servants and overtly comic scenes.

11. Smith, *Tenth Muse*, 69: "With Zeno, the *opera seria* achieved a more or less stereotyped form. . . . There was one main theme (always accompanied by the secondary one of love), upon which the librettist rang changes for three, four or five acts."

12. Braden, "Drama," 261.

13. Ibid.; Russell, "Spanish Literature," 358. On casuistry in Golden Age Spanish literature, see 314.

14. The Spanish influence finds its way to France, where it is evident in, for example, Corneille's *Le Cid* (1637), in which Don Rodrigo is faced with the prospect of taking vengeance for an insult to his father by the father of the woman he loves. If he fails to challenge and defeat the perpetrator of the insult, he will not only dishonor his own family but also lose the respect of his beloved, even though by killing her father he becomes her enemy. *Le Cid* is Corneille's overtly Spanish-style play, but *Cinna* (1640), his drama about Cornelius Cinna's plot on the life of the emperor Augustus, displays a similar fascination with moral conundrums (see chapter 8). Zeno inherits the casuistical arguments most directly from Boccabadati, although he elaborates upon them.

15. On neo-Stoicism in Italy and Venice, see Oestreich, *Neostoicism and the Early Modern State*, 104–5.

16. Russell, "Spanish Literature," 334–37.

17. Arnold, *Roman Stoicism*, 308–9.

18. Vedrò anche il mondo al tuo valor sommesso, / Or che con tanto amor, vinto hai tè stesso.

19. Ancient sources on Cato the Younger include Plutarch, *Cato*. For modern analyses, see Gelzer, "Cato Uticensis"; and Goar, *Legend of Cato Uticensis*.

20. Theobald, *Life and Character of Marcus Portius Cato Uticensis*, 4–5.

21. Plutarch, *Cato* 52.4–5, reports that Caesar in his *Anticato* called the transaction an act of venality, calculated to bring Cato Hortensius's considerable fortune. Plutarch goes on to deny that this could be the case, "for it is like reproaching Herakles for cowardice to accuse Cato of shameful greed."

22. *Purgatorio*, C.1.85–90, trans. John Ciardi, *The Purgatorio* (New York: New American Library, 1957).

23. The compliment to Elizabeth Christina was even more marked in Zeno's *Atenaide*, the opera paired in 1710 with *Scipione nelle Spagne* in Barcelona. See Sala di Felice, "Zeno," 82–84.

24. Boccabadati's equivalent character to Sofonisba is Nisida, Principessa di Celtiberi, so again the choice is Zeno's. The name Elvira is also taken from Boccabadati, but the equivalent character to Zeno's Elvira in Boccabadati is named Irene (i.e., "Peace"), Principessa de Celtici. Her maidservant is Elvira. As we will see below, the change is appropriate for what Zeno does with the character.

25. Cardenio's name, too, was familiar from seventeeth-century Spanish fiction,

including Cervante's *Don Quixote* (Pt.1, chapter 24). See, for example, Powell, *Cardenio und Celinde*, lxxv.

26. Livy 26.49; Polybius, *Histories* 10.18.

27. Michel de Montaigne, "Of the Inconsistency of Our Actions," in Montaigne, *Complete Essays*, 241. Montaigne's point is not quite the same as Zeno's. He goes on to say that he learned later that the woman was not "so hard to come to terms with" and concludes that though you may not have any luck with a lady, that does not mean she is inviolably chaste.

28. Möbius, *Woman of the Baroque Age*, 147, fig. 117.

29. The scene in the opera is Zeno's creation; Scipione is not present in Boccabadati's version.

30. This passage appears to be a reassertion of the Platonic notion of love as a means to higher reality, famous from the *Symposium* and repeated often in opera at its early Neoplatonic stages. See chapter 2.

31. Ergiti, amor, sù vanni; / E prendi ardito il volo / Senza abbassarti più. / Perchè con nuovi inganni / Tù non ricada al suolo, / Lo sosterrà virtù.

32. The difference between Zeno and his source is instructive here. Boccabadati invented Luceio's final refusal to take his beloved from Scipio, as well as the choice of Irene/Elvira as arbiter by a process of elimination. But Irene's choice in Boccabadati's play has not the moral authority of Zeno's Elvira, as Irene has no equivalent soliloquy to Elvira's aria in which she describes her love as flying toward heaven.

33. Matsche, *Die Kunst im Dienst der Staatsidee* 1:274–75.

34. Ariosto, *Orlando Furioso*, c. 15.22, trans. Sir John Harington (1634), cited in Yates, *Astraea*, 53. For this imagery as it continued to be applied to Philip II of Spain, see Tanner, *Last Descendant of Aeneas*, 137.

35. Matsche, *Die Kunst im Dienst der Staatsidee* 1:212–18.

36. The equation of Astraea with the Virgin Mary goes back to the time of Constantine. See Tanner, *Last Descendant of Aeneas*, 31–32 and n. 41.

37. Below, chapters 6 and 9.

38. Francis, *First Peninsular War*, 292.

39. Zeno was already working with the themes that became important to Charles's program in his early *drammi per musica*, and thus he was especially suited to service with the Habsburgs. See Sala di Felice, "Zeno," passim, but especially 87 with the chart of Zeno's favored themes on 114.

40. The Habsburg appropriation of the Romans on the operatic stage had been going on for decades. It included operas by Minato, and was continued by Stampiglia, whose reform librettos on Roman themes had been produced for Vienna since 1705.

41. *Lettere*, no. 13, vol. 1, p. 24.

42. Zeno negotiated for several months for agreeable conditions for his move to Vienna, and his own sense of his worth is summed up in his assertion in a letter to Marchese Giorgio Clerici (Jan. 22, 1718) that he ought to be maintained at the court in Vienna "with that decorum and propriety that is appropriate to the Monarch's dignity, to the honor of the position, and if I may be permitted to say so, to my own birth and condition" (*Lettere*, no. 412, vol. 2, p. 402). In the same letter he refuses to write comic drama, but he also will not write anything except

dramas and nominates his friend Pariati to be a second poet in the court for other purposes. His demands were met. On April 9, 1718, he wrote to Salvino Salvini, "My summons to Vienna is solidly confirmed (*verissima*). The conditions offered me have been so respectable and advantageous that I haven't been able to refuse them" (*Lettere,* no. 419, vol. 2, p. 416).

43. Sala di Felice, "Zeno," 87–88.

44. Zeno set out an appreciation of the limits and possibilities of his art in *Lettere,* no. 756, vol. 4, pp. 276–80, to Marchese Giuseppe Gravisi (Nov. 3, 1730).

45. Francis, *First Peninsular War,* 286. Compare Zeno, *Lettere,* no. 1119, vol. 6, p. 95, to Domenico Vandelli (Dec. 30, 1740): "I have composed about fifty dramas on various occasions and in various places. Those I wrote in the service of my August Patron, of glorious memory—and for me, a memory always cherished and sorrowful—were the most tolerable."

46. According to Negri, *Vita di Apostolo Zeno,* 118, Charles was so pleased with the librettos that he sent copies back to his brother, the emperor Joseph, with the boast, "[T]hus do my poets serve me!"

47. Ed in lui rispettate / Quanto di grande unqua formar gli Dei. / Il suo nome in alto grido / Mare, lido, / E Cielo acclama. / Solo il cor / È maggior / De la sua fama.

48. The licenze dedicated to Charles at the end of *Ormisda* and *Venceslao* also celebrate him through his *nome,* but that does not negate its particular relevance to the material here.

49. Horace, *Epistles* 2.1 (*Epistle to Augustus*), 156–57.

50. Matsche, *Die Kunst im Dienst der Staatsidee* 1:276.

Chapter 6. The Problem of Caesar

1. Sallust, *Bellum Catilinae,* 10, is the clearest statement of the idea; see also Sallust's *Bellum Iugurthinum,* 41; Polybius, 31.25; Livy, *Praefatio* to books 1–5, and 39.6.

2. Widdows, *Lucan's Civil War,* xix. For a more extended analysis see Caesar as Lucan's demon and Stoic villain, see Marti, "Meaning of the Pharsalia," 362–67.

3. The music was supposedly by Cavalli for a Venetian production, but it is lost and possibly was never composed or performed. See Rosand, *Opera,* 108 and n. 99.

4. Letter of Pope to John Caryll, April 30, 1713, in Sherburn, *Correspondence of Alexander Pope,* 175.

5. On the question of a dedication, see Smithers, *Life of Joseph Addison,* 265–66; and Loftis, *Politics of Drama,* 60.

6. "Cato Examined: or, Animadversions on the Fable or Plot, *Manners, Sentiments* and *Diction* of the New Tragedy of Cato, with a Comparison of the Characters of the *Dramatical* and *Historical* Hero," which is included with the 1713 edition of *Cato* (London: John Pemberton). This aversion to factionalism was a preoccupation in contemporary political writing (Smith, *Handel's Oratorios,* 186–87).

7. Rand, *Berkeley and Percival,* 114.

8. *Spectator,* no. 18, March 21, 1711, in Bond, *Spectator,* vol. 1, p. 81.

9. The reference may be to a story that Cato left a theater in Rome when he realized that his forbidding presence was hampering the crowd's enjoyment of the customary indecencies performed at the Floralia festival: Valerius Maximus, *Memorable Deeds and Sayings,* 2.10.8; Seneca, *Moral Epistles* 97.8; Martial, *Epigrams,* book 1, introductory epistle.

10. *Spectator,* no. 39, April 14, 1711, in Bond, *Spectator,* vol. 1, pp. 163–64. See also Smithers, *Life of Joseph Addison,* 259–60. Smith, *Handel's Oratorios,* especially 52–80, elucidates attitudes toward stage and music that ultimately led Handel and his librettists to create the English oratorio as a music drama that better embodied the ideals of the age.

11. Berkeley to Percival, May 7, 1713, in Rand, *Berkeley and Percival,* 115–16; Pope to Caryll, April 30, 1713, in Sherburn, *Correspondence of Alexander Pope,* 174–75; G. Smalridge to Addison, August 2, 1713, in Graham, *Letters of Joseph Addison,* 483–84.

12. Noce, "Early Italian Translations of Addison's *Cato.*"

13. See Litto, "Addison's *Cato* in the Colonies," especially 440–47.

14. "But *Cato* itself has increased the evils of the present time, how many poetasters have since then infested the world with wild notions of liberty and patriotism!" The essay, in *The Universal Spectator,* April 10, 1731, is signed "Crito." See Loftis, *Essays on the Theatre,* 17; and Loftis, *Politics of Drama,* 82.

15. The original libretto of 1724 is available in Harris, *Librettos of Handel's Operas* 4:1–93. The score has most recently been edited and published by Dean and Fuller, *Giulio Cesare.*

16. Handel revived *Giulio Cesare* in London in 1725, 1730, and 1732. A concert version was performed in Paris in 1724 and staged versions in Brunswick (1725, 1727, and 1733) and thirty-nine times in Hamburg between 1725 and 1737. Dean and Knapp, *Handel's Operas,* 500–507; Dean and Fuller, *Giulio Cesare,* x–xi.

17. Knapp, "Handel's *Giulio Cesare in Egitto,*" 389. The unusual care in preparation of the score for the premiere in 1724 and the close collaboration of librettist and composer that can be observed makes it somewhat easier in the case of this opera to talk about dramatic purpose and intended effect than others from the Baroque period. On the process of composition in 1724, see Burrows, *Handel,* 136–37; and Dean and Knapp, *Handel's Operas,* 508–16.

18. The production in Munich and Peter Sellars's at Purchase, New York, were hugely successful because they respected Handel's score and the humanity emerges irresistibly, sometimes because of and sometimes despite scenic concepts. For descriptions and reactions, see the following: Munich, 1994: *Opernwelt* 5 (May 1994): 18–21; *Opera* (England) 45 (June 1994): 718–20; *Musical Opinion* 117 (Summer 1994): 205; Houston Grand Opera, 2003–4: *Newsletter of the American Handel Society* 23.3 (Dec. 2003): 1, 3; *Opera* (England) 55 (Jan. 2004): 78–80; *Opera News* 68 (Feb. 2004): 57–58. On the PepsiCo Summerfare at Purchase, 1985: *New Yorker* 61 (July 15, 1985): 21–23, and 61 (July 29, 1985): 70–72; on the video version, *Opera Quarterly* 10.4 (1994): 118–21.

19. I am not alone in this opinion. See Monson, "*Giulio Cesare in Egitto,*" 322–23; and Kubik, "Die angenehme," especially 51–53.

20. Imperialistic conquest in the interest of mercantile gain was not without its detractors, however. See Smith, *Handel's Oratorios,* 244 with n. 28.

21. Ruth Smith, in program notes on *Giulio Cesare* for the 2005 Glyndebourne season ("Playing with History for a Discerning Audience") and in a paper titled "Shaping Caesar for Senesino's Audience" at the American Handel Festival 2007 (Princeton, April 21) noted that the 1723–24 season in London was a remarkably "Roman" season: In addition to *Giulio Cesare* and *Cato*, there were productions of Shakespeare's *Julius Caesar*, Dryden's *All for Love*, Bononcini's opera *Calfurnia*, and three operas by Ariosti: *Vespasiano, Coriolano*, and *Aquilio consolo*. See "Season of 1723–24," *London Stage*, pt. 2, vol. 2, 735–84.

22. Elioseff, *Cultural Milieu*, 77. Compare Russell, *Voltaire, Dryden and Heroic Tragedy*, 59: "A more prosaic age of morality and social decorum began with the coming of William and Mary. Heroic romances were not approved, and tragedians turned to Republican Rome for their heroes."

23. Addison in *Spectator*, no. 18, March 21, 1711, in Bond, *Spectator*, vol. 1, p. 81.

24. On Handel's audience, see Hunter, "Patronizing Handel." On the disturbances over the singers, see Burrows, *Handel*, 102–33, but especially 112–14 for the period around 1724. It is true that there were sometimes political issues as well. The consequences of an opera plot injudiciously presented were seen in Handel's 1721–22 *Floridante*, where a royal father-son rivalry looked too much like the current tensions between the king and the prince of Wales (Burrows, *Handel*, 110). For what appears to be a more positive approach to a similar situation, see the discussion of Handel's *Arminio* in chapter 7.

25. A translation of Bussani's libretto along with Sartorio's score has been edited and published by Monson in Sartorio, *Giulio Cesare in Egitto*.

26. "Col guardo, / Meglio, ch'egli non fece / Col capo di Pompeo, / Cesare obligherò." The translations of *Giulio Cesare* given here come from the 1724 libretto. They are not literal but usually do not stray too far. Important exceptions are noted.

27. This is a considerable expansion from Bussani's II.iv, which merely has "Lydia" sing "V'adoro pupille, saette d'Amore" offstage to lure Caesar to the garden of Adonis in a later scene.

28. In Bussani the aria is different. After his initial horror, Caesar in recitative dismisses Achilla and comments that Tolomeo has robbed the Roman standard of its most noble thunderbolt, but that he pardons him because of his youth and inexperience (I.iii; Monson, no. 7). The Naples version adds a brief aria in which he reflects on the mutability of Fate.

29. Translation by Bernadotte Perrin, *Plutarch's Lives*, vol. 7 (London: Heinemann, 1928), 555, 557.

30. For example, I.xvii (Monson, no. 44): "This heart will always be / Enchained as your prisoner." And II.iv (Monson, nos. 7 and 9): "I am a prisoner of the naked archer"; and "This heart is condemned / To imprisonment by a lock of hair. . . . Freedom, I have already released you. / I stand adoring my chains / Of growing bulk."

31. Alma del gran Pompeo / Che al cener suo d'intorno / Invisibil t'aggiri, / Fur ombra i tuoi trofei / Ombra la tua grandezza, e un' ombra sei. / Così termina alfine il fasto umano. / Ieri chi vivo occupò un mondo in guerra, / Oggi risolto in polve un' urna serra. / Tal di ciascuno, ahi lasso, / Il principio è di terra e il fine è un sasso. / Misera vita, oh quanto è fral tuo stato! / Ti forma un soffio, e ti distrugge un fiato.

32. Stat magni nominis umbra / qualis frugifero quercus sublimis in agro / Exuvias veteres populi sacrataque gestans / Dona ducum nec iam validis radicibus haerens / Pondere fixa suo est, nudosque per aera ramos / Effundens trunco, non frondibus, efficit umbram; / Et quamvis primo nutet casura sub Euro, / Tot circum silvae firmo se robore tollant, / Sola tamen colitur. Sed non in Caesare tantum / Nomen erat nec fama ducis, sed nescia virtus / Stare loco, solusque pudor non vincere bello. The 1994 Munich production (above, note 18) included in its opening scenes a towering *Tyrannosaurus rex* that slowly collapsed after the death of Pompey. (For the images, see *Opernwelt* 5 [May 1994]: 18–21.) I do not know if they had this passage of Lucan in mind, but if I am right about the debt of "Alma del gran Pompeo" to Lucan, then the Munich production's conception is on the right track.

33. Further inspiration for the passage may come from the end of Lucan's book 8, when a faithful slave has given Pompey's headless body a meager burial on the Egyptian seashore, Lucan reflects that the shade (*umbra*) still lies in exile from Rome; lines 855–72 reflect on the impermanence of the ash and stone that mark Pompey's poor resting place.

34. The scene is very different from Bussani's III.vi: Haym developed two recitative lines of Curione, who has rescued Cesare, and Achilla, Sesto, and Cornelia are all on stage. Haym's adaptation gives Senesino another aria, but that motivation does not change how we view what Haym and Handel chose to do with it dramatically.

35. Translation by Bernadotte Perrin (see note 29), 561. Cf. [Caesar], *Alexandrian War*, 21; Suetonius, *Caesar*, 64; and Cassius Dio, *Roman History*, 42.40. This battle (although not Caesar's heroic swim) is the last surviving episode in Lucan's *Pharsalia*, and one of the moments when he at once admires and mocks Caesar's "demonic energy."

36. See especially the first of the two essays titled "On the Fortune or the Virtue of Alexander the Great," *Moralia* 336c–333c. On the popularity and widespread availability of the works of Plutarch after antiquity, see Russell, *Plutarch*, 143–63.

37. 328b.4, and cf. 332e–f. Translation by F. C. Babbitt, *Plutarch's Moralia*, vol. 4 (Cambridge, Mass., 1936), 392.

38. The English interprets rather than translates the Italian: V'adoro pupille / Saette d'amore, / Le vostre faville / Son grate nel Sen. / Pietose vi brama / Il mesto mio Core, / Che ogn'ora vi chiama / l'amato suo ben.

39. J. M. Rysbrack created a similar image of George I in Roman imperial dress, dated c. 1739, now at the Cambridge University Law Library.

40. Ketterer, "Handel's *Scipione.*"

41. As noted above, there were at least six Italian translations of *Cato* available. See note 12, and Brunelli, *Tutte le opere di Pietro Metastasio*, 1:1397.

42. In Matteo Noris's *Catone Uticense* for Venice, 1701, Cato appeared onstage mortally wounded but exits after swooning in Caesar's arms and blessing the union between his son Floro and Caesar's sister (see chapter 1, figure 3).

43. Both passages quoted in Brunelli, *Tutte le opere di Pietro Metastasio*, 1:1399n8. The text of the libretto is quoted from Brunelli's edition.

44. *Il trionfo della libertà*, an opera on the Lucretia story by Frigimelica-Roberti for Venice in 1707 (music by Scarlatti) included Lucretia's death but was not a

success. For other experiments in tragic denouements early in the eighteenth century, see Strohm, "Antonio Salvi's *Amore e maestà* and the *funesto fine* in Opera," 169–70.

45. Warburton, *Catone in Utica*, ix–xii.

46. *Argomento*, p. 5, *Catone in Utica*, Drama per Musica, Del Signor Abbato Pietro Metastasio, Da rappresentarsi ne Famoso Teatro dell' Accademia Filarmonica di Verona. Nella Fiera di Maggio, 1737 (Venezia: Girolomo Savioni), cited in Bellina, *I libretti vivaldiani*, 47.

47. Strohm, *Die italienische Oper*, 13–15; Strohm, *Dramma per musica*, 5–6. Burt "Opera in Arcadia," 145–6, describes Metastasian opera as a kind of esthetic *lingua franca* of "stupefying popularity."

48. Ah, prima degli dei / Piombi sopra di me tutto lo sdegno / Ch'il sangue d'un indegno / Infami il sangue mio, che a me congiunto / Io soffra un traditore, un che di Roma / Ha quasi già nel suo furor sepolta / L'antica libertà!

49. Livy, 1.13.1–5: "Then the Sabine women, on account of whose outrage the war had arisen, . . . dared to put themselves between the flying weapons, and with a rush on the flank, to split apart the hostile ranks of battle and to put an end to their fury. They were begging their husbands on the one side and their fathers on the other not to splatter themselves with the impious blood of fathers-and sons-in-law, nor to stain their own offspring—the children of the one and grandchildren of the other—with slaughter of their kindred." I owe this point to Richard Tarrant.

50. Quoted in Giazotto, *Antonio Vivaldi*, 255–56, who suggests that Vivaldi was thinking of Italy in terms of a unified political entity rather than simply a geographical feature.

Chapter 7. Arminius and the Problem of Rome

1. *Annals* 2.88: "Liberator haud dubie Germaniae." A continuous narrative of the lives of Arminius and his family is in *Annals*, book 1, written sometime in the early second century C.E., and so about one hundred years after the events narrated. We learn more details about the slaughter of Varus's troops in the Teutoburger Forest from Velleius Paterculus, who wrote Roman history during the reign of Tiberius and may have known Arminius personally. Strabo's *Geography* was also written during Arminius's lifetime and provides us with the name Thusnelda for Arminius's wife as well as a list of Germans who were displayed in Germanicus's triumph in Rome. Further details are also provided in Cassius Dio, book 56.

2. There is now significant bibliography on the site at Kalkriese, postulated as the location of the battle by Theodore Mommsen in 1885 and confirmed by excavations starting in 1987. See Schlüter, "Battle of the Teutoberg Forest"; Wells, *Battle That Stopped Rome*; and Murdoch, *Rome's Greatest Defeat* for summaries of the history, tradition, and archaeological finds.

3. J. C. Rolfe, trans., *Suetonius*, vol. 1 (Cambridge, Mass.: Harvard University Press, 1998), 181, 183.

4. Tacitus, *The Annals of Imperial Rome*, rev. ed., trans. Michael Grant (London: Penguin Books, 1996), 119.

5. Dihle, *Greek and Latin Literature*, 219–20.

6. Kuehnemund, *Arminius*, 37.

7. Ibid., 54–110. See also the summary of the literary development and use of the Arminius/Hermann legend in Murdoch, *Rome's Greatest Defeat*, 155–80. Neither author refers to the Arminius operas.

8. Agrippina the Elder was the mother of the Agrippina of Handel's opera in chapter 4.

9. *Arminius, an Opera, as It Is Acted at the Queen's-Theatre in the Hay-Market* (London: Jacob Tonson, 1714). Strohm, "Handel and His Italian Opera Texts," 73 and n. 108, identifies it as a *pasticcio* by Haym that included music by Vivaldi, Orlandini, Ristori, Lotti, and others. Pace Strohm, there is no relation between this libretto and the Antonio Salvi text that Handel used in 1737 (discussed later in this chapter). Any slight similarities may be due to a shared familiarity with Campistron's play. There may have been an earlier Italian exemplar for the 1714 *Arminius*, but I have not been able to identify it.

10. Quotations are from the libretto's English translation.

11. Sambrook, "Godolphin [née Churchill], Henrietta [Harriet]."

12. There may be another, more personal connection here between the opera's plot and the dedicatee. The Countess Godolphin, although married to Sidney Godolphin's son Francis in 1698, began a long-term affair with the playwright William Congreve, perhaps as early as 1703. The affair, as well as Henrietta's patronage of the arts, was an ongoing source of strife with her strong-minded parents, especially with her mother Sarah, the Duchess of Marlborough. The sympathetic depiction in this opera of the stubborn Ismena and her faithful adherence to Arminius despite her father's wishes may have Henrietta as its point of reference, although whether such an association would be read as respectable might be open to question.

13. Quotations are from the libretto's English translation, available in Harris, *Librettos of Handel's Operas* 7:1–43. The only modern published score is Chrysander's 1882 edition. There is a brief discussion of *Arminio*'s libretto, score, and history in Dean, *Handel's Operas: 1726–1741*, 349–61.

14. Al par della mia sorte / E forte questo cor. / Coll' involarmi rigida / E vita, e libertà / Misero mi farà, non traditor.

15. Kilburn, "Frederick Lewis, Prince of Wales," especially the sections titled "Marriage" and "Opposition to Walpole"; see also Black, *Hanoverians*, 105–6.

16. Sedgwick, *Lord Hervey's Memoirs*, 42–43, quoted in Burrows, *Handel*, 180. Professor Burrows pointed out to me the possible links between the opera's subject and the situation in the royal family. The Blues and Greens to which Hervey refers were chariot-racing teams associated with political factions in Byzantium.

17. Burrows, *Handel*, 192. Frederick's support for Handel was interrupted for only two years, 1734–36, and so any hostility that existed did not go very deep. See Taylor, "Handel and Frederick, Prince of Wales."

18. Strohm, "Handel and His Italian Opera Texts," 73.

19. The English is scarcely high poetry, but in this case it actually improves upon the Italian, inherited from Salvi, which descends to incoherent exclamations: Fermate! O Padre! O Amore! / Oh! sangue! oh! Arminio! oh! oh! Sorte! / Oh! Ramise! oh! Sorella! oh! affetti! oh! Morte!

20. The assessment is Anthony Hicks's in "Arminio," *Grove Music Online* (accessed Dec. 4, 2006).

21. Harris, *Librettos of Handel's Operas*, vol. 8, vii–viii. But *Arminio* was produced before the formal split; *Faramondo* came after it, in 1737–38, at Haymarket, written for Heidegger and possibly for Opera of the Nobility (8:vii).

22. A capir tante dolcezze / Troppo angusto è 'l nostro cor. / Cangia in goia le tristezze / Generoso un bel valor.

23. For example, Lippmann says, "The republican spirit of ancient Rome is expressed in no verses of Metastasio, not even in *Catone in Utica*, so powerfully as in *Giunio Bruto* or *Gli Orazi e i Curiazi.*" Lippmann, "Über Cimarosas Opere Serie," 33. See further chapter 9.

24. On marriage as an important theme in neoclassical art and its relation to contemporary operas, see Rice, "Sarti's *Giulio Sabino*," 184.

Chapter 8. Clemencies of Titus

1. Metastasio's remark in the chapter epigraph begins the *Argomento* to *La Clemenza di Tito*. Arteaga's question was posed in his *Le Rivoluzioni del teatro musicale italiano dalla sua origine fino al presente*, 3 vols. (1783; reprint, Bologna: Forni, 1969), 1:347, quoted in Neville, "Moral Philosophy," 43n11.

2. Lists of productions may be found in Brunelli, *Tutte le opere di Pietro Metastasio*, 1:1498–99. The libretto is on pages 692–750.

3. For a different description of the period of opera history that I treat in my final two chapters, see Feldman, *Opera and Sovereignty*. (See my chapter 1, note 3.) Our conclusions sometimes differ, most notably in regard to what I call the myth of the clement prince, which in some respects corresponds with Feldman's "myths of sovereignty." What I describe in the next chapter as the end of the myth of the clement prince and the gradual triumph of the myth of liberty, Feldman sees as a continuation and transformation of the myth of sovereignty (see, for example, Feldman's *Opera and Sovereignty*, 227 and 437–41).

4. Suetonius, *Titus*, 9.

5. Buttini, "*Il Vespesiano*," traces the opera's fortunes as indicated by the title, though she does not note the connection with the Berenice story.

6. On the debt to French tragedy, see Moberley, "Influence of French Classical Drama," 288–89; and Rice, *La clemenza di Tito*, 21–26. Seidel, "Seneca—Corneille—Mozart," 117–21, discusses the differences between *Cinna* and Metastasio's text. Sala di Felice, "Segreti, menzogne, e coatti silenzi," discusses the philosophical underpinnings for Metastasio's drama, which she believes include Aristotle's *Nichomachean Ethics* as well as Seneca's *De Clementia*.

7. Cassius Dio Cocceianus, *Dio's Roman History*, vol. 8, trans. Earnest Cary (Cambridge, Mass.: Harvard University Press, 1968), 298.

8. Seidel, "Seneca—Corneille—Mozart," 117–19.

9. Metastasio's lines, "Or che diranno / I posteri di noi? Diran che in Tito / si stancò la clemenza, / Come in Silla e in Augusto / la crudeltà," adapt Seneca's *De Clementia* (1.11.2), which calls Augustus's *clementia* "cruelty exhausted" (*lassa crudelitas*). I owe this point to Richard Tarrant.

10. Sia noto a Roma / Ch'io son l'istesso, e ch'io / Tutto so, tutti assolvo e tutto oblio.

11. Je suis maître de moi comme de l'Univers: / Je le suis, je veux l'être. O

Siècles, ô Memoire, / Conservez à jamais ma dernière victoire, / Je triomphe aujourd'hui du plus juste courroux / De qui le souvenir puisse aller jusqu'à vous."

12. Seidel, "Seneca—Corneille—Mozart," 120–21.

13. Joly, "De Metastase à Mazzola," 12.

14. Algarotti's objection is in Strunk, *Source Readings* 5:178, with a larger selection of the essay reproduced on 175–88. The unease with serious historical figures was not a new one. See Sbarra's preface to *Alessandro, il vincitore di se stesso* with Crescembeni's remarks on Cavalli's *Giasone* in Rosand, *Opera*, 275–77.

15. For the reform movement described in this paragraph and the next, see Kimbell, *Italian Opera*, 216–37; Bauman, "Eighteenth Century," 45–51.

16. On marriage as an important theme in neoclassical art, see chapter 7, note 24.

17. For these trends, see Kimbell, *Italian Opera*, 243–4, 397. Their application in specific cases is observed by Weiss, *Morte di Cesare*, xi–xii; and Quétin, "'Lucio Silla'," with discussion, 597–600.

18. The most complete account of the opera is in Rice, "Sarti's *Giulio Sabino*," 182–92. On authorship of the libretto, see 183n6; on subsequent performances of the opera, see 182n4. The undated published score from Vienna (1781–84?) has been republished in facsimile (Bologna: Forni, 1969).

19. The story is told in Tacitus (*Histories* 4.55 and 67), Plutarch ("Erotikos", 25 *Moralia*, 770C–771C), and Cassius Dio (65.3 and 65.16).

20. *Dio's Roman History*, trans. Cary, 8:293.

21. Plutarch, *Moralia*, vol. 9, trans. W. C. Helmbold (Cambridge, Mass/: Harvard University Press, 1961), 441. Plutarch also says that the boys survived to manhood and that he had met one of them, so the family's story may not have ended as tragically as the sources elsewhere suggest.

22. The full details of this list are in Rice, "Sarti's *Giulio Sabino*," 183n6.

23. "Il Gallo, Il Germano / Del Lazio il nemico / A Cesare amico / La fè giurerà." Note however that this is sung in duet by the Romans Tito and Annio, not by the Gauls.

24. For further details on *Giulio Sabino* as a progressive libretto, see Rice, "Sarti's *Giulio Sabino*," 185–91.

25. Real revolutionary opera was yet to come. See discussions in chapter 1 and chapter 9.

26. Boadicea (more properly Boudicca) led a briefly successful rebellion of the East Anglian tribes against Roman forces in Britain in the first century C.E. but was defeated and took poison (Tacitus, *Annals* 14.31–37; *Agricola* 16.1–2; Cassius Dio 62.1–12).

27. On the popularity of "Cari figli," see Rice, "Sarti's *Giulio Sabino*," 190–91.

28. On the setting, see Rice, "Sarti's *Giulio Sabino*," 185–87, and his plate 3 for Sabino's underground hideout.

29. Of the possible sources, the *Argomento* mentions only Plutarch: "Sabinus was the father of two little boys (one of which Plutarch says he knew)." The libretto's dependence on the *Moralia* seems confirmed by a significant element of the plot that is only mentioned by Plutarch (770D): After burning his castle and

feigning suicide, Sabinus might have escaped to the Germans but was prevented from doing so by his attachment to Epponina.

Chapter 9. The Revolution and the End of a Myth

1. On the historical Lucius Cornelius Sulla (dictator, 82–79 B.C.E.), see chapter 1. A series of operas on "Lucio Silla" included a *L. C. Silla* by Handel, perhaps performed in London in 1713, and a 1771 *Lucio Silla* for Milan by the young Mozart, about which more is said below. In both these examples, the title role's last-minute repentance was validated by the historical fact that after imposing his stern and violent will on Rome, he retired from public life and died at his villa a private citizen. On the Sulla operas, see Quétin, "'Lucio Silla'," 594 and n. 3; Ketterer, "Senecanism."

2. De Gamerra's *Argomento* to the libretto for 1771 says that Metastasio "with his rare affability has deigned to honor the present dramatic composition with his fullest approval." The libretto is reproduced by Angermüller in *W. A. Mozart*; and Warburton, *Librettos of Mozart's Operas* 1:261–334. The score is available in Hansell, *Lucio Silla*, pt. 2.

3. For reproductions of the designs for the *luogo sepocrale* and act I ruins, see Hansell, *Lucio Silla*, pt. 1, lvi–lvii.

4. Other tragic elements in *Lucio Silla* hark back to Senecan and Shaksperaean drama. See Quétin, "'Lucio Silla'," 598–99; and Ketterer, "Senecanism," 226–33.

5. The most important narratives are in Livy 2.3–5; Dionysius of Halicarnassus, *Roman Antiquities* 5.6–8; and Plutarch, *Publicola* 3–6.

6. *Giunio Bruto. Dramma per musica da rappresentarsi in Camerino nel Luglio del 1749. Dedicato all Nobil Donna Signora Contessa Virginia Bandini Tesei in Camerino 1749,* libretto by Mariangiola Passari "tra gl'Arcadi Gelmarania Dianea," music by Nicolà Logroscino, "Maestro di capella Napolitano." I have not seen Passari recognized as the source for Pindemonte in the scholarship on the opera.

7. In addition to the Metastasian model, there may also be influence from Matteo Noris's 1697 libretto *Tito Manlio,* based on a similar story of a Roman commander who executes his son for indulging in the heroics of single combat and killing his enemy, despite orders that there is to be no engagement. The ancient story about Titus Manlius Torquatus is another object lesson in the importance of the Roman state as a corporate body over personal and family feeling. Noris's libretto rescues the younger Titus in the final scenes as the indignant army led by a subordinate officer arrives to assert the young man's worth and heroism. "It makes the severity of the plot more pleasing, adapting it to a happy ending," he says in his *Argomento.* A notable version of *Tito Manlio* was set by Vivaldi in 1719 for Mantua.

8. I have been unable to see the 1781 libretto; a tragic ending is attested in Gordana Lazarevich, "Giunio Bruto," Grove Music Online (accessed Dec. 4, 2006). The Pisa libretto is *Giunio Bruto. Dramma tragico per musica d'Eschilo Acanzio P. A. della Colonia Veronese da rappreseantarsi nel nuovo teatro de' Nobili Sigg. Fratelli Prini della Città di Pisa. La Primavera dell'Anno 1783.* The London li-

bretto is *Giunio Bruto; a new serious opera, as performed at the King's Theater in the Hay-Market. The Music by several eminent composers, under the direction of Signor Bertoni* (London, 1781).

9. Frema pur quel rè superbo, / E minacci guerra, e morte; / Sorgerà sempre più forte / La Romana libertà / Ed al nome solo un giorno / Del gran Popolo Latino / Ogni re sul suo destino / Ogni gente tremerà.

10. Concerning Alfieri's influence on libretto writing, see Angermüller, "Grundzüge des nachmetastasianischen Librettos," 202–206; Lippmann, "Über Cimarosas Opere Serie," 32–33; and Kimbell, *Italian Opera*, 245–46. Bauman, "Society of La Fenice," 350, notes an "idealistic sympathy with the French Revolution" that affected the generation of *opera seria* librettists at the end of the century.

11. A reprint of the original libretto of *La Clemenza di Tito* is in Warburton, *Librettos of Mozart's Operas* 4:115–70. The score is conveniently published in the Dover Press reprint (1993) of the 1882 Breitkopf edition.

12. The reception of the opera in Prague is described and evaluated by Rice, *La clemenza di Tito*, 62–65.

13. The young Mozart's earliest dramatic experience was in a Latin play in which he had a part when he was five (Deutsch, *Mozart: Die Dokumente seines Lebens*, 15–16). On Mozart's education and the classics, see Koch, "Mozart und die Antike," especially 24–28. On Mozart's desire to write *opera seria*, see Rushton, *Mozart*, 38.

14. Rice, *La clemenza di Tito*, 8–9.

15. The operas that show a debt to *La congiura* were on classical themes: *Meleagro* (anon., 1798), *Il trionfo di Clelia* (Sografi, 1798), *Clitennestra* (Salfi, 1801), and *I Manli* (Sografi, 1802). See Nocciolino, "Il melodramma nella Milano napoleonica," 7–8.

16. Legouvé, *Oeuvres Complètes*, vol. 1, 87–171.

17. On Tarchi, see Dennis Libby, Marita McClymonds, "Tarchi, Angelo," Grove Music Online (accessed Dec. 4, 2006). On Salfi, see Serpa, *Francesco Saverio Salfi*, 6–11.

18. For a description of the characteristics of operas performed during the Terror, see Bartlet, "New Repertory at the Opéra," especially 124–32. See also Dean, "Opera under the French Revolution."

19. *La Morte di Cesare, dramma per musica del Signor Abate D. Gaetano Sertor, da rappresentarsi nel Nobilissimo teatro di San Samuele. Il Carnovale dell' Anno 1789*. The libretto and facsimile of the score are in Weiss, *Morte di Cesare*. Weiss's introductory essay (ix–xxxiii) includes a survey of the death of Caesar onstage in the early modern period.

20. Brunelli, *Tutte le opere di Pietro Metastasio*, 1:1384–85.

21. On the "Morte" operas, see McClymonds, "La Morte di Semiramide" 3:288–89.

22. For a more detailed view of this issue in *La congiura* and Cimarosa's *Gli Orazi e i Curiazi*, see Ketterer, "Roman Republicanism and Operatic Heroines."

23. See chapter 7, note 23.

24. Morelli and Surian, *"Gli Orazi e i Curiazi,"* xv–xvi.

25. Republished in facsimile in Morelli and Surian, *"Gli Orazi e i Curiazi."*

26. Rossini, "Opera classicista nella Milano," especially 127–31, summarizes

the characteristics of classicizing Italian opera in the early nineteenth century and notes the ongoing value of Roman history in these texts.

27. Rice, *La clemenza di Tito,* 113; Cowgill, "Mozart Productions," 148–52.

28. Kimbell, *Italian Opera,* 409–10, on Mercadante. He quotes F. Florimo, *La scuola musicale di Napoli,* vol. 3 (Naples, 1880–84), 16.

29. Michael Rose, "Mercadante, Saverio, 1. Life" and "Works," Grove Music Online (accessed Dec. 4, 2006).

30. Kimbell, *Italian Opera,* 396. The decline in interest corresponds with a general decline in the use of Plutarch as a model for the upper classes, noted by Russell, *Plutarch,* 161–62.

31. Directed by Jürgen Flimm, conducted by Tomas Netopil, scene design by Christian Bussmann, costume design by Birgit Hutter, lighting design by Fabio Barettin.

32. The singers, on the other hand, ranged from adequate (in one case) to superb: Annick Massis as Giunia, Monica Bacelli as Cecilio, and Julia Kleiter as Celia were especially notable. Tomas Netopil's conducting brought out the best in the adolescent Mozart's score.

33. The original Milanese production, with its shadowy ruins designed by Galliari (above, note 3), were shabby, too, but had a stylish profusion of detail in the manner of Piranesi's prints.

34. Shaw returns to the economic issue, continuing, "This is of course quite a tentative view argumentatively; but it is not the understanding upon which the public pays for its seats." Shaw, *Music in London* 3:284; originally in *The World* (8 August 1894).

35. Similar thoughts on modern production of Handelian opera have been expressed by Jones, "Performing Matters," especially 278 and 280–81.

36. Rice, *La clemenza di Tito,* 11–12, with n. 13.

BIBLIOGRAPHY

Abert, Anna Amalie. *Claudio Monteverdi und das musikalische Drama.* Lippstadt: Kistner & Siegel, 1954.

Allen, Christopher. "Ovid and Art." In *The Cambridge Companion to Ovid.* Ed. Philip Hardie. 336–67. Cambridge: Cambridge University Press, 2002.

Angermüller, Rudolph. "Grundzüge des nachmetastasianischen Librettos." *Analecta Musicologica* 21 (1982): 192–235.

——, ed. *W. A. Mozart: Lucio Silla. Facsimiledruck des Librettos von G. de Gamerra. Mailand 1772.* Munich: E. Katzbichler, 1975.

Arnold, Denis, and Nigel Fortune, eds. *The New Monteverdi Companion.* Boston: Faber & Faber, 1985.

Arnold, Edward V. *Roman Stoicism.* New York: Humanities Press, 1958.

Axelrad, A. José. *Le thème de Sophonisbe dans les principales tragédies de la littérature occidentale.* Lille: Bibliotèque Universitaire, 1956.

Barbier, Patrick. *The World of the Castrati.* Trans. Margaret Crosland. London: Souvenir Press, 1996.

Barkan, Leonard. *The Gods Made Flesh.* New Haven, Conn.: Yale University Press, 1986.

Bartlet, M. Elizabeth C. "The New Repertory at the Opéra during the Reign of Terror: Revolutionary Rhetoric and Operatic Consequences." In *Music and the French Revolution.* Ed. Malcolm Boyd. 107–56. Cambridge: Cambridge University Press, 1992.

Bauman, Thomas. "The Eighteenth Century: Serious Opera." In Parker, *Oxford History of Opera.* 32–56.

——. "The Society of La Fenice and Its First Impresarios." *Journal of the American Musicological Society* 39.2 (1986): 332–54.

Bellina, Anna Laura, Bruno Brizi, and Maria Grazia Pensa. *I libretti vivaldiani.* Florence: Olschki, 1982.

Bellori, Giovanni Pietro. *The Lives of Annibale and Agostino Carracci.* Trans. Catherine Enggass. University Park: Pennsylvania State University Press, 1968.

——. *Le vite de' pittori, scultori et architetti moderni.* Parte prima. Facsimile dell' edizione di Roma del MDCLXXII. Rome: E. Calzone, 1931.

Bianconi, Lorenzo, and Thomas Walker. "Production, Consumption and Political Function of Seventeenth-Century Opera." *Early Music History* 4 (1984): 209–96.

Black, Jeremy. *The Hanoverians: The History of a Dynasty.* London: Hambledon and London, 2004.

Boccabadati, Giovanni Battista. *Scipione, overo Le Gare Eroiche.* Modona: Antonio Capponi, 1693.

Bond, Donald, ed. *The Spectator.* 4 vols. Oxford: Clarendon Press, 1965.

Braden, Gordon. "Drama." In *The Legacy of Rome: A New Appraisal.* Ed. Richard Jenkyns. 243–68. Oxford: Oxford University Press, 1992.

Brown, Howard Mayer, ed. *Italian Opera Librettos, 1640–1770.* 16 vols. New York: Garland, 1978–84.

Brown, J. W. "On the Road with the 'Suitcase Aria': The Transmission of Borrowed Arias in Late Seventeenth-Century Italian Opera Revivals." *Journal of Musicological Research* 15 (1995): 3–23.

Brunelli, Bruno, ed. *Tutte le opere di Pietro Metastasio.* 5 vols. Verona: Mondadori, 1953.

Buller, Jeffrey. "From *Clementia Caesaris* to *La Clemenza di Tito.*" In *Qui Miscuit Utile Dulci.* Ed. Gareth Schmeling and Jon D. Mikalson. 69–85. Waukanda, Ill.: Bolchazy-Carducci, 1998.

Burrows, Donald. *Handel.* Oxford: Clarendon Press, 1994.

Burt, Nathaniel. "Opera in Arcadia." *Musical Quarterly* 41.2 (1955): 145–70.

Butler, H. E., and H. H. Scullard, eds. *Livy.* Book XXX. London: Methuen, 1939.

Buttini, Francesca Menchelli. "*Il Vespesiano* da Venezia (1678) a Napoli (1707). Un contributo sull'opera a Napoli nel primo Settecento." *Rivista italiana di musicologia* 30.2 (1995): 335–58.

Calcagno, Mauro. "Censoring *Eliogabalo* in Seventeenth-Century Venice." *Journal of Interdisciplinary History* 36.3 (2006): 355–77.

Carter, Tim. *Monteverdi's Musical Theatre.* New Haven, Conn.: Yale University Press, 2002.

———. "The Seventeenth Century." In Parker, *Oxford History of Opera,* 1–31.

Cavalli, Francesco. *Scipione Africano.* Facsimile ed., with an introduction by Howard Mayer Brown. New York: Garland, 1978.

Chafe, Eric T. *Monteverdi's Tonal Language.* New York: Schirmer, 1992.

Clausen, Wendell V. "Callimachus and Latin Poetry." *Greek, Roman and Byzantine Studies* 5 (1964): 181–96.

Clément, Catherine. *Opera, or the Undoing of Women.* Trans. Betsy Wing. Minneapolis: University of Minnesota Press, 1988.

Cody, Richard. *The Landscape of the Mind.* Oxford: Clarendon Press, 1969.

Conte, Gian Biagio. *Latin Literature: A History.* Trans. J. B. Solodow. Revised by D. Fowler and G. W. Most. Baltimore: Johns Hopkins University Press, 1994.

Copley, Frank O. *Exclusus Amator: A Study in Latin Love Poetry.* Madison, Wis.: American Philological Association, 1956.

Corneille, Pierre. *Théâtre Complet,* 3 vols in 6. Ed. Alain Niderst. Paris: Presses Universitaires de France, 1986.

Cowgill, Rachel. "Mozart Productions and the Emergence of *Werktreue* at London's Italian Opera House, 1780–1830." In Marvin and Thomas, *Operatic Migrations.* 145–86.

Curtis, Alan, ed. *Monteverdi: L'incoronazione di Poppea.* London: Novello, 1989.

———. "*La Poppea impasticciata;* or, Who Wrote the Music to *L'incoronazione* (1643)?" *Journal of the American Musicological Society* 42 (1989): 23–54.

Dandelet, Thomas J. *Spanish Rome, 1500–1700.* New Haven, Conn.: Yale University Press, 2001.

Dauge, Yves A. *Le Barbare: Recherches sur la conception romaine de la barbarie et de la civilisation.* La Collection Latomus, vol. 176. Brussels: Latomus, 1981.

Davidson, James. "Domesticating Dido: History and Historicity." In *A Woman Scorn'd: Responses to the Dido Myth*. Ed. Michael Burden. 65–88. London: Faber & Faber, 1998.

Dean, Winton. *Handel and the Opera Seria*. Berkeley and Los Angeles: University of California Press, 1969.

———. *Handel's Operas: 1726–1741*. Woodbridge, Suffolk: Boydell, 2006.

———. "Opera under the French Revolution." In *Essays on Opera*. By Winton Dean. 106–22. Oxford: Clarendon Press, 1993.

Dean, Winton, and Sarah Fuller, eds. *G. F. Handel: Giulio Cesare in Egitto*. Oxford: Oxford University Press, 1998.

Dean, Winton, and J. Merrill Knapp. *Handel's Operas, 1704–1726*. Rev. ed. Oxford: Clarendon Press, 1995.

Deutsch, Otto. *Mozart: Die Dokumente seines Lebens*. Kassel: Bärenreiter, 1961.

Dihle, Albrecht. *Greek and Latin Literature of the Roman Empire from Augustus to Justinian*. Trans. Manfred Malzahn. London: Routledge, 1994.

Dizionario biografico degli Italiani. Rome: Istituto della Enciclopedia Italiana, 1960–. 68vv.

Donington, Robert. *Opera and Its Symbols: The Unity of Words, Music and Staging*. New Haven, Conn.: Yale University Press, 1990.

———. *The Rise of Opera*. London: Faber & Faber, 1981.

Drebes, Gerald. "Monteverdis 'Kontrastprinzip,' die Vorrede zu seinem 8. Madrigalbuch und das 'Genere concitato.'" *Musiktheorie* 6 (1991): 29–42.

Elioseff, Lee A. *The Cultural Milieu of Addison's Literary Criticism*. Austin: University of Texas Press, 1963.

Fabbri, Paolo. "New Sources for 'Poppea.'" *Music & Letters* 74.1 (1993): 16–23.

———. *Il secolo cantante: Per una storia dei libretti d'opera in Italia nel Seicento*. Bologna: Il Mulino, 1990.

Fantham, Elaine. *Comparative Studies in Republican Latin Imagery*. Toronto: University of Toronto Press, 1979.

Fears, J. Rufus. "The Cult of the Virtues and Roman Imperial Ideology." *Aufstieg und Niedergang der Römischen Welt* 2.17.2 (1981): 827–948.

Fehr, Max. *Apostolo Zeno (1668–1750) und seine Reform des Operntextes*. Zurich: Tschopp, 1912.

Feldman, Martha. "Magic Mirrors and the *Seria* Stage: Thoughts toward a Ritual View." *Journal of the American Musicological Society* 48.3 (1995): 423–84.

———. *Opera and Sovereignty*. Chicago: University of Chicago Press, 2007.

Fenlon, Iain, and Peter N. Miller. *The Song of the Soul: Understanding Poppea*. London: Royal Music Association, 1992.

Foley, Helene P., ed. *The Homeric "Hymn to Demeter": Translation, Commentary, and Interpretive Essays*. Princeton: Princeton, N.J. University Press, 1994.

Francis, Alan D. *The First Peninsular War, 1702–1713*. London: E. Benn, 1975.

Freeman, Robert S. "Farinello and His Repertory." In *Studies in Renaissance and Baroque Music in Honor of Arthur Mendel*. Ed. Robert L. Marshall. 301–30. Kassel: Bärenreiter, 1994.

———. *Opera Without Drama: Currents of Change in Italian Opera, 1675–1725*. Ann Arbor: UMI Research Press, 1981.

Frye, Northrop. *Anatomy of Criticism: Four Essays*. Princeton, N.J.: Princeton University Press, 1957.

Garrard, Mary D. *Artemisia Gentileschi.* Princeton, N.J.: Princeton University Press, 1989.

Gelzer, Matthias. "Cato Uticensis." *Die Antike* 10.1 (1934): 59–91.

Giazotto, Remo. *Antonio Vivaldi.* Turin: ERI, 1965.

Giuntini, Francesco. "L'amore trionfante nell' 'Incoronazione di Poppea.'" In *Claudio Monteverdi: Studi e prospettive.* Ed. Paola Besutti, Teresa M. Gialdroni, and Rodolfo Baroncini. 347–56. Florence: Olschki, 1998.

Glover, Jane. *Cavalli.* New York: St. Martin's Press, 1978.

Goar, Robert J. *The Legend of Cato Uticensis from the First Century B.C. to the Fifth Century A.D.* La Collection Latomus, no. 197. Brussels: Latomus, 1987.

Grafton, Anthony. *Rome Reborn: The Vatican Library and Renaissance Culture.* Princeton, N.J.: Yale University Press, 1993.

Graham, Walter, ed. *The Letters of Joseph Addison.* Oxford: Clarendon Press, 1941.

Green, Peter. *Alexander to Actium: The Historical Evolution of the Hellenistic Age.* Berkeley and Los Angeles: University of California Press, 1990.

Grove Music Online. Ed. Laura Macy. http://www.grovemusic.com/.

Haley, Shelley P. "Livy, Passion, and Cultural Stereotypes." *Historia* 39 (1990): 375–81.

Hanning, Barbara R. "Glorious Apollo: Poetic and Political Themes in the First Opera." *Renaissance Quarterly* 32.4 (1979): 485–513.

Hansell, Kathleen K., ed. Mozart: *Lucio Silla.* 2 vols. Kassel: Bärenreiter, 1986.

Harbison, Robert. *Reflections on Baroque.* Chicago: University of Chicago Press, 2000.

Hardie, Philip, ed.: *The Cambridge Companion to Ovid.* Cambridge: Cambridge University Press, 2002.

Harris, Ellen, *Handel and the Pastoral Tradition.* London: Oxford University Press, 1980.

———, ed. *The Librettos of Handel's Operas.* 13 vols. New York: Garland, 1989.

Heller, Wendy B. *Emblems of Eloquence: Opera and Women's Voices in Seventeenth-Century Venice.* Berkeley and Los Angeles: University of California Press, 2003.

———. "The Queen as King: Refashioning *Semiramide* for Seicento Venice." *Cambridge Opera Journal* 5.2 (1993): 93–114.

———. "Tacitus Incognito: Opera as History in *L'incoronazione di Poppea.*" *Journal of the American Musicological Society* 52.1 (1999): 39–96.

Henke, Robert. *Pastoral Transformations: Italian Tragicomedy and Shakespeare's Late Plays.* Newark: University of Delaware Press, 1997.

Heriot, Angus. *The Castrati in Opera.* London: Caldar and Boyers, 1975.

Heslin, P. J. *The Transvestite Achilles: Gender and Genre in Statius' Achilles.* Cambridge: Cambridge University Press, 2005.

Hill, John W., ed. *Domenico Lalli—Antonio Vivaldi: Ottone in villa.* Milan: Ricordi, 1983.

Holzer, Robert. "'Ma invan la tento et impossibil parmi,' or How *guerrieri* Are Monteverdi's *madrigali guerrieri*?" In *The Sense of Marino: Literature, Fine Arts and Music of the Italian Baroque.* Ed. Francesco Guardiani. 429–50. New York: Legas, 1994.

Hoxby, Blair. "The Doleful Airs of Euripides: The Origins of Opera and the Spirit of Tragedy Reconsidererd." *Cambridge Opera Journal* 17.3 (2005): 253–69.

Hunter, David. "Patronizing Handel, Inventing Audiences." *Early Music* 28.1 (2000): 32–49.

Hutchinson, G. O. *Hellenistic Poetry.* Oxford: Clarendon Press, 1988.

Joly, Jacques. "De Metastase à Mazzola." *Avant-Scène Opera* 99 (June 1987): 12–18.

Jones, Andrew V. "Performing Matters: Staging a Handel Opera." *Early Music* 34.2 (May 2006): 277–88.

Jones, Christopher P. *Plutarch and Rome.* Oxford: Clarendon Press, 1971.

Kallendorf, Craig. *Virgil and the Myth of Venice: Books and Readers in the Italian Renaissance.* Oxford: Clarendon Press, 1999.

Ketterer, Robert C. "Handel's *Scipione* and the Neutralization of Politics." *Newsletter of the American Handel Society* 15.1 (April 2001): 1, 4–8.

——. "*Militat Omnis Amans*: Ovidian Elegy in *L'incoronazione di Poppea.*" *International Journal of the Classical Tradition* 4.3 (Winter 1998): 381–95.

——. "Neoplatonic Light and Dramatic Genre in Busenello's *L'incoronazione di Poppea* and Noris' *Il Ripudio d'Ottavia.*" *Music & Letters* 80.1 (1999): 1–22.

——. "Roman Republicanism and Operatic Heroines in Napoleonic Italy." In Marvin and Thomas, *Operatic Migrations.* 99–124.

——. "Senecanism and the 'Sulla' Operas of Handel and Mozart." *Syllecta Classica* 10 (1999): 215–34.

——. "Why Early Opera Is Roman and Not Greek." *Cambridge Opera Journal* 15.1 (2003): 1–14.

Kilburn, Matthew. "Frederick Lewis, Prince of Wales." *Oxford Dictionary of National Biography.* Online ed., Oxford University Press, May 2005. http://www.oxforddnb.com/. (Accessed Oct. 24, 2006.)

Kimbell, David. *Italian Opera.* Cambridge: Cambridge University Press, 1991.

Kirkendale, Ursula. "The War of the Spanish Succession Reflected in the Works of Antonio Caldara." *Acta Musicologica* 36.4 (1963): 221–33.

Knapp, J. Merrill. "Handel's *Giulio Cesare in Egitto.*" In *Studies in Music History: Essays for Oliver Strunk.* Ed. Harold Powers. 389–403. Princeton, N.J.: Princeton University Press, 1968.

Koch, Klaus-Dietrich. "Mozart und die Antike." *Mitteilungen der Internationalen Stiftung Mozarteum* 45.3–4 (1997): 21–52.

Konstan, David. "Clemency as a Virtue." *Classical Philology* 100.4 (2005): 337–46.

——. *Roman Comedy.* Ithaca, N.Y.: Cornell University Press, 1983.

Kretzschmar, Hermann. "Monteverdi's *Incoronazione di Poppea.*" *Vierteljahrschrift für Musikwissenschaft* 10 (1894): 483–530.

Kristeller, Paul O. *Eight Philosophers of the Italian Renaissance.* Stanford, Calif.: Stanford University Press, 1964.

Kubik, Reinhold. "'Die angenehme, abgemessene, . . . doch auch nicht verwirrte Rührung.' Bemerkungen zum 'Dramatischen' in Händels 'Giulio Cesare.'" In *Aufführungspraxis der Handel-Oper.* Ed. Hans Joachim Marx. 43–54. Laaber: Laaber-Verlag, 1990.

Kuehnemund, Richard. *Arminius, or the Rise of a National Symbol in Literature, from Hutten to Grabbe.* Chapel Hill: University of North Carolina, 1953.

Lancel, Serge. *Carthage: A History.* Oxford: Blackwell, 1995.

Leclerc, Hélène. "Du mythe platonicien aux fêtes de la Renaissance." *Revue d'histoire du théâtre* 11.2 (1959): 107–71.

Legouvé, Gabriel. *Oeuvres Complètes*, 3 vols. Paris: L. Janet, 1826–27.

Lindberg, David C. *Theories of Vision from Al-Kindi to Kepler*. Chicago: University of Chicago Press, 1976.

Lippmann, Friedrich. "Über Cimarosas Opere Serie." *Analecta Musicologica* 21 (1982): 21–60.

Litto, Frederic M. "Addison's Cato in the Colonies." *The William and Mary Quarterly*, ser. 3, 23 (July 1966): 431–49.

Loftis, John C. *Essays on the Theatre from Eighteenth-Century Periodicals*. Los Angeles: William Andrews Clark Memorial Library, 1960.

———. *The Politics of Drama in Augustan England*. Oxford: Clarendon Press, 1963.

The London Stage, 1660–1800. 5 vols. in 11. Carbondale: University of Southern Illinois Press, 1960–68.

Lucas, Hans. "Recusatio." *Festschrift Johannes Vahlen*. Ed. W. von Hartel. 319–33. Berlin: G. Reimer, 1900.

Malipiero, Gian Francesco, ed. *Tutte le opere di Claudio Monteverdi*. 17 vols. in 22. Vienna: Universal, 1926–68.

Marti, Berthe M. "The Meaning of the Pharsalia." *American Journal of Philology* 66 (1945): 352–76.

Marvin, Roberta M., and Downing Thomas, eds. *Operatic Migrations: Transforming Works and Crossing Boundaries*. Burlington, Vt.: Ashgate, 2006.

Matsche, Franz. *Die Kunst im Dienst der Staatsidee Kaiser Karl VI: Ikonographie, Ikonologie und Programmatik des "Kaiserstils."* 2 vols. Berlin: Walter de Gruyter, 1981.

May, Georges. *D'Ovide à Racine*. New Haven, Conn.: Yale University Press, 1949.

Mazzali, E. ed. Torquato Tasso: *Opere*. Vol. 1. Naples: Rossi, 1969.

McClymonds, Marita P. "'La Morte di Semiramide ossia La Vendetta di Nino' and the Restoration of Death and Tragedy to the Italian Operatic Stage in the 1780s and 90s." *Atti del XIV Congresso della Società internazionale di musicologia*. 3:285–92. 3 vols. Turin, 1990.

McKeown, J. C., ed. *Ovid: Amores: Text, Prolegomena and Commentary in Four Volumes*. Liverpool: F. Cairns, 1987.

McLauchlan, Fiona. "Giulio Cesare in Egitto." *Music & Letters* 82.1 (2001): 160–64.

Mellers, Wilfrid. *The Masks of Orpheus: Seven Stages in the Story of European Music*. Manchester: Manchester University Press, 1987.

MGG: Die Musik in Geschichte und Gegenwart: Allgemeine Enzyklopädie der Musik. Ed. L. Finscher. 26 vols. Kassel: Bärenreiter, 1994–98.

Migiel, Marilyn. "Clorinda's Fathers." *Stanford Italian Review* 10.1 (1991): 93–121.

Moberley, R. B. "The Influence of French Classical Drama on Mozart's 'La Clemenza di Tito.'" *Music & Letters* 55.3 (1974): 286–98.

Möbius, Helga. *Woman of the Baroque Age*. Trans. Barbara Chruscik. Montclair, N.J.: A. Schram, 1984.

Monson, Craig, ed. Antonio Sartorio: *Giulio Cesare in Egitto*. Madison, Wis.: A-R Editions, 1991.

———. "'Giulio Cesare in Egitto': From Sartorio (1677) to Handel (1724)." *Music & Letters* 66.4 (1985): 313–43.

Montaigne, Michel de. *The Complete Essays*. Trans. Donald M. Frame. Stanford, Calif.: Stanford University Press, 1958.

Morelli, Giovanni, and Elvidio Surian, eds. "Domenico Cimarosa, *Gli Orazi e i Curiazi.*" *Tragedia per musica in tre atti di Antonio Simeone Sografi*. Vol. 2. *Facsimile dell' edizione Imbault, Parigi 1802*. Milan: Suvini Zerboni, 1985.

Moscovich, M. James. "Cassius Dio on the Death of Sophonisba." *Ancient History Bulletin* 11.1 (1997): 25–29.

Moses, Gavriel. "Tasso to Monteverdi: Intertextual Poetics." In *Studies in the Italian Renaissance: Essays in Memory of Arnolfo B. Ferrulo*. Ed. Gian-Paolo Biasin, Albert N. Mancini, and Nicholas J. Perella. 245–61. Naples: Società Editrice Napoletana, 1985.

Muir, Edward. *Civic Ritual in Renaissance Venice*. Princeton, N.J.: Princeton University Press, 1981.

Muraro, Michelangelo. *Venetian Villas: The History and Culture*. Photographs by Paolo Marton. New York: Rizzoli, 1986.

Murdoch, Adrian. *Rome's Greatest Defeat: Massacre in the Teutoburg Forest*. Gloucestershire, UK: Sutton Publishing, 2006.

Murgatroyd, P. "Militia Amoris and the Roman Elegists." *Latomus* 34 (1975): 59–79.

Negri, Francesco. *La Vita di Apostolo Zeno*. Venice: Alvisopoli, 1816.

Neville, Don. "Moral Philosophy in the Metastasian Dramas." *Studies in Music from the University of Western Ontario* 7.1 (1982): 28–46.

Nocciolino, Monica. "Il melodramma nella Milano napoleonica: Teatro musicale e ideologia politica." *Nuova rivista musicale italiana* 29 (1995): 5–30.

Noce, Hannibal S. "Early Italian Translations of Addison's *Cato.*" In *Petrarch to Pirandello: Studies in Italian Literature in Honour of Beatrice Corrigan*. Ed. Julius A. Molinaro. 111–30. Toronto: University of Toronto Press, 1973.

Oestreich, Gerhard. *Neostoicism and the Early Modern State*. Cambridge: Cambridge University Press, 1982.

Ossi, Massimo. *Divining the Oracle: Monteverdi's Seconda Prattica*. Chicago: University of Chicago Press, 2003.

Palisca, Claude V. *Baroque Music*. 3rd ed. Englewood Cliffs, N.J.: Prentice Hall, 1991.

Panofsky Erwin. *Hercules am Scheidewege und andere antike Bildstoffe in der neueren Kunst*. Leipzig: B. G. Teubner, 1930.

Parker, Roger, ed. *The Oxford History of Opera*. Oxford: Oxford University Press, 1996.

Pelling, C. B. R., ed. *Plutarch, Life of Antony*. Cambridge: Cambridge University Press, 1988.

Pigler, Andor. *Barockthemen: Eine Auswahl von Verzeichnissen zur Ikonographie des 17. und 18. Jahrhunderts*. 3 vols. Budapest: Akadémia Kiadó, 1974.

Plutarch. *The Lives of the Noble Grecians and Romanes*. Trans. Thomas North. 8 vols. Boston: Shakespeare Head Press, 1928.

Poggioli, Renato. *The Oaten Flute: Essays on Pastoral Poetry and the Pastoral Ideal*. Cambridge, Mass.: Harvard University Press, 1975.

Poriss, Hillary. "Making Their Way Through the World: Italian One-Hit Wonders." *Nineteenth-Century Music* 24.3 (2001): 197–224.

Powell, Hugh, ed. *Andreas Gryphius: Cardenio und Celinde*. Leicester: Leicester University Press, 1961.

Powers, Harold S. "Il Serse trasformato." *Musical Quarterly*, Pt.1 47.4 (1961): 481–92; Pt.2: 48.1 (1962): 73–92.

Quétin, Laurine. "'Lucio Silla,' un livret à la hauteur de la partition?" *Mozart-Jahrbuch* Teil. 2 (1991): 594–600.

Rand, Benjamin, ed. *Berkeley and Percival.* Cambridge: Cambridge University Press, 1914.

Ricci, Charles. *Sophonisbe dans la tragédie classique italienne et française.* Geneva: Slatkine Reprints, 1970.

Rice, John A. "Sarti's *Giulio Sabino*, Haydn's *Armida*, and the Arrival of *Opera Seria* at Esterháza." *Haydn Year Book* 15 (1984): 181–98.

———. *W. A. Mozart: La Clemenza di Tito.* Cambridge: Cambridge University Press, 1991.

Rime degli Arcadi. Tomo settimo. Rome: Antonio de Rossi, 1717.

Robb, Nesca A. *Neoplatonism of the Italian Renaissance.* New York: Octagon Books, 1968.

Rosand, David. *The Myths of Venice: The Figuration of a State.* Chapel Hill: University of North Carolina Press, 2001.

Rosand, Ellen. *Monteverdi's Last Operas: A Venetian Trilogy.* Berkeley and Los Angeles: University of California Press, 2007.

———. "Monteverdi's Mimetic Art: *L'incoronazione di Poppea*." *Cambridge Opera Journal* 1.2 (1989): 113–37.

———. *Opera in Seventeenth-Century Venice: The Creation of a Genre.* Berkeley and Los Angeles: University of California Press, 1991.

———. "Seneca and the Interpretation of *L'incoronazione di Poppea*." *Journal of the American Musicological Society* 38.1 (1985): 34–71.

Ross, David. *Aristotle.* 5th ed. London: Methuen, 1964.

Rossini, Paolo. "L'opera classicista nella Milano napoleonica (1796–1815)." In *Aspetti dell' opera italiana fra Sette e Ottocento: Mayr e Zingarelli.* Ed. Guido Salvetti. 127–71. Lucca: Libreria Musicale Italiana, 1993.

Rouvière, Olivier. "L'équation vénitienne." *L'avant Scène Opéra* 216 (2003): 89–91.

Rushton, Julian. *Mozart.* Oxford: Oxford University Press, 2006.

Russell, Donald A. *Plutarch.* New York: Charles Scribner's Sons, 1973.

Russell, P. E. "Spanish Literature (1474–1681)." In *Spain: A Companion to Spanish Studies.* Ed. P. E. Russell. 265–380. London: Methuen, 1973.

Russell, Trusten W. *Voltaire, Dryden and Heroic Tragedy.* New York: Columbia University Press, 1946.

Rutherford, R. B. *The Meditations of Marcus Aurelius: A Study.* Oxford: Oxford University Press, 1989.

Sala di Felice, Elena. "Segreti, menzogne e coatti silenzi nella 'Clemenza di Tito' del Metastasio." In *Pietro Metastasio: Il testo e il contesto.* Ed. Marta Columbro and P. Maione. 187–201. Naples: Altrastampa, 2000.

———. "Zeno: Da Venezia a Vienna. Dal teatro impresariale al teatro di corte." In *L'opera italiana a Vienna prima di Metastasio.* Ed. M. T. Muraro. 65–114. Florence: Olschki, 1990.

Sambrook, James. "Godolphin [née Churchill], Henrietta [Harriet]." *Oxford Dictionary of National Biography.* Online ed., Oxford University Press, May 2005. http://www.oxforddnb.com/. (Accessed Oct. 24, 2006.)

Sandbach, Francis H. *The Stoics.* New York: Norton, 1975.

Sartori, Claudio. *I libretti italiani a stampa dalle origini al 1800*. 6 vols. in 7. Cuneo, Italy: Bertola & Locatelli, 1990–94.

Saslow, James. *The Medici Wedding of 1589: Florentine Festival as Theatrum Mundi*. New Haven, Conn.: Yale University Press, 1996.

Saunders, Harris Sheridan, Jr. "Handel's 'Agrippina': The Venetian Perspective." *Göttinger Händel-Beiträge* 3 (1989): 87–98.

Sawyer, John E. "Irony and Borrowings in Handel's 'Agrippina.'" *Music & Letters* 80.4 (1999): 531–59.

Schlüter, Wolfgang. "The Battle of the Teutoberg Forest: Archaeological Research at Kalkriese near Osnabrück." In *Roman Germany*. Ed. J. D. Creighton and R. S. A. Wilson. 125–59. Portsmouth, R.I.: *Journal of Roman Archaeology*, Supp. 32, 1999.

Scullard, Howard H. *Scipio Africanus: Soldier and Politician*. Ithaca, N.Y.: Cornell University Press, 1970.

Seidel, Wilhelm. "Seneca—Corneille—Mozart: Ideen- und Gattungsgeschichtliches zu 'La Clemenza di Tito.'" In *Musik in der Antike und Neuzeit*. Ed. Michael von Albrecht and Werner Schubert. 109–28. Frankfurt: P. Lang, 1987.

Selfridge-Field, Eleanor, ed. *Pallavicino, Messalina*. Milan: Ricordi, 2001.

Serpa, Rosanna. *Francesco Saverio Salfi: Teatro giacobino*. Palermo: Palumbo, 1975.

Shaw, George Bernard. *Music in London: 1890–1894*. 3 vols. London: Constable, 1932.

Sherburn, George W., ed. *The Correspondence of Alexander Pope*. Oxford: Clarendon Press, 1956.

Skippon, Sir Philip. *Journey through the Low Countries, Germany, Italy and France*. 1682. Reprint, London, 1752.

Smith, Patrick J. *The Tenth Muse: A Historical Study of the Opera Libretto*. New York: Knopf, 1970.

Smith, Ruth. *Handel's Oratorios and Eighteenth-Century Thought*. Cambridge: Cambridge University Press, 1995.

Smithers, Peter. *The Life of Joseph Addison*. 2nd ed. Oxford: Clarendon Press, 1968.

Steinby, Eva M., ed. *Lexicon topographicum urbis Romae*. Rome: Edizioni Quasar, 1993–2000.

Sternfeld, Frederick W. *The Birth of Opera*. Oxford: Clarendon Press, 1993.

Strohm, Reinhard. "Antonio Salvi's *Amore e maestà* and the *funesto fine* in Opera." In *Dramma per musica: Italian Opera Seria of the Eighteenth Century*. By Reinhard Strohm. 165–76. New Haven, Conn.: Yale University Press, 1997.

———. *Die italienische Oper im 18. Jahrhundert*. Willhelmshaven: Heinrichshofen, 1979.

———. *Dramma per musica: Italian Opera Seria of the Eighteenth Century*. New Haven, Conn.: Yale University Press, 1997.

———. "Handel and His Italian Opera Texts." In *Essays on Handel and Italian Opera*. By Reinhard Strohm. 34–79. Cambridge: Cambridge University Press, 1985.

———. "Händel in Italia: Nuovi contributi." *Rivista italiana di musicologia* 9 (1974): 152–74.

Strong, Roy C. *Splendour at Court: Renaissance Spectacle and the Theater of Power*. Boston: Houghton Mifflin, 1973.

Stroup, Thomas B., and Arthur L. Cooke, eds. *The Works of Nathaniel Lee*. 2 vols. Metuchen, N.J.: Scarecrow Reprint, 1968.

Strunk, Oliver. *Source Readings in Music History*. Rev. ed. Vol. 4, *The Baroque Era*. Ed. Margaret Murata. New York: Norton, 1998.

———. *Source Readings in Baroque History*. Rev. ed. Vol. 5, *The Late Eighteenth Century*. Ed. Wye J. Allenbrook. New York: Norton, 1998.

Syme, Ronald. *Tacitus*. 2 vols. Oxford: Clarendon Press, 1959.

Tamburini, Elena. *Due teatri per il principe: Studi sulla committenza teatrale di Lorenzo Onofrio Colonna (1659–1689)*. Rome: Bulzoni, 1997.

Tanner, Marie. *The Last Descendant of Aeneas: The Hapsburgs and the Mythic Image of the Emperor*. New Haven, Conn.: Yale University Press, 1993.

Taylor, Carole. "Handel and Frederick, Prince of Wales." *Musical Times* 125. 1692 (1984): 89–92.

Theobald, Lewis. *The Life and Character of Marcus Portius Cato Uticensis . . . Designed for Readers of Cato, a Tragedy*. London: B. Lintott, 1713.

Tomlinson, Gary. *Monteverdi and the End of the Renaissance*. Berkeley and Los Angeles: University of California Press, 1987.

Trevor-Roper, H. *Princes and Artists: Patronage and Ideology at Four Habsburg Courts, 1517–1633*. London: Thames and Hudson, 1976.

Walbank, Frank W. "The Scipionic Legend." In *Selected Papers: Studies in Greek and Roman History and Historiography*. Ed. F. W. Walbank. 120–37. Cambridge: Cambridge University Press, 1985.

Walsh, Patrick G. *Livy: His Historical Aims and Methods*. Cambridge: Cambridge University Press, 1961.

Warburton, Ernest, ed. *J. C. Bach, Catone in Utica: Opera Seria in Three Acts*. New York: Garland, 1987.

———, ed. *The Librettos of Mozart's Operas*. 7 vols. New York: Garland, 1992.

Weiss, Piero, ed. Gaetano Sertor–Francesco Bianchi: *La Morte di Cesare*. Milan: Ricordi, 1999.

Wells, Peter. *The Battle That Stopped Rome: Emperor Augustus, Arminius, and the Slaughter of the Legions in the Teutoberg Forest*. New York: Norton, 2004.

Widdows, Paul F., trans. *Lucan's Civil War*. Bloomington: Indiana University Press, 1988.

Wimmel, Walter. *Kallimachos in Rom*. Wiesbaden: F. Steiner, 1960.

Wiseman, Thomas P. *The Myths of Rome*. Exeter: University of Exeter Press, 2004.

Wolff, H. C. "L'opera comica nel xvii secolo a Venezia e l' 'Agrippina' di Händel." *Nuova rivista musicale italiana* 7 (1973): 39–50.

Yates, Frances A. *Astraea: The Imperial Theme in the Sixteenth Century*. London: Routledge & Kegan Paul, 1975.

Zeno, Apostolo. *Lettere di Apostolo Zeno, Cittadino Veneziano, Istorico e Poeta Cesareo*. 2nd ed. 7 vols. Venice: Francesco Sansoni, 1785.

Zimmerman, Mary. *Metamorphoses: A Play*. Evanston, Ill.: Northwestern University Press, 2002.

INDEX

Page numbers of the principal discussions of individual operas are italicized. Ancient passages quoted or cited in the text and footnotes are listed by author in the Index Locorum.

INDEX LOCORUM

ROBERT C. KETTERER is professor of Classics at the University of Iowa. He has devoted his career to the study of ancient drama and revivals of ancient Rome in theater and music. His articles have appeared in the *Cambridge Opera Journal, Music & Letters, Renaissance Latin Drama in England,* and *Crossing the Stages: The Production, Performance and Reception of Ancient Theater.*

The University of Illinois Press
is a founding member of the
Association of American University Presses.

Composed in 9.5/12.5 Trump Mediaeval
with Trump Mediaeval display
by Celia Shapland
at the University of Illinois Press
Manufactured by Sheridan Books, Inc.

University of Illinois Press
1325 South Oak Street
Champaign, IL 61820-6903
www.press.uillinois.edu